KT-478-559

CHOSEN WORDS

PAST AND PRESENT PROBLEMS
FOR DICTIONARY MAKERS

EXETER LINGUISTIC STUDIES

General Editor: R.R.K. Hartmann

Understanding Semantics
by D. Connor Ferris, 1983

The ESP Classroom: Methodology, Materials, Expectations
edited by Gregory James, 1984

Workbook on Lexicography
by Barbara Ann Kipfer, with Jennifer Robinson (glossary), Henri Béjoint, A.P. Cowie, R.R.K. Hartmann, Lesley Jeffries, W.J.R. Martin and N.E. Osselton (exercises), 1984

Applied Text Linguistics
edited by Alan Turney, 1988

Lexicographers and their Works
edited by Gregory James, 1989

Lexicography in Africa
edited by R.R.K. Hartmann, 1990

Dictionary Workbooks. A Critical Evaluation
by Martin P. Stark, 1990

Sound Change in Progress: a Study of Phonological Change and Lexical Diffusion, with Reference to Glottalization and R-Loss in the Speech of Some Exeter Schoolchildren
by Anthea E. Sullivan, 1992

CHOSEN WORDS

PAST AND PRESENT PROBLEMS FOR DICTIONARY MAKERS

N.E. OSSELTON

UNIVERSITY
of
EXETER
PRESS

First published in 1995 by
University of Exeter Press
Reed Hall, Streatham Drive
Exeter, Devon EX4 4QR
UK

British Library Cataloguing in Publication Data
A catalogue record of this book is available
from the British Library

ISBN 0 85989 419 3

Printed and bound in Great Britain
by Short Run Press Ltd, Exeter

Contents

List of Figures

List of Abbreviations

(For further details see Bibliography)

COBUILD	*Collins Cobuild English Language Dictionary*
COD	*Concise Oxford Dictionary*
DB	Bailey, *Dictionarium Britannicum*
DWB	Grimm, *Deutsches Wörterbuch*
GAN	*Glossographia Anglicana Nova*
IJL	International Journal of Lexicography
JK	J[ohn] K[ersey], *A New English Dictionary*
LDOCE	*Longmans Dictionary of Contemporary English*
OALD	*Oxford Advanced Learner's Dictionary*
ODEP	*Oxford Dictionary of English Proverbs*
OED	*Oxford English Dictionary*
UEED	Bailey, *Universal Etymological English Dictionary*
WNT	*Woordenboek der Nederlandsche Taal*

Preface and Acknowledgements

The sixteen essays printed in this volume cover a range of practical and theoretical problems which may arise whenever anyone sets about compiling a dictionary. When I began writing on the history of the English dictionary in the 1950's there was little scholarly interest in the matter in America, and virtually none in Europe. Now, dictionary research of all kinds is a flourishing academic industry, our lexicographers at last enjoy professional status, and the canons of dictionary criticism have come to form the subject of lively debate. I hope that the papers brought together here from various books and journals published over the past thirty years may serve the convenience of scholars, and also contribute something to current discussions. Two of the papers have not been published before.

The texts are here reprinted with minor corrections. Certain typographical adjustments have also been made so as to achieve greater uniformity of appearance in the book, and the eight illustrations which have been added were chosen for their relevance to recurring topics within the whole collection. The bringing together of articles written over a long period of years on quite closely related topics has inevitably resulted in some duplication of material. I have however made no attempt to edit out minor repetitions, since each chapter may still be read as an independent study. Immediately following each chapter title, the original date of compilation or publication is given in square brackets, so that the reader may be alerted at the outset to the passage of time. Scholarship moves on, and in the *End Notes* to the chapters, I have provided references to later work in the same field.

The common theme running through the essays is that of a shared past in dictionary-making. The choices confronting a modern compiler—of what words to put in, or of how to treat the words that are put in—often worried early dictionary-makers too. Dictionaries are by their nature derivative works, they copy to the point of plagiarism, so that it even makes sense to talk of a common text, a basic list of English words, handed down and modified from generation to generation. I hope that this collection of essays may serve to show that not only the word-list is inherited, but so too are the problems of lexicographical choice which go with it.

I owe thanks to a number of people for their support while I was putting this collection of essays together: Simon Baker, Secretary of the Exeter University Press, for his patience and excellent advice; my colleagues at Newcastle University, Hermann Moisl, who taught me all I know about computers and word-processing, Ken Nott, who so cheerfully sorted things out whenever the machines got the better of me, and Rowena Bryson for always being ready to help with producing the camera-ready copy. In particular, my thanks go to Reinhard Hartmann, of the Dictionary Research Centre in Exeter, for the original suggestion that it all might make a worthwhile book, as well as for his continued interest throughout. I also wish to acknowledge the generosity of the many publishers (noted elsewhere) who have given me permission to reprint material of which they hold the copyright. The pages from the dictionaries of Elisha Coles and Henry Cockeram shown in Figures 2 and 7 are reproduced here by courtesy of the Librarians of Durham and of Newcastle Universities respectively. Other illustrations are from volumes in my private collection, except that of Figure 6, for which I am indebted to the Bodleian Library in Oxford.

Finally I wish to thank my wife, who has not only lived through the making of these essays over the past thirty years, but has been willing to go through them all again: without her bibliographical and linguistic expertise, many more errors would have crept into the book than the ones which the attentive reader will undoubtedly find.

Durham, May 1995 N.E. Osselton

1

The Character of the Earliest English Dictionaries

[1990]

The first century and a half of English dictionary making saw the evolution of three main types of work: the compact 40,000-word reference dictionary best typified by Bailey's *Universal Etymological English Dictionary* (1721); a more encyclopaedic volume such as that of Kersey-Phillips (1706), giving a wider range of information for the leisurely and educated user; and in Johnson (1755), the first scholarly inventory of the English language. With the evidently rapid expansion of the demand for monolingual works, some 22 different dictionaries came on the market during the period, and others were planned (Segar 1931, Alston 1974 Vol.V; see also chapter 11 below). Many of them (Bullokar 1616, Cockeram 1623, Coles 1676, Bailey 1721) were to run to ten or more editions, and there was never a gap of more than a few years between one publication and the next. There were false starts and stops as compilers cast about to find their public and shake themselves free of the bilingual tradition they inherited. But by the end of the period the proper bounds of the dictionary seem to have become pretty well generally accepted, and from men of different professions (schoolmaster, barrister, calligrapher, doctor, mathematician, etc.), there emerged in Kersey and Bailey (and also in Johnson) something near to the professional lexicographer. Starnes and Noyes (1946) provide the fullest account of the dictionaries before Johnson, and modern scholarship has been focused especially on the nomenclature, the sources and the interrelationships of the early dictionaries (Murray 1900, Mathews 1933, Kolb and Sledd 1953, Hulbert 1955, Osselton 1983). The evolution of dictionary structure and of lexicographical techniques (Hayashi 1978) has been the subject of little research so far.

Size The English dictionary had small beginnings, even though it evolved in a period when large bilingual models were available. Thus the first English dictionary, that of Cawdrey (1604), has only 2543 entries (Schäfer 1989, 51), Bullokar (1616) has 4249, and even the enlarged fifth edition of the folio Phillips dictionary (1696) no more than 17,000. The gradual increase thereafter in the size of dictionaries for general use may be judged from the statistics given by Starnes and Noyes for the editions of Bailey UEED in 1721 (40,000 entries), 1728 (42,500 entries), 1770 (44,000 entries) and 1783 (50,000 entries). The first edition of Johnson (1755) has, with 55,000, rather fewer than Bailey's *Dictionarium Britannicum* (1730), upon the second edition of which he is known to have drawn, though the treatment of them is of course far more extensive. In terms of letter-tokens, the corresponding figures are approximately as follows:

Cawdrey	100,000
Bullokar	310,000
Blount	1.5m
Bailey UEED	4.2m
Bailey DB	7.25m
Johnson	26m.

Alphabetization Presentation of the nomenclature in a single fully alphabetized list is the norm from the start, though Cawdrey still felt the need to explain this system in his address to the reader, and in the work itself reveals himself to be less than fully competent in the application of it (see further in chapter 12 below). In all dictionaries of the period, I/J is treated as a single letter for the purposes of alphabetization, as is also U/V. There was a tendency to deviate from strict alphabetical order when dealing with derivations, so that Blount (1656), for instance, gives *epidemy* before *epidemical* and brackets *nugal* and *nugatory* before entries for *nugator* and *nugation*. Most of the early works reveal a tendency towards *dégroupement*, with separate senses, compounds and idiomatic phrases accorded lemma status: there are for example 50 entries for the word *angle* in Kersey-Phillips (1706). Improvement came only with the imposition of

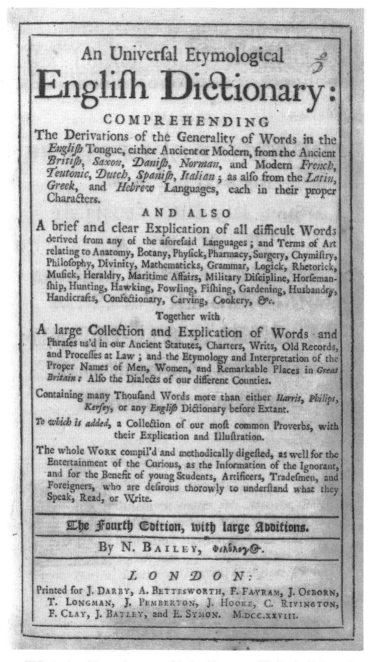

An Univerſal Etymological

Engliſh Dictionary:

COMPREHENDING

The Derivations of the Generality of Words in the *Engliſh* Tongue, either Ancient or Modern, from the Ancient *Britiſh*, *Saxon*, *Daniſh*, *Norman*, and Modern *French*, *Teutonic*, *Dutch*, *Spaniſh*, *Italian*; as alſo from the *Latin*, *Greek*, and *Hebrew* Languages, each in their proper Characters.

AND ALSO

A brief and clear Explication of all difficult Words derived from any of the aforeſaid Languages; and Terms of Art relating to Anatomy, Botany, Phyſick, Pharmacy, Surgery, Chymiſtry, Philoſophy, Divinity, Mathematicks, Grammar, Logick, Rhetorick, Muſick, Heraldry, Maritime Affairs, Military Diſcipline, Horſemanſhip, Hunting, Hawking, Fowling, Fiſhing, Gardening, Husbandry, Handicrafts, Confectionary, Carving, Cookery, &c.

Together with

A large Collection and Explication of Words and Phraſes us'd in our Ancient Statutes, Charters, Writs, Old Records, and Proceſſes at Law; and the Etymology and Interpretation of the Proper Names of Men, Women, and Remarkable Places in *Great Britain*: Alſo the Dialects of our different Counties.

Containing many Thouſand Words more than either *Harris*, *Philips*, *Kerſey*, or any *Engliſh* Dictionary before Extant.

To which is added, a Collection of our moſt common Proverbs, with their Explication and Illuſtration.

The whole WORK compil'd and methodically digeſted, as well for the Entertainment of the Curious, as the Information of the Ignorant, and for the Benefit of young Students, Artificers, Tradeſmen, and Foreigners, who are deſirous thorowly to underſtand what they Speak, Read, or Write.

The Fourth Edition, with large Additions.

By N. BAILEY, Φιλόλογος.

LONDON:

Printed for J. DARBY, A. BETTESWORTH, F. FAYRAM, J. OSBORN, T. LONGMAN, J. PEMBERTON, J. HOOKE, C. RIVINGTON, F. CLAY, J. BATLEY, and E. SYMON. M.DCC.XXVIII.

FIG. 1. An eighteenth-century blurb: title-page of Bailey's *Universal Etymological English Dictionary* (4th edn 1728).

greater semantic discipline by Martin (1749) and Johnson. Cockeram (1623) is experimental in presenting his nomenclature in three separate alphabetical lists, one containing the 'choicest' words explained in everyday language, one of common words with more learned equivalents, and a third list consisting of proper names and other encyclopaedic matter. His example was not followed, and the most that ensuing compilers permit themselves is modest appendices, such as the collection of 189 'barbarous words' listed at the end of Phillips (1678). William Lloyd (1668) provides the most interesting structural experiment in the dictionaries of the period (Dolezal 1985, Hüllen 1986) if indeed his work is to be classed as a dictionary in the narrow sense: it is often regarded as a precursor of Roget's *Thesaurus* (1852). In it there are no direct definitions for most monosemous words, and the alphabetical list depends very largely on use in conjunction with the Philosophical Tables in the book by Bishop Wilkins to which it is appended.

Front Matter As with books of other kinds in that period, elaborate title-pages must often have done service as a blurb. Bailey, for instance, proclaims on the title-page of the UEED (1721) that

> the whole WORK [is] compil'd and Methodically digested, as well for the Entertainment of the Curious, as the Information of the Ignorant, and for the Benefit of young Students, Artificers, Tradesmen, and Foreigners, who are desirous thorowly to understand what they Speak, Read, or Write

and he boasts that it contains 'many Thousand Words more than either *Harris*, *Philips*, *Kersey*, or any *English* Dictionary before Extant' (see Figure 1).

The early prefaces, on the other hand, were underdeveloped in their functions. They may be valuable to us today as evidence for the sociology of early dictionaries, but must have served their readers poorly; in the seventeenth-century works, criticism of predecessors and anecdotal notes on the genesis of the book tend to outweigh practical guidance on contents and use. Here again it is Martin and Johnson who excel, and Johnson's renowned Preface—foreshadowed by his *Plan of a Dictionary of the English Language* (1747)—must be ranked as a classic, alike as an introduction to a dictionary, and as an exposition of lexicographical theory (Weinbrot 1972b). Johnson's inclusion of a history of the English language in his front matter was not unexampled (even Phillips 1658 had a rather sketchy one); it also fitted in well with his historical approach to the English vocabulary, and was followed by some later compilers such as Barclay (1774). Johnson has a grammar, too. Grammars had long been common in bilingual dictionaries, and from Dyche and Pardon (1735) onwards were to become a staple component of front matter throughout the eighteenth century; though whether such grammatical outlines were really functional (or continue to be functional) must be doubted.

Nomenclature There is a steady evolution in the range and types of vocabulary deemed to be appropriate for inclusion in the monolingual dictionary. The early works were (and called themselves) 'hard-word' books—serving to expound the new scholarly (especially Latinate) vocabulary of Renaissance English. Thus, nearly all the words in Cawdrey will be found to have entered the English language only in the fifteenth and sixteenth centuries, and most (though not all) of them are 'hard words' (Noyes 1943). Blount's *Glossographia* (1656) is a classic work in this vein, with sequences of entries such as *macilent, macritude, macrocosmus, macrology, mactator, maculatures, maculate, madidate, madifie*; here the learned (and especially abstract) vocabulary is very little relieved by other matter, though (see chapter 6 and Figure 3 below) it is to Blount's credit that he was in part basing his selection on real usage.

It is fair to say that with the exception of the work by John Wesley (1753) all monolingual English dictionaries down to and including Johnson belong to the hard-word tradition in some measure: it reflected the great lexicographical need of the age.

In the nature of things a sizeable part of this learned vocabulary consisted of technical terms (or 'Terms of Art' as they were then called), and the list of fields covered forms the centre-piece of many a title-page such as that of Bailey's UEED as shown in Figure 1. Phillips (1658) claims to have used external consultants for his technical terms, but his list (including Robert Boyle for chemistry and Izaak Walton for fishing) must be treated with some reserve. The actual entries for technical terms in some of the early works (especially Kersey-Phillips 1706 and Bailey 1730) tend to be of disproportionate length. But with the coming of specialist technical dictionaries such as John Harris's *Lexicon Technicum* (1704) the pressure to cover a wide range of such terms in general dictionaries can be seen to decline, and Johnson is sparing of them.

Attitudes to encyclopaedic matter varied (Roe 1977); in particular, the inclusion of geographical and personal names has had a chequered history in the English dictionary: Cawdrey (1604) had none, Blount (1656) eschewed them on the whole, but his rival Phillips in his grander and more encyclopaedic work favoured especially the names of classical, historical or biblical interest. Like many of the bilingual dictionaries of the period, his text aimed at helping readers of poetry and polite letters (Starnes 1940). Coles (1676) extended the coverage to personal names and the names of English towns (*Ilia* 'daughter of Numitor King of the Albanes', *Iliades* and *Ilium* are preceded by *Ilchester* and *Ilfracombe*). Bailey and his reviser Scott (Scott-Bailey 1755) followed suit, but the more linguistically orientated Martin (1749) omitted them, leaving a delicate balance of decision to Johnson, whose policy of excluding names was to have its effect on British dictionaries for two centuries to come.

The focus on learned and technical terms went with a neglect of common words and idioms. The first attempt to include the ordinary words of English systematically in a monolingual English dictionary was by John Kersey (JK 1702) though it seems that an effective source for these may have been hard to come by (see chapter 3 below), and certainly for the common phrasal verbs of English (*give up, set down*, etc.) we have to wait until Johnson before any reasonably full coverage is given—a matter dealt with more fully in chapter 10 below.

Cant and slang terms on the other hand make an early entry into English dictionary nomenclature with Coles (1676), who explains that they may 'save your Throat from being cut, or, at least, your Pocket from being pick'd'. With the appropriate cautionary labelling, some of these words (such as *booze*) have retained an assured peripheral status in English dictionaries ever since. Dialect comes in at this stage too. Monolingual dictionaries of English appear on the scene too late for there to be any question of what region was to be associated with the polite standard. But the convention of including a scattering of regional (especially northern) words is established by Coles in 1676 and has survived since then (see chapter 4 and Figure 2 below).

Diachronically the matter was more complex. Because of their excessive resort to the works of predecessors the early dictionaries tend more and more to retain elements of vocabulary no longer current. Dialect and legal terms were often felt to be archaic anyway, and the inclusion of 'old' or Chaucerian words (such as *clepe, eld, ifere*) from Bullokar (1616) onwards shows that even long before Johnson the dictionary was by some compilers being designed as a help to the reader of earlier as well as of current literature (Simon 1960, Kerling 1979, Schäfer 1982; also chapter 5 below). Johnson's own definition of the chronological limits to his nomenclature—in effect, words from writers of the two preceding centuries—had to do especially with the literary function which the dictionary fulfilled.

Evolution of the Lemma Between Cawdrey (1604) and Johnson (1755) the entry in monolingual English dictionaries evolved pretty well into the form which is generally expected today. In Cawdrey, the average length of the lemma is under five words, and it is very hard to find entries running to more than twenty words. In Johnson, the article for the verb *to set* has 88 sections, and runs to some five pages folio. The variety of structural devices used by compilers within the lemma increased correspondingly in the same period.

Definition The earliest dictionaries depended largely on single synonymy, often pairing a learned foreign term with a native one as in '*ignify* to burn'. Where multiple equivalents are given, the semicolon is from the start used alongside commas, but accuracy in observing major and minor sense distinctions comes only gradually, and it is not until Martin (1749) that numbered definitions are presented in a pre-determined order. Definitions in many of the earlier works are often unhelpful, and may even be misleading to the modern user seeking guidance on seventeenth- and eighteenth-century words (Riddell 1974). The definitional techniques which evolved were generally aimed at (though they often fell short of) logical or insertible equivalents, as in '*quotidian* done daily, that happens every day, ordinary' (Blount 1656). Some early works break away from the stiffer conventions: Coles (1676) devises concatenated entries for clusters such as *ignitible – ignition – ignited* (on these see chapter 12 below), and the *Glossographia Anglicana Nova* (1707) adopts what would now probably be recognized as a discourse approach: '*Becalm'd*, is when the Water is so very smooth, that the Ship has scarce any Motion, or moves but slowly'; '*Mademoiselle*, answering to Mistress in *English*, is a Title given to ...'. Johnson was clearly indebted to his predecessors (McCracken 1969) and has been much criticized for the excessive Latinity of his defining metalanguage (Congleton and Congleton 1984). But the disciplined precision of his definitions has been universally admired, and he differed radically from the compilers before him in arranging his senses chronologically so as (in part at least) to illustrate the semantic development of the word.

Typographical Devices Italic was available from the start to set off the entry-word against the definition in roman (or vice-versa), and black letter was used for headwords at least as late as Kersey-Phillips (1706). These type faces tended to give way to capitals in the eighteenth century (e.g. in the Bailey dictionaries), and Johnson was the first to make use of large and small capitals to distinguish between main and derivative entry-words (see further in chapter 12 below).

The usefulness of brackets and braces as lexicographical space-savers was realized early, as in *Cavalry* 'the hors[men] in an army' (Coles 1676). Use is however inconsistent, and there were less successful experiments, such as Cawdrey's invention of (k) for 'kind of' as in '*crocodile*, (k) beast'. Asterisks to mark 'old' words occurred as early as Bullokar in 1616 (Kerling 1979), and before that, Cawdrey had prefixed the symbol § to many of his entries of French origin. The extensive use of the obelisk or dagger (†) for words of doubtful acceptability reached a peak in Bailey's 'Vol. II' in 1727 (see chapter 13 and Figure 8 below) but died out in the English tradition with Martin (Osselton 1958). Martin was however the initiator of another and longer-lasting typographical device: that of using italic capitals to pick out unassimilated foreign loan-words.

Illustrations Two rather crude heraldic woodcuts in the text of Blount (1656) represent the beginnings of dictionary illustration in English. He had few imitators. GAN (1707) went further with heraldic items, and in his larger dictionary Bailey saw the value of the device to support the more technical definitions such as those for *isosceles* and *orrery*—though he was clearly limited by the range of cuts available to his printers. Johnson set his face against illustrations and sought by verbal dexterity to overcome the need for them.

Etymology Given the very mixed character of the English vocabulary we should perhaps expect etymology to be recognized early as a lexicographical need, and indeed the beginnings of it are to be found in Cawdrey (1604): a letter (g) is placed after some entry-words of Greek origin—a technique extended later to a range of other languages in Coles (1676). Blount (1656) goes further, commonly giving the root word (as in '*Tithing*

[Sax. Teothung] ...') and adding other useful bits of information—of *Tobacco* he says 'sic vocatur in omnibus linguis'. The anonymous *Gazophylacium Anglicanum* (1689) was the first explicitly etymological dictionary of the language to be published in English, but it is Bailey (1721) who first attempts any systematic statement in a general dictionary of both the immediate source and the remoter analogues of English words. For *clergy*, for instance, he records French, Latin and Greek, and he devotes much of the introduction of his dictionary to an explanation of the principles adopted. Like his predecessor Edward Phillips he makes some alarming blunders, but then they and all the compilers of the period (including even Johnson) were unhappily dependent on the existing imperfect reference works such as Somner, Verstegan, Junius and Skinner. Bailey's work no doubt did much to establish the inclusion of etymology as a valid option for the monolingual dictionary compiler: from his time on, the more serious English dictionaries commonly gave etymologies (including the term in their titles too, in many cases) whereas the quick reference books did not; and things have stayed that way ever since. For Johnson, however, etymology was an essential prop to the historically structured presentation of words and their meanings.

Pronunciation Little was done about pronunciation in English dictionaries before Johnson or indeed by Johnson (Bronstein 1986). No doubt the need for guidance existed in this period of intense interest in the spoken word (Dobson 1957). Coles (1676) even prefixes to his dictionary a traditional list of homophones (such as *sloe – slow – slough,* and *ware – wear – were*). But an effective method of representing the pronunciation of individual words had not yet been devised, and so the dictionaries themselves get no further than a bare indication of word stress—first in 1727 in both parts of Bailey's 'Vol. II' (see chapter 13 and Figure 8 below) and later, with added guidance on syllabification, in Dyche and Pardon (1735), followed by Martin, who even says that to teach an accepted pronunciation is 'the principal use of a Dictionary next to the explication of words' (Martin 1749, Introduction, 26).

Grammar, Collocation, Idiom Though formal grammars came to be prefixed to some of the early works, structural information about English was slow to establish a place for itself in the body of the monolingual dictionary. Word-class was generally indicated only incidentally through definitions, or else in the form of the entry (*fine, a fine, to fine*), until Dyche and Pardon (1735) initiated the modern convention of including a note of word class (*v* for verb, *a* for adjective, etc.) for every entry. Morphology is likewise largely a blank until the eighteenth century. J.K.(1702) seems to be the first compiler to enter noun plurals and verb forms such as *mice* and *rang*. This spreads to later dictionaries such as the second edition of Bailey's DB (1736) which, for instance, has *women* in its proper alphabetical sequence and notes it also as '*Ir[regular] Pl[ural]*' under the main entry for *woman*. Derivations and compounds, when they are entered at all in these early dictionaries of English, generally have lemma status, but coverage of compounds is extremely skimpy compared with what was already on offer in the bilingual dictionaries of the time. Johnson (who has 16 compounds for the word *foot*) is an exception here (Stein 1984), as he is also in the very full coverage of phrasal verbs (see chapter 10 below). Idiomatic phrases, with the notable exception of proverbs (Starnes and Noyes 1946, 104-6, 122-3), are likewise not well represented, though the large Bailey dictionary of 1730 finds room for a good number of items such as *to learn without book* and *to keep in touch with one*. Here Johnson's dictionary stands apart, and especially through its inclusion of quotations it must always rank as a major record of English idiomatic usage, as well as of the grammatical structures current at the time.

Style and Register Labels The monolingual dictionaries in English were from the start strong in 'Terms of Art', and the need to distinguish specialized technical senses was often satisfied incidentally within the definition: '*Operation* (Lat.) a labouring or working. 'Tis frequently used in Chymistry and Surgery, and signifies ...' (GAN 1707). Shorter bracketed notes such as '(in gunnery)', '(in hunting)' were adopted by many compilers, including Martin and Johnson. As a further stage of compression on his three-column pages, Coles (1676) entered 'c' for 'canting' and 'o' for 'old word' alongside various dialect indicators such as 'Che[shire]', 'E[ssex]', 'We[st-Country]'. But the major innovator of abbreviated labels was John Kersey, who printed a list of 46 at the beginning of his *Dictionarium Anglo-Britannicum* (Kersey 1708) including items such as

H.T. = Hunting-Term
P.T. = A Term in Physick, or Pharmacy
P.W. = Poetical Word

Sc. = Scotch

S.L. = Statute-Law

S.T. = Sea Term.

The list was taken over largely unchanged by Bailey (1721) and the device has continued in vigorous use down to our own times. The adoption of abbreviated labels for items entered but felt to be marginal may be seen as a refinement upon the use of typographical devices (asterisks and daggers) referred to above, and it is to be set against the individual verbal condemnations such as 'a barbarous term in husbandry' which were favoured by Johnson (Allen 1940).

Illustrative Quotations and Reference to Sources Though plagiarism was clearly the norm, and there are even some contemporary accusations of it (Starnes and Noyes 1946, 51-6) there are also early instances of honest acknowledgement: Blount lists Cotgrave, Dasypodius and Hexham among ten source-books, and says disarmingly 'I profess to have done little with my own Pencil' (Blount 1656, sig. A5^{r}). Bailey (1721), like Johnson (1755), acknowledges the use of Skinner and Junius for etymologies. Blount is also the first of the English compilers to record non-dictionary sources in the text proper, drawing especially heavily on Lord Bacon and Sir Thomas Browne (see further in chapter 6 below). From Phillips (1658) onwards a tradition develops of acknowledging words of Chaucerian origin (Kerling 1979), and the anonymous compiler of GAN (1707) lists on his title-page some of the 'best Modern Authors' he claims to have drawn on, including Tillotson, Evelyn and Dryden. Dr Johnson's acknowledgement of literary and other sources is therefore not unexampled even in the English tradition, though his mode of compilation certainly was. In particular, the practice of providing quotations for all (or nearly all) words has nothing like it in the works of his predecessors, and it underlies the whole principle upon which his dictionary was set up. The process by which he assembled them has received much attention (Read 1935, Stenberg 1944, Wimsatt and Wimsatt 1948, Wimsatt 1951, Kolb and Kolb 1972, Clifford 1979, DeMaria 1986). His quotations are drawn from major writers of the preceding two centuries—with Shakespeare, Dryden, Milton, Addison, Pope and Bacon accounting for almost half of all quotations (Osselton 1958, 133)—and they are arranged chronologically so as to illustrate the semantic development of individual words. It was through the very presence of the quotations that Johnson's dictionary became elevated into that exemplary compendium of good usage which his contemporaries had long craved.

Audience The first English dictionaries professed to cater especially for the semi-educated: 'all Persons that would rightly understand what they discourse, write, or read' (Phillips 1658). There are many early references to women (Cawdrey 1604, Defoe 1735), to young students (Cockeram 1623), artificers, merchants, and 'persons ignorant of the learned languages' (J.K. 1702). The monolingual dictionary in the seventeenth century was conceived as a prop for the linguistically insecure, baffled by the highly heterogeneous vocabulary of their native language. The need to cater for this humbler public continues through into the eighteenth century, as is shown by the appearance of the Defoe dictionary, the *Pocket Dictionary* (1753), Wesley (1753) and the numerous editions of J.K. down to 1772 (Alston 1974 Vol. V, nos. 77-85). Meantime the notion of the dictionary as an instructive and readable work had become established, and the folio volumes of Phillips and Bailey will certainly have served for the 'Entertainment of the Curious' (Bailey 1730). It is known that William Pitt the Elder found Bailey's dictionary profitable reading (Starnes and Noyes 1946, 100), and there can be no doubt that Johnson's dictionary was intended to be both instructive and morally improving among the upper ranks of society (DeMaria 1986), even though it was not universally acclaimed in its own time (Rypins 1925, Noyes 1954).

Circulation and Adaptations The demand for monolingual dictionaries in English was clearly a steady one from the start, though circulation figures are generally lacking. In the case of Johnson, we know that some 6000 copies of the folio were printed by 1784, and the octavo edition, with 40,000 copies produced down to 1786, must be classed as a bestseller (Sledd and Kolb 1955, 113-14). Evidence for the popularity of earlier works must lie in the frequency of reprints and revisions. Bullokar, for instance, went through 19 editions between 1616 and 1775 (by which time it must have been completely out of date in contents) and Bailey's smaller dictionary saw 28 editions from its publication in 1721 down to the end of the eighteenth century (Alston 1974 Vol. V, nos. 5-29, 94-126). The first abridged dictionary of English (Kersey 1708) was no commercial success, but the large number of abridged and miniature versions of Johnson (Alston 1974 Vol. V, nos. 37-41) shows that a new market had been created.

Johnson also came to be drawn on heavily for pronouncing and foreign-language dictionaries (Sledd and Kolb 1955, 156-64). As well as his own revisions there were later reworkings such as those of Todd (1818) and Latham (1866). Numerous supplementary vocabularies were also produced, and Johnson has remained a focus of scholarly interest down to our own times (Clifford and Greene 1970, 213-25; Congleton and Congleton 1984).

Sources The immediate and most important source for the nomenclature of the earliest English dictionaries was unquestionably the Latin-English dictionaries of the late Middle Ages and the Renaissance, most fully described in Starnes (1954) and Stein (1985a). The initial 'hard-word' vocabulary derived from them is seen at its fullest in Blount (1656), and because of the plagiarizing habits of the compilers it was slow to die away (Starnes and Noyes, *passim*) so that some purely 'dictionary' words have led a ghost existence right down to our own times. Dependence on Latin-English dictionaries should however not be overstated: there were also direct borrowings from literary works, and especially in technical terms the vocabulary was usefully extended from glossaries appended to learned vernacular publications of the time (Schäfer 1970, 1984, 1989), and important additions were made even in the seventeenth century from specialist dictionaries and glossaries of legal terms, cant and dialect (Noyes 1941, Bately 1967). For their etymologies compilers were also able to turn to outside works such as Skinner (1671). It seems likely that the alphabetical lists of words in spelling-books may also have been drawn on, though this is hard to prove. It has been shown that even for the everyday words of the language J.K. (1702) may have turned again to the bilingual dictionaries, where the need for them had existed from the start (see chapter 3 below). Studies in the defining methods of bilingual dictionaries (Stein 1985b, 1986) show a line of development to the monolingual works, and it is clear that foreign models must have been a constant source of new lexicographical and typographical techniques, though little research has been done on this so far. The dictionaries of the French Academy and the Italian Academy were constantly admired at the time, and we know that Johnson possessed copies of these as well as of numerous other foreign dictionaries in his library. Even as late as 1749 we find Martin admitting in his Preface that he found it helpful to confront his amanuensis with Ainsworth's Latin dictionary so as to bring home the semantic complexity of the English words he was to define. The direct input from literary sources begins with Blount and reaches its apogee with Johnson, though it has been shown that even Johnson at times resorted to secondary borrowing (Keast 1957).

Influence In structure and content the first 150 years of lexicographical endeavour undoubtedly created a fairly stable pattern for later compilers. Bailey's volume of 1721 would not have looked unduly antiquated even to Victorian users, and of Johnson, Noah Webster said in 1807 that his writings 'had, in Philology, the effect which Newton's discoveries had in Mathematics, to interrupt for a time the progress of this branch of learning' (Wells 1973, 24). Johnson's scholarly achievement was such that there were still ideas of revising and supplementing his dictionary even in the 1850's (Aarsleff 1967, 247-8), and when the OED did come, the editors did him the honour of taking over many of his definitions.

Whether native-language dictionaries have any long-term effect on the vernacular must always be hard to make out. But in the period down to 1750 it seems almost certain that the dictionaries will have affected English spelling, especially by mediating the printers' conventions and establishing a norm in private use, as well as public (see chapter 9 below). Though there are large numbers of lexical items in the early dictionaries which never existed outside of them, it has been argued that dictionaries may have contributed also to the establishment of both technical and other uncommon words in the general language (Sledd 1949). Argument for any influence on semantic development must be speculative, but there seems no reason to doubt that then, as now, dictionaries will have been resorted to as arbiters of acceptable meaning, and (in Johnson's case) of good taste in usage.

END NOTE

Originally published in 1990 with the title 'English lexicography from the beginning up to and including Johnson' in Hausmann et al. *1989-91, Vol. II, pages 1943-53, and reprinted here by courtesy of Walter de Gruyter & Co., Berlin. The same volume contains companion articles on English lexicography after Johnson and down to 1945 (Simpson 1990), and on present-day British lexicography (Ilson 1990). Béjoint (1994) reflects upon the conservatism of English dictionaries in practice and the possibilities for future innovation in them. A useful bibliography of recent publications on the early English dictionaries has been provided by Gabriele Stein in the re-issue in 1991 of the standard work by Starnes and Noyes. The English (and European) tradition in lexicography is set in a wider context in Boisson* et al. *(1991).*

2

Figurative Words: Modern Practice and the Origins of a Labelling Tradition

[1986]

A study of the widely conflicting practices in the marking of items as 'figurative' in current monolingual English dictionaries suggests that the label is hard to justify on linguistic grounds; that the use of it appears to be on the decline; and that arguments for its retention are best sought in the cultural and historical context out of which it arose in the first place.

Any attentive user of modern dictionaries must be aware of striking differences in the treatment of figurative senses. The following entries from the *Concise Oxford Dictionary* (COD 1982) will serve as a general illustration:

> **locust**: any of various African and Asian short-horned edible grasshoppers of the family *Acrididae*, migrating in swarms and consuming all vegetation of districts; *(fig.)* person of devouring or destructive propensities.

> **wolf**: 1. erect-eared straight-tailed coarse-furred tawny-grey fierce usu. gregarious carnivorous doglike mammal of the genus *Canis*, esp. *Canis lupus*, preying on sheep etc. or combining in packs to hunt larger animals ... 2. Rapacious or greedy person.

In each case the animal sense is given first, with detailed technical specification, and the personal sense follows. The difference lies in the marking of *locust* as being used figuratively for a destructive person, whereas *wolf* (if we are to accept the logic of the labelling) is used for a rapacious person without thought of those real or supposed qualities of the animal which have been transferred to the human context.

It is hard to discover any reason for this: most English people, if they call a man a 'wolf' because he is rapacious, must surely at least be in mind of the potential comparison with the traditionally greedy animal. Here are two words, each designating an animal, and each also designating a person: why should one of them enjoy the usage label *fig.* but the other one not? The fact that the *Chambers Twentieth Century Dictionary* (Chambers 1983) agrees with the COD in the allocation of the label suggests that it is not a random error. One might argue that the association with the animal kingdom is simply stronger in the one case than the other. Does it make sense to talk of *degrees* of figurativeness, rather than to suggest (as the device of a label does) that all meanings are either figurative or not, and that there is no half-way house?

It certainly seems that the lexicographer, once committed to the use of the label, must take pretty crude decisions. Thus, to refer once again to the COD (1982), we find that *to torpedo (a policy, institution, etc.)* meaning 'to paralyse it or make it ineffective' is said to be a figurative usage, as is also *to shoot down (a proposal)*; but *to undermine (a person's reputation)* is not. Perhaps World War I forms a chronological barrier for such military metaphors. To say of an accent that you can *cut it with a knife* is given as a figurative use of the word, but *get your knife into a person*, *stab in the back* and *hit below the belt* are not. Other parallel cases, one marked, one unmarked, are

Figurative	**Unmarked**
battle royal	*battleaxe* (domineering woman)
to cold shoulder	*to throw one's weight about*
crooked (not straight-forward, dishonest)	*twister* (untrustworthy person, a swindler)
pilgrimage (mortal life viewed as a journey)	*the vale of tears* (the world as scene of life, trouble, etc.)
smell out (find out by investigation)	*smell a rat*
a thin excuse	*have a thin time*
vestal virgin	*weaker vessel*
see how the wind lies	*straws in the wind*

Given such a high degree of unpredictability within so well-established a dictionary as the COD, it is not surprising to find that different dictionaries do not agree with each other in indicating that particular usages are to be considered figurative. The words *magnetic* and *myopic*, for instance, are commonly used in reference to human relations and attitudes ('magnetic personality', 'myopic minds') and we get this interesting cross-pattern in the COD (1982) and the Longman *Dictionary of Contemporary English* (Longman 1978):

	COD	**LDOCE**
magnetic (person, etc.)	*figurative*	*unmarked*
myopic (mind, etc.)	*unmarked*	*figurative*.

Examples such as this show that it is not merely a matter of the frequency with which the label is used: our lexicographers also contradict each other in the selection of items for marking as figurative.

A Superfluous Usage Label? The internal and external inconsistency thus illustrated must lead to the question of whether 'figurative' should not simply be dropped from the dictionary maker's battery of conventional usage labels, as indeed it has been in Collins (1979) and Longman (1984). Various arguments can be adduced, of which the evident difficulty of avoiding inconsistency is one. Another, related to it, is reader-orientated: because of their educational or social or personal backgrounds, people will simply differ in their perception of figurative senses. At a reference to 'the brow of a hill' one person will recognise a pleasant conceit, perhaps thinking of the mountains dozing in the afternoon sun. But for another reader 'the brow of a hill' will no more convey a picture than 'the head of a valley' or the foot of a waterfall or the mouth of a river. For one woman, *crow's feet* round the eyes will derive part of their meaning from a primary sense in the ornithological world. Another will never even have thought of it. It may be argued that such matters are altogether too subjective to be pinned down by the *yes:no* crudity of a dictionary label. No doubt informant reaction tests might be devised to discover a level of awareness of figurative senses for certain items, but it must remain questionable whether they could lead to much improvement in ways of dealing with the problem.

If we consider the matter purely from the point of view of lexicographical technique, it is clear that the label *fig.* is very unlike other conventional labels such as *theat.* for 'theatrical' or *her.* for 'heraldry'. With these you are dealing with, or striving to delineate, something like a closed class. There may be fuzziness at the edges; nevertheless there is a recognisable corpus of specialist theatrical and heraldic words in the language. But using words figuratively is in part an imaginative or even a creative process involving —potentially at least—just about all the nouns, verbs and adjectives in the language, so that the line between the established and the occasional can never be drawn. On a fundamentalist view of the lexicographer's duty, it may be argued that the label *fig.* is completely unnecessary anyway; if *vitriol* means 'poison' and it also means 'severe criticism' then it is the dictionary compiler's business to list those meanings, and not to parade speculations about doubtfully perceived connections between them.

Order of Definitions One subsidiary matter of lexicographical technique which doubtless has to do with unspoken feelings about the status of figurative and literal senses is the order of definitions. Even from early times there has been general agreement that the literal should be entered first, and then the figurative. This is logical enough: if one is felt to be a derivative from the other it is quite natural to give the prime meaning to start with. In a dictionary such as the COD (1982) this is still generally the practice. Under the verb *hamstring* we find first 'cripple (person, animal) by cutting the hamstrings', and then '*(fig.)* destroy activity or efficiency of', even though this second sense must surely be the normal or most common one today; likewise with *slipshod* the literal sense of 'having shoes down at heel' comes before 'negligent, careless, unsystematic', which is for many people the only meaning which the word carries. It is a curious fact that even in dictionaries which have given up the label 'figurative', the literal sense is often still given a seemingly undeserved priority: Longmans (1984) have 'cutting the tendons' first for *hamstring* and only then do they go on to refer to 'teachers hamstrung by excessive teaching schedules'.

Some Functions of the Label 'Figurative' The use of the label may then seem hard to justify on rational grounds and it may be regarded as superfluous in lexicographical principle. But given the recognition that one's users will not on the whole be irritable searchers after logic, it is still possible to discern certain practical advantages in retaining it.

For one thing, it may be economical of space. Under *win the day*, the COD (1982) gives the explanation 'be victorious in battle' and then adds in brackets '*lit. or fig.*', which saves a great deal of repetition; so also *exile* for 'exiled person *(lit. or fig.)*'. A less successful attempt is *hot spot*, entered as 'small region that is relatively hot *(lit. or fig.)*'.

The argument from economy of space must also clearly be a strong one in bilingual dictionaries. The English word *bottleneck*, for instance, shares its literal and figurative meanings with the Dutch *flessehals*. For many hundreds of such items in a bilingual dictionary space can be saved by entries in the style '*bottleneck* flessehals *(ook fig.)*'—that is, 'including figurative sense'. It is noteworthy that though Collins do not use the label in their monolingual English dictionary (Collins 1979), it is used in the bilingual English-German (Collins 1980), where we find for instance (with a bi-directional label) '*horse-trading* n *(fig.)* Kuhhandel'.

A more subtle justification for retaining the label may perhaps be deduced from the COD (1982) treatment of *twist a person's arm* ('coerce him by moral pressure') and *pull a person's leg* ('deceive him jokingly'). Only the former is said to be figurative, and this may look to be somewhat arbitrary. On the other hand we should perhaps consider that twisting a person's arm to hurt him physically is part of daily experience (for some people at least); whereas, though it would be perfectly possible to perform the act of pulling a person's leg, this is not an event anyone experiences or would then wish to talk about. The *fig.* label on the former therefore presumably serves to relate the metaphor to one's experience of the real world. There are many other such instances in COD (1982) of marked items standing in relation to known literal meanings, but other figurative meanings left unmarked because they stand on their own. On this general principle, one could presumably argue that *crocodile tears* ('hypocritical grief') should not be marked as figurative, because crocodiles do not weep.

With many figurative or potentially figurative items such as *aftermath*, *slack hand*, *slipshod* and *to vet*, it is probably true to say that for most people no 'second meaning' is present. Yet all are entered as figurative in the COD (1982). Even more striking is *slapstick* 'boisterous knockabout comedy', since hardly anyone save those with a special interest in the history of the theatre would know that in sixteenth-century performances the character Harlequin would carry with him on the stage a kind of flexible divided lath with which he could make a loud slapping noise—literally a stick for slapping. Here, the use of the label *fig.* seems an almost desperate,

Canute-like attempt at preserving an original or 'proper' or 'real' meaning of the word. The function of the label here is quasi-etymological, and a critical user might well wonder whether it is really a part of the lexicographer's business thus to bolster a folk memory of nearly lost allusions.

The label *fig.* appears often to serve as an alternative to other possible usage labels. In COD (1982) *pill* for 'tennis ball' is for instance given not as 'figurative' but as 'slang or jocular'. *Pillbox* in its obviously figurative sense is noted as 'military'. The word *wolf* for 'man who pursues women' is said to be slang, as also is *bun-fight*. *Battleaxe* is given as 'colloquial'. Very often, where one dictionary enters a word as figurative others produce differing labels for it: *jellyfish* ('spineless person') is given as *fig.* in COD (1982), but appears as *informal* in Collins (1979), and this may prompt the thought that the label *fig.* is at times being used in a mildly apologetic or admonitory way. At any rate, it seems to operate as merely one of a battery of alternatives between which stylistic judgements are made.

Alternative Strategies If the label 'figurative' is dropped—and clearly there is a tendency on the part of modern lexicographers to do so—how is one to compensate for the loss of information this may entail? One way is to indicate awareness of the literal sense by building it into the wording of the definition:

> **network**: arrangement ... *recalling* that of a net
> **pilgrimage**: mortal life *viewed as* ... a journey
> **net**, vb.: to catch with *or as if with* a net.

Thus, for the learner confronted with a sentence such as 'he netted a cushy job', the four words *or as if with* in this last example (taken from Collins 1979) will very adequately suggest that it took a fisherman's skill, patience and perhaps cunning to do so.

Such built-in indications of the literal sense may provide the best solution to the problem of figurative meanings in dictionaries, though of course there will still be uncertainty about how far to go: are you going to do the same thing with 'land a good job', or make reference to a croupier in defining the verb 'rake in'?

The Genesis of a Lexicographical Habit It is worth enquiring how we became saddled with this label 'figurative', which some major English lexicographical houses now evidently wish to get rid of. The dictionary as we know it is the product of a late medieval and renaissance tradition, and I believe the extensive practice of marking out figurative meanings in dictionaries can be related to the debates about nominalism conducted in that period, to the feeling that all confusion in language might be avoided if only men could get back to the real, tangible objects which lie behind words. There was, especially in the seventeenth century, a great distrust of figurative language. The philosopher Hobbes says that metaphors and tropes of speech 'can never be true grounds of any ratiocination' (Hobbes 1651: I,4). Bishop Wilkins, who above all others wanted a language with a sharply and logically defined lexical system, proposed in his *Essay towards a Real Character and a Philosophical Language* that there should be a distinct mark for all metaphorical items, so that 'common Metaphor may be legitimated' (Wilkins 1668). The very choice of the word 'legitimated' here suggests the feeling that metaphorical senses were somehow improper, even dangerous to use. This was a view commonly held among the new scientists, who were generally antagonistic to all kinds of picturation, and demanded a language as bare and literal as could be.

It is then not surprising that in this great formative age for European dictionaries figurative senses should have come to be at best tolerated, and in many cases marked down in them. An example may be given from a bilingual dictionary by Boyer (1699):

> **Un esprit brillant*, *a sparkling wit
> **Eau dormante*, still, standing or stagnant water.

Here an asterisk is used to mark *expressions figurées* in the native language as well as in the target language. In other works, such as the revision by Buys of Sewel's Dutch and English dictionary (1766), an inverted dagger is to be found, warning the reader against all figurative senses (see further chapter 8 and Figure 4 below).

Another technique already evolved in the early dictionaries is that of deliberately relegating figurative senses to second place. Even in 1650 we find Robert Sherwood in his address 'To the English Reader' prefixed to the English-French Cotgrave dictionary providing a clear statement of such an intention: 'In giving the French interpretation to the English words, I have, for the most part, observed to set down first the Proper, then, the Translated and Metaphoricall' (Cotgrave 1650). Benjamin Martin, the first English compiler to use numbered definitions, says specifically in his preface that he has taken care to place first the 'truly Etymological or Original' meanings, then the 'General or Popular significations' and only after these the 'Figurative or Metaphorical Uses' (Martin 1749, viii).

Dr Johnson clearly intended something similar. When he wrote the *Plan* of his dictionary he illustrated the technique for dealing with such items by stating what was needed for a definition of *to arrive*:

> to exhibit first its natural and primitive signification, as ... He arrived at a safe harbour ... Then to give its consequential meaning ... as, he arrived at his country seat ... Then its metaphorical sense ... as he arrived at a peerage (Johnson 1747, 22).

But he was less specific than this in the preface when the dictionary was published in 1755, and was later to be taken to task by Lord Monboddo for his failings in this very respect : 'I should, however, have praised this labour of the Doctor's more ... if, in the account he has given us of words, he had distinguished between the proper and original signification of the words, and the figurative and metaphorical' (Monboddo 1774-92, V, 265-75).

By the early nineteenth century the general pattern of compilers' procedures had become pretty much settled, and the label *fig.* has been in extensive use since then, however hard it may be to justify. The OED marked an interesting development, since the editors operated the further distinction between 'figurative' and 'transferred' senses. This generally seems to involve the opposition physical:non-physical. Thus *stream* meaning 'a flow of water' is literal; a *stream of persons* (where the sense has become attached to other physical objects) is said to be transferred, but a *stream of words* or a *stream of events* is classified as figurative, since words and events are intangibles. I am not sure the distinction works very well, though it is carried on into the new Supplement where we find, for instance, *infighting* given as 'transf. and fig.' There are many instances such as 'spring of life *(fig.)*' and 'evening of life *(transf. and fig.)*' where labelling seems hesitant and uncertain. The double system employed in the OED has in any case not found general acceptance, and Zgusta (1971, 56-9) offers a rather different analysis of the meaning carried by the two terms.

It seems to me that the retention and use of a label for figurative meanings in many modern dictionaries is best understood in the historical perspective set out above. It is a part of what has been called our 'empiricist legacy': an attitude of hostility to metaphor, running from Hobbes and Locke, through Berkeley and down to the twentieth-century positivists (Mackenzie 1985, 59). The original hope of distinguishing all metaphorical senses has of course long been abandoned, and if we use the label 'figurative' today, we use it as some sort of rhetorical device. The alternative and more rigorously semantic approach is to drop it altogether, because there can in the end be no linguistic rule for distinguishing the figurative from the non-figurative. The decision of the individual lexicographer on whether to use the label, or how much to use it, must depend on the extent to which he sees the dictionary as a vehicle for preserving a continuity of rhetorical tradition.

END NOTE

Originally published in Symposium of Lexicography III. Proceedings of the Third International Symposium on Lexicography May 14-16, 1986 at the University of Copenhagen, *ed. K. Hyldgaard-Jensen and A. Zettersten (1988, 239-49), and reprinted here by permission of Max Niemeyer Verlag, Tübingen. The edition of the COD used throughout the above study was that of 1982, and readers may care to note that in the more recent eighth edition (1990) the use of the label* fig. *has been drastically reduced. Further discussion of the English label 'figurative' is to be found in Ayto (1988). Drosdowski (1989) deals with the general principles involved and provides a historical survey of the treatment of metaphorical senses in major German dictionaries. Some references to the marking of figurative use in Richelet (1680) are contained in Bray (1990). The ordering of concrete and abstract (including figurative) senses in historical dictionaries is examined in Zgusta (1989, 208-13). On foreign learners' difficulties with the representation of figurative meanings in dictionaries, see Nuccorini (1988).*

3

Common Words: John Kersey and the First General Dictionary of English

[1979]

When common words of everyday use—words such as *earth*, *up* or *seven*—were first included in the early dictionaries of English, they were not taken (as has been generally supposed) from the elementary spelling-books of the day. They came from two sources: English-Latin dictionaries and English-French dictionaries, the Latin and French definitions being simply left out. It may seem surprising that an English compiler in the eighteenth century should have needed to turn to bilingual works to find the ordinary words of his own language; the very unlikelihood of such a procedure perhaps explains why this has not hitherto been noticed. But the fact that it did happen had far-reaching consequences for the selection of words and phrases that was made, and for the way in which common words came to be treated in English dictionaries before Johnson. It also places the work of the native English dictionary makers even more firmly within the European lexicographical tradition than we had hitherto believed it to be.

J.K.'s *New English Dictionary*, published in 1702, is generally acknowledged (e.g. Starnes and Noyes 1946, chapter 9, Wells 1973, 19) to be the first to break with the 'hard-word' tradition established by early compilers such as Cawdrey (1604), Blount (1656) and Phillips (1658). Actually, anyone troubling to look for common words in dictionaries in the seventeenth century would have found a fair sprinkling of them in the second part of Henry Cockeram's *English Dictionarie*, originally published in 1623 (see Figure 7 in chapter 12). This lists 'vulgar' terms and their more refined and elegant equivalents: words such as *cup*, *dwell*, *hair*, *large*, *tavern*, *twin* and *yellow* are all there; even more are to be found in the *Gazophylacium Anglicanum*, published anonymously in 1689—for instance, *above*, *best*, *ear*, *easy*, *floor*, *inch*, *last*, *obey*, *pert*, *twirl* and *yes*. 'J.K.', now usually taken to be John Kersey (Heddesheimer 1968, 444-5, Alston 1969, prefatory note), has then perhaps been given rather more credit for the 'ordinary' words than he deserves, though it remains true that he puts in a greater number of them than any English dictionary compiler before him, and that he does it more systematically.

Kersey is also the first man to state his reasons for doing so: earlier dictionaries, he says, such as those of Bullokar (1616) and Coles (1676), contained so many learned or exotic words that they would tend to discourage 'a plain Country-man, in looking for a common *English* Word'. He thus hopes that his book will be favourably received because of the assistance it will give to 'young Scholars, Tradesmen, Artificers and others, and particularly, the more ingenious Practitioners of the Female Sex; in attaining to the true manner of Spelling of such Words, as from time to time they have occasion to make use of' (Preface, sig. A3^{r}).

Kersey and the Spelling-Books The assumption by P.W. Long (1909, 30) that Kersey's dictionary of 1702 was an 'outgrowth of the spelling-book' may have owed something to the emphasis which Kersey himself gives in the passage just quoted. Starnes and Noyes quote Long's dictum with approval, and add that the compiler 'possibly ... drew up his basic word-list' from school texts such as Richard Browne's *English-School Reformed* (1700); they then go on to say that 'the influence of the spelling-books upon the technique of definition was regrettable' (Starnes and Noyes 1946, 72).

In fact it seems doubtful to me whether in the nature of things there would have been any such influence. For one thing, most spelling-books (including the one by Browne) are divided up into lists of 'Words of one syllable', 'Words of two syllables', and so on to 'Words of six or seven syllables'; this would be an initial inconvenience to any compiler of an ordinary dictionary bent on lexical plunder. Secondly, such lists, forming the bulk of a spelling-book, generally contain no definitions whatsoever.

The place where definitions are to be found in some spelling-books is the homophone list, giving words that 'agree (somewhat) in sound, but differ in sense and spelling', as Browne puts it. But the definitions or identifying phrases given there serve merely to distinguish from each other two or more words which might otherwise be confused; and in any case, even the most extensive collection of homophones would hardly have provided a compiler with a representative list of the everyday words of the language.

Thus, of the eleven words from Kersey chosen by Starnes and Noyes (1946, 73) to illustrate the spelling-book connection, only one (*arm*) occurs in any of Browne's homophone lists, and even that has a quite different definition. In Kersey the main entry reads

> *An* Arm of a man's body, *of a tree, or of the sea.*

But Browne has only 'Arm, joining to the Shoulder', thus distinguishing the word from 'Harm, or hurt'. As we shall see below, Kersey's definition here derives from the Latin dictionaries. I have found no evidence to suggest that he used the spelling-books at all, for this or for any other entries.

Kersey and the Bilingual Dictionaries Clearly what a compiler in Kersey's position needed was a substantial list running straight through the alphabet, from which he might be able to glean as he went along those common words which had been so sadly lacking in monolingual English dictionaries till then. Bilingual dictionaries would at least be likely to supply his needs, since the common words would be included as a matter of course, and since the different senses of any given word would in general be conveniently distinguished by the foreign synonyms. As we shall see, they were often distinguished by English phrases too, and this made the task of the monolingual lexicographer an even easier one.

To determine which works Kersey actually used, and to see how great his indebtedness was, a list of 87 of his 'common' words, spread through the whole alphabet, was checked against the major English, English-Latin and English-French dictionaries which could have been available to him in 1702. These were, for English, Cawdrey (1604), Bullokar (1616), Cockeram (1623), Blount (1656), Phillips (1658), Coles (1676) and the *Gazophylacium Anglicanum* (1689); for English-Latin, Huloet (1552), Rider (1589), Wase (1662), Gouldman (1664), Holyoke (1677), Coles

(1678) and Littleton (1678); and for English-French, Cotgrave (1650), Miège (1679, 1688, 1701) and Boyer (1699).

This survey made two things abundantly clear: (i) *any* English-French dictionary (even the Cotgrave of 1650) and any English-Latin dictionary (even the early Rider of 1589, or Gouldman of 1664) would have been of far more use to him as a source of ordinary words than would any of the earlier monolingual dictionaries; substantial monolingual works such as those of Blount and Phillips contain no more than a handful of the 87 words; (ii) though the dictionaries of Coles (1678), Littleton (1678), Miège (1688) and Boyer (1699) all contain over 90% of the test-group of common words, the style of definition and other details show that no one of these works was the sole source. In the following account of how Kersey used these bilingual works I shall deal first with the Latin, then with the French sources.

Latin Sources Of the many seventeenth-century English-Latin dictionaries likely to have been available to him, it is Adam Littleton's *Linguae Latinae Liber Dictionarius Quadripartitus* (1678) which comes nearest to Kersey in the representation of everyday words. For the noun *arm*, for instance, quoted above, Littleton has a total of nine entries, giving three main senses as follows:

> A mans Arm. *Brachium, laceratus.*
> An Arm of the sea. *Sinus maris, aestuarium.*
> An Arm of a tree. *Ramus, ramale.*

It is not hard to see how Kersey assembled his own three-part definition from these, leaving out the Latin while retaining the identifying phrases *of the sea*, *of a tree*. The remaining six 'arm' entries in Littleton are idiomatic phrases ('by strength of arm', 'to take one in his arms'), and compounds ('an arm-full', 'an arm-pit or arm-hole'); and it is from these that Kersey has taken over his only other entry for *arm*, 'The Arm-pit, or *arm-hole*'.

The entries of a large number of common words in Kersey, such as *cuff*, *cup*, *curl*, *earth*, *last*, are simply identical to the English wording given in Littleton. With others there have been minor changes, and the following list may serve to show how the original has been adapted:

Littleton, 1678	**Kersey, 1702**
Above an hour. *Horâ amplius.*	Above, as *above an Hour.*
Arseversie. *Praeposterè, perverse, inverso ordine.*	Arse-versy, *topsy-turvy,* or *preposterously.*
To sit a brood. *Incubare ovis.*	*To sit* abrood *upon eggs, as a bird does.*
A Chuff or country clown. *Agrestis, insubidus, rusticus.*	*A* Chuff, or *Country-clown.*
Clammy or gluish. *Glutinosus, viscosus, tenax, sequax, viscidus.*	Clammy, or *gluish.*
A fleece of wool. *Vellus, êris,* neut.	*A* Fleece *of Wooll.*
To fleece one. *Spolio, deglubo, tondeo.*	*To fleece one.*
In times past. *Quondam.*	In, *as in times pass'd.*
Large, great or ample. *Largus, latus, laxus, amplus, spatiosus, diffusus.*	Large, *great* or *ample.*
To tarry, abide or remain. *Maneo, moror, commoror.*	*To* tarry, *abide*, or *remain*; *to delay,* or *linger.*
To tarry, delay or linger. *Cunctor, moras nectere.*	
Unwise. *Imprudens, insipiens, stultus, inconsultus.*	Unwise, *imprudent,* or *indiscreet.*

Here we find Kersey taking over English synonyms (as with *chuff* and *clammy*); providing synonyms which have probably been suggested by the Latin definition (see 'imprudent' for *unwise*, 'preposterously' for *arse-versy*, and 'ample' for *large*); incorporating parts of the Latin definitions (such as 'upon eggs' in the entry for *abrood*); conflating entries from his original (*to tarry*); and at times leaving phrases with no explanation at all (*to fleece one*).

Sometimes—as with *fleece*, noun and verb—Kersey has taken over the entire semantic coverage provided by Littleton. More commonly he cuts down drastically on the original: the entry for the word *in* ('In, *as in times pass'd*') is the sole survivor from 31 *in* entries in Littleton, and it stands in rather pointless solitude as the sole piece of information provided by a lexicographer claiming to deal with the ordinary words of English.

The treatment of *in* also serves to illustrate the rather baleful influence which Latin dictionaries had. The English phrase *in times pass'd* almost certainly occurs in Kersey because it corresponds to the single lexical item *quondam* in the Latin. Here it is important to remember that the English-Latin dictionary begins as a reversal and an alphabetic reordering of the Latin-English dictionary (Starnes 1954, chapter 12); '*quondam* in times past' makes a more sensible lexicographical entry than '*in times past* quondam', and the rather erratic collection of English terms resulting from this reversal process comes to look even odder when the Latin has vanished in the purely English context of Kersey's work. Thus we find 'and not' (for *neque*), 'a pair of yarn-winding blades' (corresponding to *gyrgillus* in the Latin-English dictionaries), 'great-buttock'd' (*lumbosus*), 'south-east wind' (*altanus*). No compiler, we may assume, would ever have thought of including such items if his starting-point had been English for its own sake.

The many multiple entries illustrate still better how dependence on the Latin affected the selection of English items. For the word *basket* Kersey gives the following six compounds, all without further explanation:

A Bread-basket	*A Wicker-basket*
A Hand-basket	*A Basket-hilt*
A Table-basket	*A Basket-maker.*

Definitions are of course hardly needed, and so the question arises of why such compounds should be included at all. The case of *bread-basket* is instructive. This compound is recorded in actual use by the OED only from the year 1753; but it had had a shadowy existence in the world of Latin-English dictionaries for 200 years before that as an explanation of the Latin *panariolum*. From Huloet (1552) it passed through a succession of other dictionaries into Littleton, where it appears together with three of the other five compounds for Kersey to take over.

It seems possible that Kersey also made use of other English-Latin dictionaries, particularly that of Coles. *Cock-brain'd* and *yellow-hair'd*, for instance (the latter corresponding to the Latin *rufus*), occur in Kersey and in Coles, but not in Littleton. Coles is also particularly close to Kersey in the treatment of *abed*, *churn*, *spot*, and a number of other entries, though for some of these it may have been not the Latin but the French dictionaries that he turned to.

French Sources Such is the complex pattern of interrelationships between the bilingual dictionaries of the seventeenth century that it is often hard to tell who is taking what from whom. Kersey has, for instance, this entry for the word *flirt*:

Kersey, 1702	*A* Flirt, *or* jill-flirt, *a sorry baggage.*

The five dictionaries most likely to have been drawn on by him have entries as follows:

Coles, 1678	A Flirt [Baggage] *Scortillum.*
Miège, 1679	A Flurt, *une sotte femme, qui n'a aucun esprit.*
Littleton, 1687	A Flirt, or jilly-flirt, a baggagely woman. *Scortillum.*
Miège, 1688	Flurt, or Jill-Flurt, or a Whorish Woman, *Femme debauchée.*
Boyer, 1699	Flurt, a Jilt-Flurt (or a Crack). *Une Garce, une femme de Debauche.*

While Kersey may have been modifying Littleton (or Coles) independently, it looks far more likely that one or other of the French dictionaries was involved.

Sometimes Latin sources can be ruled out, as with neologisms under the letter B such as *banter, beau, bog-house* and *buccaneer,* all of which were available in English-French dictionaries but not (so far as I can discover) in the English-Latin ones. The word *dustman* provides another convincing illustration. The earliest instance of the word recorded in the OED is in a translation dated 1707, and this is followed by a quotation from a work written by Gay in 1714: 'The dustman's cart offends thy cloaths and eyes.' Kersey, putting the word into the dictionary in 1702, may of course have picked it up from the streets. It would be nice to think that he did, to credit him with an ear-to-the-ground for English usage which might be envied by the lexicographer of today. But the sober fact is that *dustman* had already been given in Miège in 1688 and by

Boyer in 1699—'un Bouëur, Celui qui ôte les Bouës des Rues & les Ordures des Maisons'.

The two large French dictionaries of Miège and Boyer are very close to each other in many of their definitions—Boyer has leant heavily on Miège—and one cannot always be sure about which of the two Kersey has turned to. Some of the newer words, such as *banterer*, occur only in the Boyer. In other cases it is the earliest Miège dictionary of 1679 which looks closest (providing, for instance, one of the English phrases in Kersey's definition of *upbraid* as 'twit, cast in the teeth, or reproach'; Miège (1679) has 'cast in the teeth *reprocher*'); in general, however, the larger Miège dictionary of 1688 seems to have been Kersey's main French source; words such as *bib, early or betimes, han't* ('for have not'), *inch out, pert, pest, prompt* and *twain* (for which only the larger Miège gives, like Kersey, the reference to St Matthew 27.51) are all clearly taken from it.

Information provided in the French context has often lost its point in the process of transfer to English. Thus, to give *vous* (as Miège does) not only as an equivalent of *you*, but also of *to you* ('he will write to you, *il vous ecrira*') is sensible enough; but Kersey's worn-down entry 'You, *as he will write to you*' looks pretty futile. Similarly Kersey's insertion of phrases such as *this is yours* and *I am yours* is explicable only by reference to his French source, where it is necessary to show that the word *yours* in English corresponds to more than one construction in French: 'voici le vôtre' and 'je suis tout à vous'.

With French, then, as with Latin, the effect was to skew the selection of ordinary words and ordinary phrases which went into Kersey's pioneering work; and this moment of change in the course of English lexicography cannot be understood properly without recognition of the role played by foreign dictionaries.

Nor can Kersey's part in it. He was certainly right to turn to the bilingual dictionaries; it was probably the only realistic course open to him. They provided him with a convenient alphabetical array of the commonest words, so that at least none of those need be forgotten; and the French dictionaries gave him as a bonus a sprinkling of topical, recently-established words. On the other hand, the focus of a bilingual dictionary was (and remains) different, and it is fair to say that Kersey was lacking in editorial rigour: both in the choice of words and in the modes of definition, far too much of the originals was allowed to stand.

Kersey may have provided English dictionaries with the ordinary words; but it was left to his imitators and successors to evolve a satisfactory technique for dealing with them.

END NOTE

First published in English Studies *60 (1979) 555-61 with the title 'John Kersey and the ordinary words of English', and reprinted here by courtesy of Swets Publishing Service, Lisse. Further discussion of Kersey's sources is to be found in Dolezal (1986) and Landau (1986, chapter 2). Kersey's innovation was to set the pattern for later works, but as Hausmann (1990) points out, the dictionary of hard words (*schwere Wörter, des mots difficiles*) still serves a useful purpose today, in English as in other languages.*

4

Dialect Words in General Dictionaries

[1992]

What is the case for including labelled dialect words in a general monolingual dictionary? It is normal practice to do so, and has been now for over three hundred years in the English tradition. But if one takes a closer look at a few representative works, it is hard to escape the conclusion that the scattering of dialect words to be found in them has more to do with habit and sentiment than with any settled lexicographical principles. Dictionaries should of course not be over-tightly organized on linguistic principles: their task is to do what will help the user most. But even on the score of practical utility it is difficult to justify much that is done in present-day English dictionaries in the name of dialect.

Disagreement on Items for Inclusion An argument for abandoning the label 'dialect' altogether might be found in the fact that the compilers disagree so markedly about what dialect words to put in. The following table lists all the entries labelled as dialect under MA- in recent editions of three widely-known and authoritative dictionaries of English, the *Collins Dictionary of the English Language* (1986), the *Concise Oxford Dictionary of Current English* (1990) and the *Chambers English Dictionary* (1988). Chambers, published in Edinburgh, includes very large numbers of Scots items, and for the purposes of comparison these have been excluded here. National labellings such as those discussed by Read (1962) are also omitted.

The table gives a clear thumbs-down for the notion of dialect in general dictionaries: there are 17 so-called dialect items, but only one of them (mardy 'a spoilt child') is agreed upon by all three; and only three of the other words occur as dialect even in two of the dictionaries:

Collins 1986	**COD 1990**	**Chambers 1988**
		mag
		main
		malkin
mam		mam
mammock		
mangy		
		manky
mardy	mardy	mardy
		marl
marrow		marrow
mash		mash
		math
maun		
		mauther
	mavis	
		mawk
mayst		
(8)	(2)	(12)

The statistical consensus here is appallingly low, and sampling from other parts of the alphabet has produced similar results. It is clear that either the compilers must have different notions of what dialect is, or else they are at odds about the status of particular words. Either way, the usage label looks unsatisfactory. One might guess (or hope) that a greater degree of consensus would be found with other dictionary labels such as *nautical*, or *NZ*.

Incongruities of Labelling The compiler's problem is one of selection. There will always be too great a profusion of dialectal terms available to him, and from these he needs to take only those which his users are most likely to come across. How does one 'come across' dialect terms? In travelling around the country? (for that purpose they were originally included in our English dictionaries). In one's reading? In regional television programmes? There may now be many different kinds of exposure to dialect. To give just one example of how this may affect the lexicographer's choice: if the word *bobby-dazzler* 'anything outstanding, striking, or showy, esp. an attractive girl' is given as dialect in the Collins dictionary today, then I suspect (though of course such things can never be proved) that this has something to do with the fact that the word occurs in the writings of D.H.Lawrence.

It is understandable then that opinions should differ to some degree on the selection of particular dialect items. But it is not merely a matter of inclusion or non-inclusion: there are startling disagreements too on the status of words. To keep simply to the MA- words listed above, we find that *manky*, listed as dialect in Chambers, appears in Collins as slang; *mam* occurs as colloquial, not dialect in COD; and the two items *mangy* and *mavis*, elsewhere called dialect, are entered in Chambers as perfectly normal acceptable English words. The presence of such incongruities within so short a list does not inspire confidence in the usefulness of the label, or in its definability. That lexicographers have in the past themselves instinctively recognized the difficulty of isolating dialect items for entry is to be seen also from the frequency with which the term 'dialect' enters into multiple labellings. These examples are taken from the letters W and Y in the 6th edition of the COD (1976):

poet. or dial.	wain
arch. or dial.	weasand, whist, whittle
dial. or joc.	wench
coll. or dial.	wiggle, yammer
arch. or joc. or dial.	wight
arch. or poet. or dial.	yon.

Such entries can certainly be said to have considerable descriptive utility. But the use of the conjunction *or* is revealing: to say that a word is 'colloquial and dialect' is to record a sociolinguistic fact, but to class it as 'colloquial or dialect' suggests that you have not quite made up your mind which category it belongs to.

Scale of Dialect Entries Current English dictionaries also disagree wildly as to the proportion of the nomenclature which is devoted to dialect material. The three works referred to above are of roughly comparable size, and their readership is probably very similar. But under MA- Collins has four times the number given in COD. At the very least, editorial policy must

BOR

a bull's-head.
Bonaventure, a famous Franciſcan Fryer.
Bone-breaker, an Eagle.
Bon Crêtien, f. good Chriſtian, a large French pear.
Bondy, Y. Simpleton.
Bonwell, a Well in Herefordſhire, full of little bones.
Bongrace f. good grace; alſo a kind of half bonnet to keep the Sun from the Forehead.
Bon hommes, f. good Men, viz. an order of Fryars.
Boniface, f. well-doer.
Bonifate, having good luck.
Bonjour, f. good morrow.
Bonis non amovendis, a writ ſtopping the removal of Goods.
Bonito, a leaping fiſh.
Bonium, Bangor-Monaſtery.
Bonne mine, f. a good aſpect, or Countenance.
Bonnet, a ſhort ſail to be joined to another ſail.
Boodeth, o. ſheweth.
Bolie, o. beloved.
Boom, a pole to ſpread the clew of the Sail further out.
Booming, with all ſails out.
Boon, o. a requeſt.
Boot, Cu. parlour or bed-chamber.
Boot, Bote, Sa. recompence; alſo help, advantage.
Boot of Bale, c. eaſe of Sorrows.
Booting-corn, certain rent corn.
Boothaling, No. ſtealing.
Booting, Sc. a puniſhment by pegging on an iron boot.
Boſtack, with one ſtone.
Boſtal, Sſ. a way up a hill.
Boötes, as Arctophylax.
Boöz, Boas, h. in ſtrength.
Booz, c. drink.

BOT

made of childrens Urine.
Borbonia, a French Dukedom.
Bord, c. a ſhilling.
Bordarii, Borduanni, Bores, Husbandmen, Cottagers.
Bordel, I. brothel-houſe.
Bordagium, the ſame as
Bordland, kept in the hand of Lords for maintenance of their bord.
Bordeu, a circumference drawn about the Arms
Boreal, an, belonging to
Boreas, g. North wind.
Borith, an herb uſed by fullers.
Born, c. burniſh.
Boreel h. head green; alſo rude, plain.
Borrow, o. pledge of ſurety.
Boryſthenes, a Scythian River.
Boſcage, a place full of Trees, alſo the maſt of Trees.
Boſcaria, wood-houſes, or Ox-houſes.
Boſcus, Bois, f. Wood.
Boſinuus, a rude wind Inſtrument.
Boſcobel, f. Fair Wood.
Boſenham, Boſcham, a town in Suſſex.
Boſphorus, the name of two ſeas over which Jupiter like a bull carried Europa.
Borachide, a place in Arcadia.
Botachus, Lycurgus's Nephew.
Botanical, g. belonging to herbs.
Botanomancy, g. herb divining.
Botargo, a kind of Sauſſage.
Bote, o. bitt.
Bothna, Buthna, Sc. a Park.
Botha, o. booth.
Botiler, f. Butler.

FIG. 2. *Bondy*, *Boon* and *Booz*: labelled dialect words, archaisms and canting terms in Elisha Coles, *An English Dictionarie* (1713 edn).

be an issue here. How important a component should dialect be in a general dictionary? Answers will depend upon public perception of dialect, and will certainly vary from language to language. In the first general English dictionary to give dialect words (Coles 1676) they are generally designated by county names (*Y[orkshire], Cu[mberland, Sf [=Suffolk]*, etc., see Figure 2), though there are also more general labels such as *No[rth-Country]* and *Sc[otch]*. Dialect words take up 3.25% of the entire vocabulary: an astonishing total which we should hardly tolerate today. In the standard concise dictionary of the eighteenth century (Bailey 1721) the figure is already down to a more manageable 1.11% (statistics based on the 17th edition, 1757). Then, Dr Johnson in his Dictionary (1755) cuts out dialect almost altogether, including only four 'native dialecticisms' in the whole work (Allen 1940, 215). His view on the subject can be characterized by the comment on *slippy* (meaning 'slippery') which he calls 'a barbarous provincial word'. Dr Johnson's attitude is understandable, since his Dictionary has a literary focus, and for literary purposes, dialect simply did not matter. In England then, as now, there is simply no dialect literature of any consequence. Note that here, once again, I am declining to talk about Scots. There are also other languages (for instance Dutch and Flemish) where distinctive literary traditions survive, so that the modern lexicographer may well need to devote considerable space and accord high status to regional variants. Not so with English, and indeed the retention of dialect at all in our general dictionaries after Johnson may seem surprising. Doubtless it owes much to the romanticization of folk-speech in the late nineteenth and the early twentieth century, and to the sense of historical continuity which dialect survivals can provide (Wakelin 1987, 168-72).

A survey of some 2000 lemmata in Collins (1986) under the letters E, M, P and S gave a scale of entry (0.56%) almost exactly half of that in Bailey (1721). The corresponding figures for the same sections in the alphabet in COD (1990) and Chambers (1988) were however 0.17% and 2.41%. The count was made by lemmata (including all those where any distinctive dialect meaning was listed) and this may have flattered the figure for Chambers with its heavily nested structure. But our lexicographers today clearly disagree on scale, even if not quite by a factor of 14. Such disagreements may not be new, but the need for reasoned and explicit lexicographical planning decisions in the matter of dialect is none the less clear. I confine myself here to monolingual dictionaries, but the same will be true *a fortiori* of bilingual works (Grindsted 1988).

Diatopic Specification In the above, 'dialect' has been used as a blanket term in reference to all dictionary items accorded a diatopically restrictive label (other than a national one). It is however worth looking in more detail at the various labelling conventions adopted by modern dictionaries.

COD (1990) is the most straightforward: the general label is simply 'dial.' without any explanation of what the term means, though occasionally, as with *beck* '*N.Engl*. a brook; a mountain stream', a region will be indicated. Chambers (1988) also mainly uses 'dial.', but specifies more often and more narrowly (*sprack* '(*W.Midland* and *S.W.*) *adj*. vigorous, sprightly, alert'), and also sometimes rather unaccountably opts for the term 'local', as with the word *peal* 'a grilse: a young sea-trout'. Collins (1986) is at the other extreme, with many very detailed localizations, such as *Liverpool dialect* ('our kid') *Northeastern English dialect, chiefly Durham* ('marrow'), and *Edinburgh and Northumbrian dialect* ('deek'). Inclusion of urban dialects fits in with current sociolinguistic fashions, though it entails an extension of function for what is already an overworked lexicographical label. Within the French tradition such urban items would I suspect be labelled not as dialect but as *pop*. ('populaire'). The use of this style label in French dictionaries alongside others such as *familier*, *vulgaire* and *argotique* has recently been carefully analysed by Lodge (1989). The explanation of *populaire* in *Le Petit Robert* (1986, xvii) is as follows: '*populaire*: c'est-à-dire courant dans les milieux populaires des villes, mais réprouvé ou évité par l'ensemble de la bourgeoisie cultivée'. This is specifically urban, and would fit *our kid* very well indeed.

The compilers of the Collins dictionary deserve credit for explaining their practice; regional dialects, they say 'have been specified as precisely as possible, even at the risk of overrestriction, in order to give the reader an indication of the appropriate regional flavour' (Collins 1986, xii). This impressionistic approach ('regional flavour') is refreshing, and such entries are, one imagines, based on real observation. But the reader is not always much helped. When we are told, for instance, that the imperative of *deek* (*deek that* = 'look at that!') is used in Edinburgh and in Northumbria we may well wonder about Berwick, Roxburgh, Selkirk and the whole area in between. The word is probably, or presumably, used there, but we just don't know, or at any rate we are not told. One might argue that a more general label is to be preferred in such cases.

The traditional identity-tag in English dictionaries has since Coles's time in the seventeenth century always been the county name, and this certainly corresponds to popular perceptions of dialect today. But unfortunately, county boundaries will not often correspond with the boundaries of linguistic features. Seeing this, some early compilers of general dictionaries adopted a coarser grid without county names after the fashion of John Ray in his dialect dictionary of 1674. Bailey (1721) provides a good example: he divides up his regionalisms into a mere four categories, *North Country*, *South Country, East Country* and *West Country* (with the north taking the lion's share, as always in English dialect), allowing for a very large ragbag called *Country Words* as well. It is then not altogether surprising that in our dictionaries today, one compiler will put down a county label and hope for the best, but another will play safe, say simply 'dialect' and leave everything to the reader's imagination. 'Dialect' has thus become within the English tradition a universal label for all regionalisms, a blanket term covering diatopic complexity, or geographic imprecision.

English lexicographers may in this be seen to operate with an unrefined terminology, and again it is instructive to compare their techniques with those adopted by compilers of dictionaries for other languages. In the large German Duden dictionary, for instance, very clear terminological distinctions are offered. Some items are given a stated location: *nordd.*, *Schweiz*, etc. ('Ist die Zuordnung zu einem bestimmten Sprachgebiet gesichert, so wird dieses genannt'). Others are designated by the label *regional* ('Erstreckt sich ihre Verbreitung über ein grösseres Gebiet, fehlt ein übergreifender hochsprachlicher Ausdruck, werden sie mit "regional" gekennzeichnet'). And then there is a third category, *landschaftlich*, for the ones which cannot be pinned down to a particular area ('Lässt sich das Sprachgebiet nicht genau abgrenzen, so steht der Hinweis "landsch."). The threefold classification given here (Duden 1977, 15-16) might perhaps not be entirely appropriate to the English linguistic scene, but one notices that one of the terms, 'regional', has been adopted by the American Webster dictionaries. There, *regional* is used for items common to specified areas, leaving *dialect* for 'a regional patterning too complex for summary labelling because it includes several regional varieties'. On this, and for a discussion of related German terms (including *mundartlich*, which Duden does not use), see Niebaum (1989).

The Need for Research on Common Dialect Terms Does it make sense to call a word 'dialect' (as our dictionaries do) when we cannot say what region it belongs to? Scholarly research on dialect is concerned with the regionally distinctive. It focuses on unusual items and, for the dialect lexicographer at least, one might say, the more unusual and the more tightly localized the better. But this is not going to be of much help to the general lexicographer: he needs to know about the commonest dialect words, and it seems to me that the basic research on these has never been done. The word *mizzle*, for instance, meaning 'drizzle', is both widely known and is felt to be dialect; but we don't know anything about its distribution—there are simply no reference books to tell us. How many English people know that *bait* means 'food', and how many would use it? Do the bulk of educated English speakers think of *lass* as a northernism, or merely as a more homely and affectionate term for 'girl'? More accurate scholarly information on the active and passive currency of such words is needed as a basis for any satisfactory treatment of dialect in general dictionaries.

The distance between traditional dialect research and what the lexicographer needs arises also from the fact that it is the language of the less educated which yields the readiest and richest harvest for the dialectologist. In the *Longman Dictionary of the English Language* (1984) there is a revealing explanation of how dialect is regarded by the editors. The label *dial.* for 'dialect', they say, 'indicates that a word or meaning belongs to the common local speech of several different places' (Longman 1984, xx). How common is common? The example given, 'critter ... *n, dial* a creature' is a word which many or perhaps most speakers of educated English would classify as sub-standard rather than regional. Other so-called dialect items such as *sodger*, *varmint* or *worrit* will carry similar implications. Thus the general label 'dialect' in our dictionaries today is often as much a social/educational discriminator as a vague indicator of regional use. To refer once again to French practice. The relevant label used in the Robert dictionaries is explained as follows: '*dialectal*: mot ou emploi provenant d'un dialecte, d'un patois, et qui n'est pas employé comme un mot français normal' (Robert 1986, xxiv). It is the inclusion of the term 'patois' which is most striking here. *Patois* is defined in the dictionary itself as being a local dialect spoken by a population 'peu nombreuse, souvent rurale et dont la culture, le niveau de civilisation sont jugés comme inférieurs à ceux du milieu environnant (qui emploie la langue commune)'. The American linguist Allen Walker Read (Read 1962, 224) was shocked to find that Martinet proposed to use *patois* 'with its built-in prejudice' as a regular linguistic term. Prejudice or not, the Robert definition does at least openly acknowledge a common perception of dialect ('niveau de civilisation jugé comme inférieur') which is suppressed elsewhere. Certainly English compilers would never be caught saying this kind of thing, but similar judgements to those of the Robert dictionaries must surely underlie their dialect selections. Research of the kind I am indicating on the current distribution of the commoner dialectal words could, if carefully structured, yield valuable results for sociolinguists as well as for compilers of general dictionaries.

A Typology of Dialect Entries Dialect information given to the user of the general dictionary has in English at least always been extremely varied in character, from words of very general meaning such as *pend* 'to hang', to highly specific items such as *Easter-ledge pudding* 'a pudding made from the young leaves of the bistort'. When it comes down to offering the user a recipe for a pudding, the question must surely be raised of what types of dialect words are most needed. As we have seen, compilers differ wildly in their selection of words for inclusion. But certain characteristic groupings can be discerned among dialect entries, and the following list of some of the main types may shed light on the often conflicting motives which have led to selection:

a. **General terms.** *Aye* 'yes', *champion* 'excellent', *mickle* 'much', *owt* 'anything', *nowt* 'nothing'. Entries for dialectal terms such as these can be justified by the very high frequency within the area where they occur, and often by widespread use.

b. **Dialectal synonyms for familiar objects, common verbs.** This is perhaps the commonest type of dialectal entry in general dictionaries. Examples are *bairn* 'child', *clout* 'rag', *dinge* 'to dent', *fadge* 'to succeed', *ken* 'to know', *kist* 'chest', *laik* 'to play', *redd* 'to tidy up'.

c. **Abstract terms with no precise semantic equivalent in the standard language.** The adjective *mim* is given in Collins as 'prim, modest, or demure', and the entry is of a type especially valuable because of its decoding function: the non-dialect speaker will very often not be able to derive the meaning from the context in which this type of word occurs. Similar items (also from Collins) are *jannock* 'honestly, truly, genuinely', *pawky* 'having or characterized by a dry wit' and *peart* 'lively, spirited, brisk' (where, for the non-dialect speaker, association with *pert* may be misleading rather than helpful).

d. **Dialect survivals.** *Pend*, referred to above, was generally current in Shakespeare's time, and English compilers often seem to favour the inclusion of words surviving (or just surviving) in dialect use, but which are of historical interest. Other examples are *make* 'mate', and *makeless* 'matchless'. Chambers give the aphetic *sponsible* (for 'responsible') as 'now dial.', and Collins record *hadst* and *mayst* as being dialectal as well as archaic.

e. **Dialect pronunciations.** In Collins there is an entry for *yawl* '*Brit. dialect.* to howl, weep, or scream harshly; yowl'. It is thus a mere phonetic variant of the well-established *yowl*, and may seem surprising, since no compiler can presume to cope with the multifarious ways in which words are pronounced locally. Such regional renderings should be of concern to the general lexicographer only where a conventionalized spelling exists (Tennyson uses *yawl*). Collins also enter *dee* and *faither*, Scots variants of 'die' and 'father'.

f. **Local products and artefacts.** *Nog* or *nogg* '*East Anglian dialect.* strong local beer', and *coble* '*Scot. and northern English.* a small single-masted flat-bottomed fishing boat' (in Collins) are distinctive local products with distinctive local names: if you are going to talk about a coble you cannot properly call it anything else. General dictionaries tend to contain (or retain) considerable numbers of such local technical terms. It is no accident that Ray (1674; 2nd edn 1691)—the first English dialect dictionary proper—contains a postscript on various local trades such as tin smelting in Cornwall and the making of salt in Lancashire.

g. **Flora and fauna.** *Spod* is a northern word for a second-year salmon, and *jibbons* a southwest British dialect word for spring onions. Items such as these (from Chambers and Collins respectively) form an appreciable part of the dialectal take-up in general dictionaries of English. Other examples are: *bagy* 'turnip', *mawk* 'maggot', *spinning-jenny* 'crane-fly'. Such items represent only a tiny fraction of the countless local terms which occur. It is a class of words which I believe to be over-represented in our general dictionaries, and here again it is worth noting that Ray (1674) incorporated long lists of birds and fishes.

h. **Geographical features.** *Brow* 'steep slope of a road', *fleet* 'creek', *hag* 'firm spot in a bog', *knap* 'crest of a hill' and *tump* 'a small mound' are examples of entries giving local names for geographical features, many of which will also occur as place-name elements. With some of the better-known ones (*coomb*, *dale*, *glen*, *mull*, *tor*) it is doubtful whether they should be classified as dialect or not, though popular associations will be with particular parts of the country.

j. **Rural items.** Dialect has traditionally been associated with the countryside, and dialect entries generally seem to favour rural and especially agricultural life: *jag* 'a small load of hay', *math* 'a mowing', *midden* 'dunghill', *spuddle* 'dig lightly', *windlestraw* 'dried grasses'. These are 'Country Words' of the type which Bailey was giving us 250 years ago, and our dictionaries have not shaken them off yet.

The above list of nine characteristic types of English dialect entries could of course easily be extended. But even as it stands it may serve to show that in his build-up of a dialectal nomenclature for a general dictionary of English, the compiler is confronted by complex and often conflicting choices. It is not only a matter of what their number should be, and of what battery of labels will serve best (dialect?, regional?, local?, all three?) and how these are defined. There are also workface problems such as the privileging of plant names, sentiment about 'old' dialect words, whether to touch at all on pronunciation, whether dialect words without a synonym in the standard language have for that reason a stronger (or maybe less strong) claim for inclusion. Such matters are all of consequence to the user. They are never (so far as I have observed) touched on in the front matter, and perhaps do not need to be. But defining one's attitude towards them must surely be an essential part of dictionary planning in the future, if we are to have general dictionaries of English which agree better with each other on what dialect is, and on what dialect words can most usefully be put in.

END NOTE

The above study was originally delivered as a paper in 1992, and appeared in K. Hyldgaard-Jensen and V.H. Pedersen (eds) Proceedings of the Sixth International Symposium on Lexicography May 7-9, 1992 at the University of Copenhagen *1994, 103-14. It is here reprinted by kind permission of the publishers Max Niemeyer Verlag, Tübingen.*

5

Old Words: Defining Obsolescence

[1978]

Every educated speaker of English—and probably most uneducated speakers too—will know or use certain words with an awareness of their being 'old'. Thus, *maiden*, *damsel*, *maid*, *may* and *wench* all can mean, in modern English, 'young woman'; all will be felt, however, to be words of the past. But the associations of 'pastness' of, say, *damsel* and *wench* are very different: one makes you think of the Bible, the other of Falstaff and his companions at the Boar's Head. What does one then do as a compiler or reviser of a bilingual dictionary to provide equivalents for these words (or even an elucidation of them) in a target language which has no Falstaff in its literature, and of which the accepted Bible translation is very much later than 1611?

Man's awareness of the past clearly differs from one culture to another, and with that will go different feelings about obsolete elements in speech. I do not know whether any language has ever been recorded in which the notion of 'old' words simply does not exist; maybe the linguistic anthropologists could tell us some time. In any case the modes of apprehending archaic elements in different languages would form an interesting subject for sociolinguistic investigation. I am here however not primarily concerned with such theoretical considerations, but with the practical problems of obsolescence which confront the lexicographer on the job.

Old words have been marked in English dictionaries since the seventeenth century (see for instance *boodeth*, *boon* in Figure 2, chapter 4 above) and the normal way of dealing with them is of course to provide usage labels such as *archaic* or *obsolete*. The function of usage labels in any dictionary—and this includes labels of all kinds, *dialect*, *technical*, *jocular*, *heraldry*, *slang* and so on—is to enable the compiler to go a bit further than he would otherwise dare; or, to put it another way, they mean the user can be helped with the fringe vocabulary; and to put it yet another way, they mean that a dictionary can be fuzzy at the edges, and yet still retain a certain degree of linguistic respectability.

The number, and kind, of usage labels you adopt will of course depend upon the public you have in mind. An elementary pocket dictionary covering merely a basic vocabulary can very well do entirely without them. In what follows I draw on experience as an editor of *Ten Bruggencate's Engels Woordenboek (1974, 1978)*, a standard bilingual reference dictionary for English and Dutch with a coverage of the two languages roughly comparable to that of the COD; aimed, then, at an educated readership, and published in a country where English is not only the first foreign language but is also a common medium of scholarly publication: where any educated man or woman may be expected to read English books and documents regularly.

Such a dictionary may be expected to cover the ordinary reading, in both languages, of the educated user: newspapers, current books on social topics, history, politics—that kind of thing. Also, clearly, the normal usage of novelists such as Amis, Orwell or Lawrence. But then what about Trollope? *The Pallisers* was bought up and shown on Dutch television, and cheap paperback copies of this and others of the novels abounded on the railway bookstalls, from which I conclude that they were also read. The question then arises of whether or not Trollope should be counted in on the recognition vocabulary of the informed Dutch reader (or, indeed, of the informed English reader).

Should such a recognition vocabulary be taken even further than Trollope? My personal view is that if, for example, you find Thackeray using *hanker* in the sense of *loiter*, then as a synchronic lexicographer you can ignore that, since we should with reason expect a modern editor to provide a gloss; just as we should *a fortiori* expect a gloss to be provided for Milton or Shakespeare, or still more for Chaucer. The verbal catchment area of a dictionary of the kind I have to do with may then be defined as 'the educated user's non-specialist reading in unannotated texts'. The present study is concerned with such obsolescent terms as occur within that catchment area.

This definition would I think work as well for a monolingual dictionary as for a bilingual one. The difference when it comes to obsolescence is that in a bilingual one you need to be more careful and more explicit. Your readers have not grown up with English: they have received English at some time in their puberty as a kind of cultural package, and have taken it on from there. Though they may in time become very competent in English as a second language, they will have no automatic built-in awareness of the associations of words. They may not know a wench from a damsel, and there is a danger in that. You can afford to put in a word such as *blade* into a monolingual dictionary and simply tell the world that it means 'jovial, dashing, gay, etc., fellow' (COD 1976); but the foreign user looking for an explanation of the word in a bilingual dictionary may not know of the eighteenth-century associations of the word. Nor will an English user know—unless you tell him—whether or not the foreign synonym you provide shares those associations. Yet each of them has the right to be told, or to be warned.

I see then three reasons why it is not enough merely to follow blindly the labelling for obsolescence of the COD or of any other monolingual dictionary: (i) any user needs more help in the target language; (ii) labelling conventions are culturally bound (and I believe many of them to be unsatisfactory for obsolescent words); (iii) the basic principle of usage labelling is in any case different in bilingual from that in monolingual dictionaries. This last matter may be illustrated with an example from the sphere of slang, not obsolescence (the same principles apply). If you enter the English word *blotto* in an English-English dictionary you will not in general define it as 'tipsy', or 'sozzled' or 'half-seas over', or by any other slang term; you will define it as 'very drunk'. But if I were to put it into an English-Dutch dictionary I should look for an equally slangy Dutch term (needless to say, there are some). That is, whereas in the monolingual dictionary one will define marked by unmarked terms, in the bilingual dictionary one strives for stylistic equivalents. And this has important consequences for the technique of labelling.

If we accept as a lexicographical principle that a bilingual dictionary will under all circumstances aim at giving exact stylistic equivalents, one interesting conclusion is that in the hypothetical case of L1 having exactly corresponding counterparts in L2 for the whole lexicon, no labelling would be needed anywhere at all in the dictionary. Some foreign-language dictionaries do indeed make incidental use of this advantage. Thus the English *prithee* may be given as *eilieve* in English-Dutch, and *eilieve* as *prithee* in Dutch-English without a label for either entry, since each of the terms is archaic in a similar way and to a similar extent.

Problems arise since there is of course no such one-to-one match in the patterns of archaism. Thus, English has a poetic archaism *helm* for the notion 'helmet'. Dutch has no such archaic term, and the Dutch word *helm* is the regular unmarked term for protective headgear. Thus, in an entry such as (1) the label refers only to the English word preceding it, not to what follows:

(1) **helm** (*poet. arch.*) helm
(2) **lea** (*poet. arch.*) landouw.

But where there is a similarly archaic term in Dutch, as in (2), the label looks both back and forward; it refers to the whole entry.

How is the dictionary user to know in which of the two ways the label is meant to operate? In this particular case, the Dutch speaker will have no problem: he is assumed to be familiar with the verbal associations of his own language; but the English speaker will be left guessing. This kind of sloppy, illogical use of labels is very common in bilingual dictionaries; and it relates of course to the tacit assumptions which have been made about readership. In the end, the only tight and orderly solution is to have double labelling; that is, both of the word which is entered and of its equivalent in the other language. But many publishers will not take kindly to that.

It is however with the terminology that the greatest problem arises in dealing with obsolescent words. The labels *obs.*, *arch.*, *lit.*, *rhet.*, *poet.*, and *hist.* are scattered around in different ways by different compilers, and it really is rather hard at times to know what to do with them. For instance, you will find that the word *eventide* is classified as archaic in COD (1976) but as poetic in OALD (1974); as against the word *even* (in the same sense), which is said to be poetic in both of them; and the word *eve*, which COD gives as poetic and Chambers (1972) as obsolete. Something needs to be done about terminology here. The very term 'poetic', used so commonly for words such as *frore* (meaning 'frozen'), seems to me to be something of a curiosity. It works all right if you are willing to say that English poetry stops with Tennyson; and there are of course some people who in their heart of hearts still believe that. But it is at least open to question whether usage labelling should have to depend upon such literary perceptions. And we must bear in mind that if a corresponding label 'poetic' is applied to foreign-language items it is almost sure to mean something very different, since the history of poetic diction in that language will be other than the history of English poetic diction.

The term 'lit.' is open to similar objections. The word *dwell*, we are told, is 'literary'. You may have a friend who lives in Exeter. Does this mean that if you write his biography or put him into a novel he will dwell in Exeter? I don't believe it. The fact is that 'lit.' refers to 'older literature', just as 'poet.' refers to 'older poetry'.

With 'hist.' we are confronted by a different problem. I find it odd that the label 'hist.' should be attached not only to such thoroughly medieval words as *villein*, *scutage* or *pardoner*, but also to *elementary school*, *panel patient* and *College of Advanced Technology* and its abbreviation *CAT*. Here the term 'historical' seems to be used in two different ways. It is not hard to see how this has come about, for all of these terms are no longer applied to existing institutions, professions, etc. But there is still a distinction to be made. The system of *scutage* ('commutation of feudal service by paying tax') simply belongs to the past, and you cannot call it anything else. But *elementary schools* do still exist, even though we now refer to them as *primary schools*; it is the name, not the institution, which is discontinued. And under the NHS we are all panel patients now. To lump all these together as 'hist.' really will not do.

In view of this rather alarming disarray in terminology, and bearing in mind the special needs of the foreign dictionary user, it seemed worthwhile to set out the components of obsolescence, of the notions of 'pastness' in language, in a grid to see if a set of mutually exclusive categories could be established. The results are shown in the table below. In this scheme the term 'obsolete' is reserved for words which are gone for ever, which have passed out of the language, such as the Chaucerian *hoker* meaning 'disdain'; column A is the only one with a minus in the first row. Words obsolete in this sense will be excluded from any but the strictly historical dictionary.

In the second row of the diagram columns B and C have pluses, but these two categories are distinguished later in rows 4 and 7. This is the difference between a groat and a shilling: we still (1978) have shillings, though we call them 5p pieces. But groats exist only in museums, they are real history, and the label 'discontinued term' is proposed to distinguish items in category C.

Column D, 'obsolescent terms' represents what is clearly a very useful category for the bilingual dictionary (though of course there may not be full agreement about what items it should contain). 'Scavenger' in the sense of

	A	B	C	D	E	F	G	H
1 known to educated speakers	-	+	+	+	+	+	+	+
2 period reference only	-	+	+	-	-	-	-	-
3 frequent jocular use	-	-	-	-	-	-	-	+
4 exists alongside modern equivalent	-	-	+	+	+	+	+	+
5 associated with older poetry	-	-	-	-	-	+	-	-
6 associated with the past	-	+	+	-	+	+	+	+
7 replaced as unmarked term	+	-	+	-	+	+	+	+
8 modern elevated use	-	-	-	-	-	+	+	-

A: *obsolete terms* hoker
B: *historical terms* villein, scutage, hulks
C: *discontinued terms* elementary school, shilling
D: *obsolescent terms* scavenger, wireless
E: *archaisms* aviator, bottle-holder
F: *poetic archaisms* welkin, glister, lea
G: *formal archaisms* hest, enterprise (*vb*), mien
H: *jocular archaisms* wench, trencherman

'dustbin man', 'refuse collector', will serve as a type example. I do remember hearing the word being used in that sense when I was a child. It is possible that in some English towns they may have a *Municipal Scavenging Department* and that the refuse collectors are still called scavengers there. I think it is unlikely, but it is possible. What you can predict safely is that the word is on its way out. Just as—to give a less extreme example—*wireless* is being replaced by *radio*, or *PT* (= physical training) by *PE* (= physical education). The plus in the fourth row is the important one here, and of course the absence of any pluses for the rows below that.

Categories E, F, G and H—the archaisms proper—all have pluses in the fourth and seventh rows (that is, they exist alongside a modern equivalent but have been replaced as the unmarked terms). That is what archaism is about. Contrast category D with its minus in row 7: *scavenger* in the sense of 'refuse collector' has perhaps not yet been totally replaced, and furthermore if it is used it will be used as an unmarked term: *scavengers* are not romantic.

The emotive associations of archaisms are dealt with in rows 3, 5 and 8. Category E may seem surprising because of the fairly narrow definition adopted for archaism *sec.* Consider the type-example *aviator*: I do not think you can call a man an aviator nowadays, or rather, if you do, it will probably go with the adjective *intrepid* and you will think of him as wearing goggles and a leather helmet as he loops the loop in his flying machine. There are associations with the past, then, but the term is not 'poetic', not 'elevated', and not quite 'jocular'.

In all this, obsolescent phrases would have posed even greater problems than obsolescent words, a point perhaps best illustrated from category D. When D gets a plus in row 7, the word goes out of the dictionary. For simplex lexical items inclusion in the current edition of the COD (1976) may serve as a convenient basis for decisions at this point; thus, though we may have doubts, we may take their word for it that *progressionist* is still used for *progressive* (noun) in the political sense, or that *C3* is a current term meaning 'unfit, worthless'. But what is to be our guide with phrases such as *be free of the gate* or *it shall go hard but ...* ? If we suspect (as we very well may) that these phrases are no longer used, how is the matter to be checked? If they are not in COD and dictionaries of comparable size, this may be because they are felt by the editors not to be current, but it may also be because in a one-language dictionary of that size one does not pretend to cover as great a range of idiomatic phrases as a bilingual dictionary needs to do. We are then driven back to checking in *OED* and its *Supplements*. But, alas, those supplements do not consistently set about indicating later obsolescence (nor the continued existence) of every phrase or construction originally recorded in the main dictionary. The history of English phraseology is in fact far less well documented than the history of the English lexicon. And the practising bilingual lexicographer, while making thankful use of these magnificent reference works, will for obsolescent phrases all too often be driven back upon his own awareness of the languages he presumes to describe.

END NOTE

Based on a lecture given at the 1978 BAAL seminar in Exeter, and published in Hartmann 1979, 120-26 with the title 'Some problems of obsolescence in bilingual dictionaries'. Reference throughout is to the 6th edition (1976) of the Concise Oxford Dictionary, *and readers may note that the definitions and labelling of archaic material there has been substantially altered in more recent editions. The process of conflating the original OED and its supplements into the second edition of the* Oxford English Dictionary *(1989) has however left the treatment of obsolescence in a highly unsatisfactory state (Osselton 1993). For a general discussion of diachronic labelling in monolingual dictionaries see Schmidt (1989), who makes use of the term* Paläologismen *alongside* Neologismen, *and devotes much attention to the range of terms traditionally used in referring to 'old words' (e.g.* vieilli, anciennement, classique, autrefois, historique*). The functions of usage labels in bilingual dictionaries are examined by Werner (1991). Algeo (1993) discusses desuetude among new English words, and provides a useful analysis of the types of words which do not survive.*

6

Literary Words: Blount's *Glossographia* and Sir Thomas Browne

[1980]

'If vision ... be abolished, it is called *Caecitas* or blindness; if depraved, and receive its objects erroneously, Hallucination.' This piece of information in Thomas Blount's mid-seventeenth century dictionary neatly explains the physiology of hallucination ('a blindness of mind') as it was then understood, and it provides a note on synonymity which is in the best tradition of later American (if not British) lexicography. But Blount has taken over the words literally from Sir Thomas Browne's *Pseudodoxia Epidemica,* or *Vulgar Errors* (1646), and they provide a nice illustration of the special place which literary sources have had in the past (and may still have today) in the making of dictionaries.

To take another, less familiar, term from the same semantic area, Blount also includes in his dictionary an entry for *cecucienty*. This runs as follows:

> *Cecucienty* (from *caecutio*) a waxing blind, dimness of sight, purblindness, half-blindness. *Br.*

If we turn to our 'Br.' we again find a passage supporting the information given by the lexicographer. Chapter 18 in Book III of the *Pseudodoxia Epidemica* is devoted to the subject of moles, which were (and are) popularly thought to be blind. Browne points out here that moles certainly have eyes, and that it would thus not be 'incongruous unto reason' to infer that Nature intended them to see. However, the physical form of their eyes is imperfect, and so their vision is too: 'So that they are not blind, nor yet distinctly see; there is in them no Cecity, yet more then a Cecucienty, they have sight enough to descern the light, though not perhaps to distinguish of objects or colours' (Browne 1646, 220).

Both *cecucienty* and *hallucination* were (if we accept the evidence of the OED) Brownean innovations: nobody had ever used the words in English before he chose to put them in his book. We may therefore at least give Blount credit for being up to date when he inserted them in his *Glossographia*, published only ten years later in 1656. But the two words differ greatly in their later history. *Hallucination* was to survive in regular use right down to our own age, when we even have hallucinogens to stimulate the phenomenon. But the word *cecucienty* never caught on; Dr Johnson included it (with the single quotation from Browne) and it lingered in dictionaries till some time in the nineteenth century; but, so far as I can tell, Browne is the only man who has ever really used it.

How was the lexicographer Thomas Blount to know this? How can any lexicographer, even today, know that he is putting his money on the new literary words that are going to stay the course? Are quotations and attributions sometimes to be looked upon as a kind of apology for including the more doubtful runners? Clearly Blount felt it that way. He says in his preface that he has added authors' names to many entries 'that I might not be thought to be the innovator of them', and insists that he does not wish people to assume he is advocating the use of such words: 'let every ones *Genius* and the quality of the Subject they treat be their own Dictator' (*To the Reader*, sig. A4v).

There is plenty of evidence in the *Glossographia* to show that Blount was being very selective in the use of such attributions. Out of a random sample of 100 words under the letters B, C, D, I/J, L and S, all supported by reference to Sir Thomas Browne, 57 seem (like *hallucination*) not to have been used by any writer before him; and of these 57, there are 19 which (like *cecucienty*) have never been used by any writer since. The former category includes some very familiar terms such as *cylindrical*, *ignitible*, *incubation*, *locomotion* and *syndrome;* among the stillborn words are *to celestify, detenebrate, incommiscibility, latirostrous* and *semicastration.*

We may well wonder what Blount's mode of working can have been, and why it is that nearly all the words from Browne have been taken from the *Vulgar Errors* rather than from the better known *Religio Medici* (though there is the occasional entry from there). The older view of Blount's procedures was that, like so many early monolingual lexicographers, he simply anglicized words wholesale from the Latin-English dictionaries of his time, merely adding incidental references to such authors as might occur to him (Starnes and Noyes 1946, 43). This opinion has recently been discredited (Bongaerts 1978, 27), and indeed if we take the twelve words referred to above we find that only four have any corresponding entry in Blount's acknowledged Latin-English source-books: *hallucinatio*, *cylindraceus* and *incubatio* occur in Thomas Thomas (1631), and Rider (1633) has these three as well as *syndrome*. There seems little reason to doubt the sincerity of the remark in Blount's preface that the dictionary had 'taken up the Vacancy of above Twenty years'. This 'vacancy' certainly included the reading of Browne and other authors with an eye very attentive to linguistic detail.

At times virtually the whole entry is lifted from the Browne:

Browne, 1646

In Jew's ears something is conceived extraordinary from the name, which is in propriety but *fungus sambucinus*, or an excrescence about the Roots of Elder, and concerneth not the Nation of the Jews, but Judas Iscariot, upon a conceit, he hanged on this tree

Blount, 1656

Iews-eares. An Excrescence about the root of Elder, and concerns not the Nation of the Jews, as some imagine. *Br.*

In other cases the reader is simply referred to Browne for such additional encyclopaedic information. There is a full entry for the word *crystal*, for instance, and at the end of it Blount adds 'See more of the nature and properties of it in Dr Brown's Vulgar Errors. 1.2 cap.1'—this is a long chapter, which is indeed devoted entirely to the subject. Other similar references are to be found, for instance, at *locust* and *lodestone* (see Figure 3), *coral*, *dogdays* and *salamander*.

Blount sometimes makes it clear that he knows Browne's usage is idiosyncratic: 'Doctor Brown in his *Vulgar Errors*, cals Lobsters, Shrimps, crevises, *&c*, *Crustaceous animals*'; of *septuary* he says 'Dr *Br*. uses it for a week, consisting of seven days'; and *retromingents* 'is used by Dr. Brown, for such animals, as Urine or Piss backwards; such are all Femal *quadrupeds*. The same Author uses *Retromingency*, for a

LO LO 385

Local (*localis*) pertaining to a place. It ſignifies in Law, as much as tied or annexed to a place certain. Example, the thing is *local* and annexed to the freehold. *Kitch. fol* 180.

Locality (*localitas*) the being of a thing in a place.

Location (*locatio*) a placing or ſetting in a place; Alſo a letting out to hire, or ſetting out work by the great.

Loche. See *Lohoc*.

Lococeſſion (from *locus* and *cedo*) a giving place.

Locomotion (*locus* and *motio*) a moving or ſtirring from one place to another. Dr. *Br.*

Loculament (*loculamentum*) a little place of boards made with holes for Pigeons or Conies; a Coffin for a Book; alſo the ſeveral places wherein the ſeeds lie, as in Poppy heads. Dr. *Charl.*

Locupletity (*locupletitas*) abundance of wealth.

Locuplete (*locuples*) rich, wealthy, well-ſtored.

Locuſt (*locuſta*) a kind of flying inſect, or Fly (which the French term *Cigale*) of which we have none in *England*. See Dr. *Brown* in his *Vul. Err. lib.* 5. *ca.* 3. There were divers kinds of theſe; ſome hurtfull and venemous, others commodious for meat, *Mat.* 3. 4. *His meat was locuſts*, which ſome conceive to be the tops of herbs and plants.

Locution (*locutio*) a ſaying or ſpeaking.

Lodemanage, is the hire of a Pilot for conducting a ſhip from one place to another, and comes from the Dutch Loot, *i. e.* lead, and in the ſame Dutch the Pilot is called Lootſman or Piloot, the man of lead, or caſting out his lead to ſave the ſhip from danger.

Chaucer would have this word to ſignifie the skill or art of Navigation. See *Pilot*.

Lodeſtar, a Star that guids Mariners, the north ſtar.

Lodeſtone (*magnes*) a ſtone of the colour of ruſty iron, which hath an admirable vertue not onely to draw iron to it ſelf, but to make an iron on which it is rubbed, to draw iron alſo. This ſtone is found in the *Indian Sea*, and in the Country *Trachonitis*; and is of greateſt uſe in Navigation; For by it Saylers find out the certain courſe of their Voyage, the needle in the Compaſs, tempered herewith, ſtill ſtanding directly towards the North and South. Read more of this ſtone in Dr. *Br. Vul. Er. l.* 2. *c.* 2.

Lodeworks, one of the works belonging to the *Stannaries* in *Cornwal*, for which ſee *Cam. Brit.* in the title *Cornwal*. See *Stremeworks*.

Log, the name of an Hebrew meaſure, as the *Sextarius Atticus* was among the Greeks.

Logarithmes (*logarithmi*) a term in Mathematicks, ſignifying numbers, which, being fitted to proportional

Bb num-

FIG. 3. Page from Thomas Blount's *Glossographia* (3rd edn 1670) with references to Sir Thomas Browne and other writers.

staling or pissing backward.' He notes that Browne uses the Latin word *utinam* 'substantively in English, for a wish'; that he prefers *aberrancy* and *abortment* to *aberration* and *abortion*, but that on the other hand he uses both of the forms *explorement* and *exploration*.

There are also occasions when the lexicographer gets it wrong. In book I chapter III of the *Pseudodoxia Epidemica* Browne is discussing the general nature of errors among the common people, who are 'unable to weild the intellectual arms of reason'; such people, he says, are led by proverbs rather than by demonstration, and by rhetorical rather than logical arguments:

> And so from this ground in the Lecture of holy Scripture, their apprehensions are commonly confined unto the literal sense of the Text; from whence have ensued the gross and duller sort of Heresies. For not attaining the deuteroscopy, and second intention of the words, they are fain to omit their Superconsequencies, Coherencies, Figures, or Tropologies; and are not sometime perswaded by fire beyond their literalities. (Browne 1646, 27)

There is much that is typical of Browne in this, and plenty for the lexicographer to cut at. Blount copes adequately in his dictionary with *deuteroscopy* and *superconsequency*, but the entry for *literality* '(from *litera*) learning, knowledge of letters. *Br.*' shows that he failed to grasp that the sense 'literal interpretation' is intended here. Other instances of errors in interpretation occur at *signaturist*, *suffraginous* and *superfluity*.

These examples are enough to show that Blount was drawing directly on the *Pseudodoxia Epidemica* as a primary source for entries in his dictionary, and that he did so with an awareness of the oddities (but also of the usefulness) of Browne's vocabulary. He was quite exceptional for his time in producing a monolingual dictionary that was thus in part text-orientated. Alongside the 300 or so allusions to Browne there are others to Lord Bacon (about equally numerous), Chaucer, Heylin, Howell, Jonson, Sir Thomas More and Sir Henry Wotton, to name only the commoner ones. The inclusion of words from Chaucer in early dictionaries was not unknown (see Kerling 1979), but unlike some of his contemporaries Blount does not explicitly disapprove of the words which he notes as Chaucerian. He also includes occasional references to contemporary poets such as Cleveland (for the word *grotesque*, for instance), Cowley (*serenade*) and Herrick (*foliage*). All this shows him to be the most literary-minded compiler before Johnson; his dictionary is in contents less encyclopaedic than that of Phillips, but more discriminating than the comprehensive Bailey.

To Dr Johnson remains the glory of having been the first English compiler to have provided illustrative quotations systematically for all (or at least the vast bulk) of words entered; and the Johnson tradition survives through the OED to our own days. But where Johnson's general aim was to illustrate good usage, and the OED quotations are explicitly representative of an assembled corpus, Blount, as we have seen, drew on Browne (and indeed on his other sources) selectively. He chose to insert literary references when unusual words, or meanings, or forms, needed justifying; and also at times when the author being cited had himself defined a word in the original context. These two motives for including literary references certainly operated for Johnson as well (Kolb and Kolb 1972, 64-5), and Blount has never been given full credit for his contributions to English lexicographical technique; nor for the part he must have played in promoting the acceptance of many new learned terms in English which were invented or propagated by Sir Thomas Browne.

It is not hard to see why he turned to Browne, and in particular to the *Pseudodoxia Epidemica*. All dictionaries of that age were heavily Latinate, committed to explaining 'hard words'. There was on the one hand (because of the Latin-English source-books) a risk of overdoing the 'Englishing' of Latin or Greek terms, and so falling foul of purists. On the other hand, there was an unquestioned need to expound the commoner of the new technical terms in the arts and the sciences; in doing this, the dictionary had an educative function. The *Pseudodoxia Epidemica*, easily the longest of Browne's works, covers with characteristic erudition an immense range of topics—from what John the Baptist ate in the wilderness to why beer can be spoiled by lightning—about which popular beliefs might be set right by the application of the new scientific knowledge. It thus provided the dictionary compiler with a wonderful compendium of just those learned terms which the general reading public might wish him to include. Dr Johnson was later to say 'I have determined to consult the best writers for explanations real as well as verbal' (Johnson 1747, 20); if you wanted to do that in 1656, then Browne's *Vulgar Errors* was probably one of the best and most up-to-date source-books to hand.

END NOTE

This study was originally written for inclusion (under the title 'Vulgar Errors and Accepted Terms: Sir Thomas Browne and the Glossographia *of 1656') in an internal production of the Department of English at the University of Leiden (Barfoot et al. 1980, 101-8). In 'The dictionary as an aid in belles lettres' Nencioni (1989) writes on the way in which dictionaries may stimulate a consciousness of literary usage in the past. In an article on dictionaries of 'difficult' and peripheral words, Hausmann (1989) discusses the need for including these—including the more literary items—in dictionaries today.*

7

Setting up a New Bilingual Vernacular Dictionary: Henry Hexham (1647)

[1969]

The genesis and early history of bilingual dictionaries in modern European languages has attracted little scholarly attention, and this study is intended to shed light on the methods adopted by one lexicographer when he was confronted with the task of compiling a bilingual dictionary for a new combination of languages. Henry Hexham's *Copious English and Netherduytch Dictionarie* was published in Rotterdam in 1647, and the second half of his work appeared the following year under the title *Het Groot Woorden-boeck: Gestelt in't Nederduytsch, ende in't Engelsch* (for bibliographical details, see Scheurweghs 1960, Alston 1964). Before that time there had been some grammar-books containing lists of phrases and words in English and Dutch such as Le Mayre (1606), the anonymous *English Schole-Master* (1646) and various editions of De Berlaimont's *Colloquia*, a polyglot phrase-book originally published in Antwerp a century before, and still used in Hexham's time (De Berlaimont 1637). But Hexham's work is the first dictionary proper of the two languages. Further editions or reprints came out in 1660 and 1675 for English and Dutch, and in 1658, 1672 and 1678 for Dutch and English. Hexham's dictionary held the field alone until the appearance of Willem Sewel's *Nieuw Woordenboek der Nederduytsche en Engelsche Taale* over forty years later, in 1691.

In his preface Hexham explains how he came to compile the dictionary as a means of whiling away the time in his old age, having spent most of his life fighting the Spaniards as a soldier in the service of the United Provinces. He had noticed, he says (Hexham 1648, *Voor-reden aen den goedt-willigen leser*) that no dictionary of English and Dutch had ever been published, even though many theologians and students in Holland wished to learn 'our' English language.

The only indication he gives of his manner of working is in the title-page phrase 'Composed out of our best English Authours', to which he adds in the preface 'and dictionaries'. It would be pleasing to think of Hexham gathering and selecting his material while he was engaged on the miscellaneous literary work of his later years (and especially his work as a translator) but how far this is from the truth will appear in due course: it is the amplifying words 'and dictionaries' which give the real clue to the sources of his work.

Other combinations of European languages had had a much earlier start. For instance, separate dictionaries of French with Dutch, with Spanish, with Italian and with English had all appeared in the latter half of the sixteenth century (Brunot 1924-43, Vol. III, Book II, 81-94; Riemens 1921; also chapter 16 below). This was likewise a period in which dictionaries of Latin with vernacular languages flourished (Starnes 1954; Stein 1985a), and it was the products of these bilingual traditions to which Hexham turned for his word-lists. He does not seem to have drawn upon the polyglot dictionaries of the sixteenth and seventeenth centuries, though he would have found both Dutch and English in some of these, such as the French version of De Berlaimont's *Colloquia* published in 1576 which included 'un Dictionnaire en six langues: Flamen, Anglois, Alleman, François, Espaignol et Italien'. But such dictionaries of half a dozen languages or more must in any case be very limited both in their range of vocabulary and scope of definition, and would hardly provide any adequate basis upon which to build a bilingual dictionary.

The Source of the English Vocabulary List As a basis for the English-Dutch half of his dictionary, Hexham took Rider's English-Latin dictionary as revised by Francis Holyoke, and replaced the Latin definitions by Dutch ones. John Rider's *Bibliotheca Scholastica* appeared in 1589; it was the product of the very lively English-Latin lexicographical tradition associated with the names of Sir Thomas Elyot, Thomas Cooper and Thomas Thomas, and as Starnes has shown (1954, 232) very justly claims to epitomize and contract 'the learned workes of all the learnedst and best Dictionaries in England'. No new scholarly dictionary of English and Latin was to appear from then until after the Restoration; but

Rider's dictionary went through many editions and revisions during that period, and it was thus natural for Hexham to turn to one edition or another of it for his English word-list.

A comparison of the first (1589) edition of Rider's *Bibliotheca Scholastica* with Hexham's *Copious English and Netherduytch Dictionarie* shows that of Hexham's first hundred entries under the letter B all but six are to be found in Rider. If we then turn to the last edition of Rider to be published before Hexham appeared (*Riders Dictionarie, Corrected and Augmented with the addition of many hundred Words* ... by Francis Holy-Oke. London, 1640), we find that four out of these six items are there as well, two of them being similarly inserted out of true alphabetical sequence both in the 1640 dictionary and in Hexham: *Babber-lipped* after *to Babble*, and *Bale, or Balefull* after *a Ballad*. The evidence that Hexham used Holyoke's revision of Rider is overwhelming. There were several different issues of the work in 1640 (Starnes 1954, 269) and the British Library copy has been used here for the further illustration of the methods he adopted.

Hexham takes over about two-thirds of the material he finds in Rider-Holyoke: his hundred entries from *a Babe or Baby* to *a printers Bals* correspond to 154 entries in Rider-Holyoke. The process of selection may be illustrated by comparing the entries from *Bacon* to *a Badger* (consecutive entries have been spaced out for ease of comparison):

Rider-Holyoke, 1640	**Hexham, 1647 (1648)**
Bacon. 1 Lardum. 3 Laridum, n.	Bacon, *Speck.*
A flitch of bacon. 1 Succidia, f.	a flitch of Bacon, *Een zijde speck.*
The fore legs of a bacon. Petaso, petasio, m.	
A little fore leg. 1 Petasunculus, m.	
A gammon of bacon, or hinder leg of an hog. 1 Perna, f. 3 Pascala, orum, n.	a gammon of Bacon, *Een Ham-Speck.*
Bacons grease. 1 Axungia, f.	
Rusty bacon. Rancidum lardum.	rustie Bacon, *Gortigh speck.*
Bad; vide *Evill.*	Bad. *Siet* Evill.
*A **Badge** or cognizance.* Insigne, signum, n. vide *Armes.*	a Badge or cognisance, *Een teecken ofte merck van silver, ofte een wapen als boden of dienst-knechten dragen. Siet* Armes.

Rider-Holyoke, 1640	**Hexham 1647 (1648)**
A badge or token; vide *Token.*	
A badge or blazon of a Pursevant or other messenger. 1 Spinther, spinter, *m.*	
A badger beast; vide *Gray*.	a Badger, *Een das.*

Everything here in Hexham is taken over from Rider-Holyoke, even down to a simple reference-item such as *Bad*. Sometimes Hexham will add a definition to such an item for the convenience of his users (e.g. 'a Baiting place, *Een p[l]eyster-plaetse. Siet* Inne'). Sometimes (as with *a Badger*) he substitutes a Dutch equivalent; once, where he finds *Band* ... Vide *To Binde*, he inserts a separate entry for the verb *bind* entirely out of alphabetical sequence. In general, however, he takes over the rather extensive system of references in his original: there are eleven instances in the first hundred entries under B.

For the rest the group of words given above shows an intelligent selection of material. His one extended entry (*a Badge or cognisance*) is a conflation of three in the original, and the items omitted altogether would have lost their point in the process of translation had he retained them: neither English nor Dutch had any term corresponding to *petaso*, *petasunculus*, or *axungia*. This shows Hexham in a favourable light, but it must be said that elsewhere in the dictionary there are many entries which are self-explanatory both in English and in Dutch. 'A Band of ten souldiers, *Een bende van tien Soldaten*' is clearly superfluous, and only occurs because of the Latin *manipulus* that lies behind it. Other examples are these (the corresponding Latin word from Rider is added in the square bracket):

> a Banquet before supper, *Een bancket voor het avont-mael [antecoenium]*
> Barges covered, *Overgedeckte schuytjens* [emphracta]
> a barge with fifteene [r]owers on each side, *Een schuytjen met vijftien riemen aen elcke zijde* [quindeceremis]
> I should or might be, *Ick soude ofte mochte zijn ofte wesen* [forem]
> it becommeth not, *Het en betaemt niet, het en staet niet wel* [dedecet].

Elsewhere sequences such as *Mee – of mee – to mee – with mee*, or *to May, or can – not to May, or cannot* betray an imperfect adaptation of Latin source material to the needs of a vernacular dictionary.

Hexham's additions to the word-list which he found in Rider-Holyoke are, as we have noted, not very considerable in number. However, they become more frequent as he goes along; thus, of the first hundred entries under B, only two are not to be found in the source-dictionary, but about twenty-five new entries occur among the first hundred under P and under TR. Only an approximate figure can be given because he here permits himself considerably greater latitude in rearranging the material. Here are two corresponding blocks of entries under *pay* (the second-language definitions are omitted in each case):

Rider-Holyoke, 1640	**Hexham, 1647 (1648)**
1. To pay or satisfie, at a day appointed	i. to pay upon his day appointed (1)
2. To pay before the day	ii. to pay a fine
3. To pay ready money downe	iii. to pay ones welcome
4. To pay or discharge severall debts	iv. to pay cost and dammages (5)
5. To pay costs and damages	v. to pay all ones debts (4)
6. To pay often	vi. Payde or discharged (9,4)
7. They pay	vii. a payer
8. To take something in full payment, or in part of that which is due	viii. a Paying or a payment
	ix. a paying a forehand (2)
9. Payed	x. a payment with ready money (3,13).
10. Payed againe	
11. Not payed	
12. A paying, or payment of debts	
13. A paying of money in hand.	

The entries numbered 6, 7, 8, 10 and 11 in Rider-Holyoke are omitted by Hexham, who adds those numbered ii, iii and vii. Some probable relationships of his other entries to those in Rider-Holyoke are indicated by the numbers in brackets.

In the latter part of the dictionary we also find that what is new arises for the most part from what the compiler found in his original. Thus he takes *Painted out, or lively drawn*, and makes of it the three entries *to paint lively*, *to paint out*, and *painted lively*; his original has *to transmit* and *Transmutation*, he adds *a Transmission* and *to Transmute*; a great number of his additions consist of idiomatic phrases as, for instance, under *take*, where he inserts fifteen new items such as *to take courage*, *I will take heede to that*. Often he has doubtless simply drawn on his own knowledge, as when he expands the entries under *pear* by seven to include an *Empresse Peare*, *a wardon Peare*, etc. At other times it looks as if the existence of certain Dutch expressions has led to the expansion of the English list. There are, for instance, ten additions under *table*; of these, *table-keeper* is not given in the OED (though there are records of the Dutch equivalent, *tafel-houder*); *Table-beare* (*tafel-bier*, i.e. beer) is first recorded in 1643; and *table-servant* (*tafel-dienaer*, *tafel-knecht*) in 1882.

To summarize, we may say that Hexham never makes any serious attempt at changing the character of the word-list he found in Rider-Holyoke. Such additions as he does make appear to be curiously haphazard, and his deletions, though on the whole sensible ones, do not go far enough, so that the English-Dutch half of his dictionary retains too many of the marks of the sixteenth-century tradition from which it derives.

The Source of the Dutch Vocabulary List For the Dutch-English half of his dictionary Hexham turned not, as we might have expected, to a Dutch-Latin but to a Dutch-French dictionary, the French definitions of which he converted into English. A comparison of the 1636 edition of E.E.L. Mellema's *Grand Dictionaire françois-flamen ... Den Schat der Duytscher Tale* with Hexham's *Groot Woorden-boeck* of 1648 (reprinted 1658) shows that of three hundred entries in the latter (the first hundred each of B, L and TR) only seven do not appear in Mellema. Two of these (*gebackt*, *Getrocken*) are simply past participle entries for verbs already well represented. *Labeur, ofte Arbeydt* is added to *Labeur, ofte landtwerck*, and the form *Labeureren* now appears alongside *Labeuren*. The remaining three, *Een babbelaer* ('A Babler or Prater'), *Babban ofte baviaen* ('A Babian, or a great Monkey') and *een lachinge waerdigh* ('A laughing stock, or worthie to be laughed at') are entirely new.

It seems then that Hexham will have added only between five hundred and a thousand items to his original, which contains about 45,000 entries. We find here, as in the English-Dutch half, a near-total dependence on a single source, and this time the dependence is in fact the more striking because there is not even any real process of selection involved: Hexham had picked out about two thirds of what he found in Rider-Holyoke, but from Mellema he takes over practically the whole Dutch word-list. The nearness of the two works may be illustrated by the following parallel entries:

Mellema, 1636	**Hexham, 1648 (1658)**
Bachten, Derriere.	*Bachten*, After, or Behinde.
Bac, Schuyte, Petit bateau, Bac à passer l'eau, Ponton, m. Barque, Flette, f.	*een back, ofte Schuyte*, A small Trough-boate.
Bac oft Troch. Vn auge, Tronc cavé pour abruverles bestes.	*een Back ofte Trogh*, A Trough to water beasts in, or a Swines Trough.
Bacxken, Auget, m.	*een backsken*, A small Trough.
gheerne by den Bac zijn, Estre volontiers a l'auge, Faire volontiers bonne chere.	*gaerne by den back zijn*, To Have his nose alwayes in the pot, or, to make good cheere.
Bac, Backe, Bake, Vn porc, m.	*een Back, backe, ofte bake*, A Pigg, or a joung Hogg.
Bac, Beke, Vn torrent.	*een Back, ofte Beke*, A Head-spring, or a Well-spring.
Back, Beker, Gobelet.	*een Back, ofte beker*, A Goblet.
Back, Kinneback, Hacke, Machoire, f.	*Back, ofte Kinne-back*, Hacke, or the Jaw.

Here Hexham follows Mellema closely in the choice of idiom (*gaerne by den back zijn*) and of alternative spellings (*Back, backe, ofte bake*); occasionally elsewhere he will drop obsolescent or regional (especially southern) forms such as *bedeemsteren* and *bederffenisse* (as alternatives to *bedeemen* and *bedervinge* respectively), or *beassemt* and *bedelersse*, replaced by *be-ademt* and *bedelaerster*, but he generally retains the character of the Dutch word-list and uncritically takes over cross-references, occasional entries given in the plural, and so on. English definitions follow the French ones closely, as may be seen in the above examples; at times slavish imitation produces distinctly un-English idioms:

Mellema, 1636	**Hexham, 1648 (1658)**
op den Avont, Tsavonts, Sur le vespre, au soir.	*op den avondt, ofte des avondts,* Upon the evening, or at the evening.
den Dach gaet ten avontwaert, Le jour s'abaisse, Il avesprit.	*den Dagh gaet ten avontwaert,* The Day declines, or It waxeth Evening.
den Dach wtstellen, Differer ou remettre le jour.	*Den Dagh uytstellen*, To differ or adjourne the Day.

One detail which reveals how little Hexham troubled to adapt his material from the French to suit the English context is the inclusion of geographical names. In this, as in the first half of the dictionary, there are very few entries of the type we should now classify as encyclopaedic, but he does include a fair number of town, regional, and river names; here is a complete list of those given under the letter L:

Langedock	de Lippe	Losane
de Leck	Lisbonen	Lotheringe
Leuven	Lombardien	Loven
Leyden	Londen	Lubeeck
Limoges	Lore (i.e., the Loire)	Lutsenborgh
Lions	Loreyne	Luyck.

The predominantly Dutch-French character of the list had been quite appropriate to Mellema, from whom Hexham takes it over without adding or deleting any item to fit the new context of a Dutch-English dictionary.

The process of conversion has at times been carelessly carried out and mistakes have crept in, as in *Back, ofte Kinne-back* quoted above (*hack* is not recorded as an English word for the jaw), or in '*Laet*, Spade, or Late'; when Hexham gives *auweerd* as 'Indigne, angrie, Vile, or, of noe worth' (taking it from 'Indigne, c. Vil, De nul valeur') we may wonder whether he felt *indigne* to be an English word or has left it there in error.

As in the first half, where we noticed superfluous items deriving from Latin terms, so also here we find that Hexham retains entries which have lost their point in the conversion from French to English; an example is '*die een rooden Baerdt heeft*, He that hath a red Beard', which might (perhaps) be justified in the original by the existence of the French *rousseau*. There appear to be fewer such superfluous items carried over from the French than from the Latin.

The Underlying Latin Tradition Each half of the dictionary thus bears distinct traces of the particular lexicographical tradition from which it derives, and (though we have so far quoted from the version of Mellema published in 1636) the character of the Dutch word-list used by Hexham can, like his English word-list, be shown to belong to the later half of the sixteenth century.

The earliest edition of Mellema's dictionary that I have been able to discover is that published in 1618 at Rotterdam under the title *Le Grand Dictionaire Francois-Flamen ... Den Schat der Duytscher Tale*. Later editions appeared in 1624, 1630, 1636, 1640, 1643, 1651, 1663, 1684, 1694 and 1699. The word-list of the Dutch-French half appears to be practically identical in all editions down to 1643, and Hexham may have used any one of them. The title pages of the 1618 volumes imply however the existence of an earlier edition, for the work is said to be 'augmenté en cestre derniere edition d'une infinité de vocables, dictions & sentences tres-elegantes & necessaires', and again 'van nieus grootelijcx vermeerdert, verciert, ende verrijct met vele nieuwe woorden, spreucken ende sententien'. There are further difficulties about dates and authorship. Mellema was born in 1544 and was a schoolteacher at Antwerp, Haarlem and Leiden during the years 1588-90 (Van der Aa 1852-78, Vol. 12, 560-61). He must have died some time between 1591 and 1599: the British Library copy of his *Dictionaire ou Promptuaire Flameng-Francoys* contains an epistle dedicatory by Mellema dated 'De mon estude à Leyden ce premier de Novembre. L'an de nostre Redemption. 1591'; in the dedication of the *Dictionaire francois-flamen* of 1599 (a version of Sasbout, referred to below) the publisher Waesberghe refers to 'feu M. Edouard Leon Mellema'.

The dictionary, which for convenience we may continue to refer to as 'Mellema', and which is generally catalogued under his name, thus appeared only some twenty years after his death. Even then it is only in the later editions that he is clearly credited with the whole compilation, though his name had been attached from the beginning to an appendix of 'hard' words ('des mots absurds et estranges, attirants aux mots Latins, Espagnols, François, &c.'), later taken over by Hexham almost without change.

It is probably best to look upon the work as the product of the Waesberghe publishing house rather than of any particular known compiler. In the dedication (to Grotius) of the 1618 edition the publisher seems to imply this when he refers to

> ceux qui en ces Païs-bas ont premierement mis en lumiere & avec le temps augmenté ces *Dictionaires François-Flamen*, comme *M. Glaude Luiton*, *M. Gabriel Meurier*, *M. Matthieu Sasbout Iurisconsulte*, & dernierement par le docte Personnage *M. Edouard Leon Mellema*, tres-tous exhibez & imprimez

> tant par feu mon Pere Iean VVaesbergue en Anvers, que par moy so Filz ici dans la Ville de Rotterdam.

In the same spirit is the title-page of the 1624 edition, which has engraved portraits of Iaquez du Puis, M. Nicod, Ed. Mellema, Gabriel Meurier, Mathias Sasbout and I. Waesbergue. There is a whole battery of lexicographical talent and experience here. G. Luython produced a *Dictionaire en Franchois et Flameng* in 1552 (Riemens 1921, 7-9). Meurier, said to have been a difficult, irascible and disapproving character (Van der Aa 1852-78, Vol. 12, 743), appears to have been a rival of Mellema and Kilianus; he produced a *Dictionaire Flamen-Francois* in 1563, as well as Dutch-French schoolbooks. Jacques du Puys (or du Puis) was a reviser or editor of Robert Estienne's *Dictionnaire francois-latin* and treated the 1564 edition of it 'comme la sienne' (Riemens 1921, 15). Nicod (or Nicot) is one of the 'plusieurs hommes doctes' whose contribution is acknowledged on the title-page of some later versions (e.g. that of 1614) of Estienne's dictionary.

Mellema himself had previously brought out a dictionary of his own, the *Dictionaire ou Promptuaire Flameng-Francoys* of 1587. The list of Dutch words in it is practically identical to that of Mathias Sasbout's *Dictionaire Flameng-Francoys* of 1576. There also appeared in 1599 over the initials I.W. (Jean Waesberghe) a *Dictionnaire Francois-Flameng*, which is an abridged version of the French-Dutch half. Any of these may thus lie behind the reference in the title-page to the 1618 dictionary as 'ceste derniere edition', though all the earlier titles differ. The motive for retaining Mellema's name after his death may be merely commercial: he was known as a 'docte Personnage', and is indeed thought to have assisted Kilianus with the Frisian words that appeared in the *Etymologicum Teutonicae Linguae* (Molhuysen and Kossmann 1911-37, Vol 10, col. 603-4).

Mellema takes over many of his French definitions from Sasbout, as well as nearly all the geographical names which, as we have seen, were later to be adopted by Hexham. The relationship of the Mellema dictionary to those which preceded it is easy to demonstrate: all of the first sixty entries under B in Mellema are to be found either in the *Etymologicum Teutonicae Linguae* of Kilianus, first published in 1574, or in Sasbout's Dutch-French dictionary of 1576. The way in which these

Latin and French sources supplement each other can be seen from the following:

Kilianus, 1574 (1599)	**Sasbout, 1576**	**Mellema, 1636**
bad-meester		Badtmeester
	Badtcamer	Badekamer
bad-doeck	Badtdoeck	Badtdoeck
bad-stove	Badtstoue	Badtstove
bad-stoofster		Badtstoofster
Bade, bode		Bade, Bode
Bademoeme		Bademoeme
Baduyt		Baduyt
	Baeck, back oft backhuys	Baeck, Backhuys
	Baectant	Baectandt.

Sasbout acknowledges a debt only to the Robert Estienne dictionary as augmented by Du Puys in 1564, but this would only account for the French word-list. In fact we find that in the Dutch-French half of his work many of the entries (including four of the five contributed to Mellema in the above list) correspond to entries in the famous Dutch-French-Latin *Thesaurus* published by Plantin in 1573.

This process of borrowing may be illustrated by grouping together the entries for a single item from the four dictionaries involved:

Plantin, 1573
Voor t'backhuys lappen. Donner sur la joue. *Alapam dare, pugnum in malam impingere.*
Sasbout, 1576
voor t'backhuys slaen. Donner sur la iouë.
Mellema, 1636
op 't Bachuys slaeñ, Donner ou frapper sur la jouë.
Hexham, 1648 (1658)
op het backhuys slaen, To Strike one upon the cheeke, or to Give one a boxe on the eare.

Thus we can say that, with Plantin and Kilian behind the immediate sources of the Dutch word-list, and Rider-Holyoke as the basis for the English list, both halves of the first dictionary of Dutch and English lie firmly within the main Latin lexicographical tradition of the two countries.

END NOTE

Originally published in the Modern Language Review *64 (1969) 355-62, with the title 'The sources of the first Dutch and English dictionary', and reprinted here by courtesy of the Modern Humanities Research Association. Details of Hexham's life and his work as a translator and lexicographer are to be found in Osselton 1973, chapter 3. For the editions of sixteenth-century Dutch and French dictionaries referred to, see Claes 1974. A historical survey of Dutch bilingual lexicography is given in chapter 16 below. Stein (1985a) contains further information on many of the dictionaries of Latin with vernacular languages. Kabell and Lauridsen (1989) provide a facsimile of the first Danish and English dictionary and discuss similar problems which arose. For other language combinations see Steiner (1991, Spanish and English) and O'Connor (1991, Italian and English).*

8

Style Markers: Early Bilingual Dictionaries and English Usage

[1964]

Renaissance dictionary compilers were free men compared with their modern counterparts, and the value of their testimony to us is the greater, since they were able to be critics, as well as observers, of the language. Our knowledge of seventeenth- and eighteenth-century English must come in the first place from the observation of actual usage, and the most we might expect of an early dictionary is that it should provide a balanced, convenient and accurate record of this, sometimes supplementing our knowledge, especially in the realm of spoken idiom. But in fact many of them do more, and it is the compilers who take their critical function seriously whose dictionaries are the most worthy of attention today.

Cautionary Marks in Monolingual and Bilingual Dictionaries That this is so with monolingual dictionaries I have shown elsewhere (Osselton 1958). It is the object of the present study to show that the same is true of bilingual dictionaries. The most striking example is perhaps the well-known Dutch and English dictionary of the Amsterdam Quaker Willem Sewel, published first in 1691, and especially the revision of it made by Egbert Buys and published in 1766 under the title *A Compleat Dictionary English and Dutch. Volkomen Woordenboek der Engelsche en Nederduitsche Taalen*. Here, in the English-Dutch volume, some 1500 words and idioms are distinguished by marks as being unfit for general use for one reason or another. This is a number far greater than that marked by any of the monolingual English dictionaries. Bailey, the most venturesome of the English compilers, comes nearest to it with his 950 condemned words in the so-called 'Volume II' of 1727 (see Figure 8 in chapter 13), and Buys, it seems to me, must certainly rank with him as one of the most important commentators on the lexicon of eighteenth-century English.

Their positions are rather different. The Englishman Bailey, experienced schoolteacher and lexicographer, has certain natural advantages over the foreigner Buys, even though (Sewel 1766, preface) the latter had spent five years in England—presumably on diplomatic service, since on the title-page he is referred to as 'Counsellor of their Polish and Prussian Majesties'. But we must set against the advantage of the native speaker the fact that in some ways the testimony of a foreigner may be more objective. In looking at the words an Englishman condemns we must always be on the watch for any special attitudes he may hold, such as a feeling that the polite language is overburdened with technical terms, a personal distaste for dialect words, and so on; but the foreigner will presumably never set himself up as a reformer of someone else's language, since he knows that no one will listen, and the limit of his intention in marking words must be to caution his fellow-foreigners.

Colloquial Idioms in the Bilingual Dictionary Furthermore, Buys is far more interested in colloquial idiom than Bailey was in his 'Vol. II', and his book has a special value for the student of language (quite apart from its critical comments on the vocabulary) for being what was in the seventeenth century called an *idiomatology* rather than a mere lexicon. Buys tries to do what the bilingual lexicographer of today will do: to provide a representative list of current idioms under each word. This may be illustrated by a comparison of new material in different editions. In the first edition of Sewel (1691) there is a total of 74 entries from B- to BAG-. In the second edition (1708) 21 new entries are added; these include new words (*backberond, back-blow, back-yard, back-room, back-sword, back-stairs, bafts, bagnio*) and are for the rest mainly simple illustrations of words which had been given earlier (*the back of a knife, bags of wool, a sweet-bag*). By the fifth edition (1754) a further 17 entries had been added to these; still the emphasis is on new words and simple illustration (*to go backward, the back-side of a leaf*) though *to save one's bacon* and *to come off with a baffle* ('Iets met een beschaamde troni staaken') are idiomatic enough. But the additions made by Buys to his edition are as follows:

to turn one's back, *Vluchten.*

To lay all on one's back, *Iemand al de schuld opleggen.*

He has no shirt to put on his back, *Hy heeft geen hemd aan zyn lyf, hy is zeer arm.*

To clap a writ on his back, *Iemand een procês aandoen.*

You must give me something back, or back again ...

I shall be back again by one of the clock ...

The back-board, (in de Zeevaart), *Het bakboord.*

I found him a little backward in it, ... *hy wilde 'er niet aan.*

To go backward and forward, (not to be in the same story), *Zich zelf tégenspreeken.*

A bacon hog ...

He is very bad ... *hy legt op het uiterste.*

Bad fortune, *Tégenspoed.*

Sure it is not bad with you! *Ik dagt inderdaad niet dat gy zo slegt bestond.*

To keep bad (or late) hours, *Laat t'huis komen, laat te bedde gaan.*

The number of new entries is thus no greater than those added to the second edition. But here nearly all the new material consists of colloquial idiom. Much of it is very recent idiom too. Of the phrases in the brief list above, *to have no shirt to put on one's back* and *to clap a writ on a person's back* both belong to the late seventeenth century; *a bacon hog* is first recorded in the OED from the early eighteenth century; also from the eighteenth century are *to keep bad hours* (1744, Pope), *to keep late hours* (1732), and *he is very bad* (1748, Richardson). *Back* in the sense of 'come back, returned' ('I shall be back again') is not recorded in OED until 1879, and there appears to be no recorded instance of the idiom *to lay all on one's back.* Buys does also add new words (the succeeding pages yield, for example, *white-bait* 'Zeer klyne Visjes in de *Theems', baldric, bambao, bandoleer* and others) but a great proportion of the material he adds to Sewel is devoted to the illustration of everyday speech. In venturing to do this, Buys may at times as a foreign observer have got things wrong; *back-board* is an unlucky shot (his own language may have influenced him unduly here, though Bailey has the word too), and there are other 'English' items which look suspiciously Dutch. But the number of idioms given by him which are additional to those in OED, or (more significantly) antedate the OED's examples by centuries, is very great indeed. Buys will no doubt have escaped the better from the constricting traditions of eighteenth-century English lexicography because he was a foreigner; and perhaps also because he was more of an amateur than Bailey—though he did produce in 1768 (the year before his death) an impressive dictionary of technical terms.

Sources No study of the sources used by Sewel and Buys is known to me. Sewel acknowledges in the preface to the second edition (1708) that he has been influenced by François Halma, with whom he had been working during this period on the production of the literary periodical *De Boekzaal van Europa*. The two men had also collaborated in producing a Dutch and French dictionary, and Sewel says he had decided to include the gender of nouns because this had also been done there. As for the English words, he stoutly maintains that it is a completely new and independent work, having nothing in common with the dictionary of his predecessor Henry Hexham, but the presence in early editions of numerous words such as *navity* ('Naarstigheit, vlyt') and *nundinal* (''t Geene tot een jaarmarkt behoort'), which never had a currency in English outside dictionaries, argues a closer connection with the English renaissance tradition of Cockeram and Blount than the compiler is ready to admit. Such a connection is neither surprising nor reprehensible. Sewel had only been to England once, for a visit lasting ten months when he was fifteen years old (Hull 1933, 28). Apart from being the historian of the Quaker movement he is remembered especially as a formidable translator from English and other languages, and it is likely that his knowledge of these languages would have been a bookish one. In the preface to the first edition he mentions that he has inserted many words which he had come across in the best modern English authors in the course of translating them; the statement may sound conventional enough, but it is amplified in the second edition when he says he had often found that even native Englishmen had been unable to give him a satisfactory explanation of some word or expression. Anyone with experience of lexicographical work will know at once that this rings true; and the picture of Sewel deriving his knowledge from books and depending for some definitions on the advice of such native speakers as he came across is probably a true one.

Buys, in the preface to his edition of 1766, says he has made use of Littleton (1768), Boyer (1699), Marin (1717) and Halma (1708) and in the text he does occasionally acknowledge these as the source of particular definitions (e.g. *to shoot point-blank, if there be any thing of a sea, scolopendra*). His other words, he says, have come from his own reading, and from a collection that he made during his stay in England of countless words which were not in Sewel. Buys does not mention any English lexicographers as a source for his entries. There seems to be no evidence that he used Dr Johnson or the smaller of Bailey's dictionaries (Bailey 1721). But Bailey's *Dictionarium Britannicum* (1730) has clearly been a major source of material (e.g. among the early entries for B: *a bargain is a bargain, the barrel of a watch* and *to bast flints with butter*—a proverbial phrase which is not in OED, ODEP or Tilley 1950). He has also made close use of the second edition (1754) of Martin's *Lingua Britannica Reformata*. How close will be clear from a comparison of the entries for *bale* and *balk:*

Martin	**Buys**
BALE (of *bale*, fr.) 1 a pack of merchandize. 2 the handle of a pail.	BALE, *Een baal.* BALE, *Het hengsel van een emmer.*
BALK 1 a piece of ground left unplowed. 2 a beam in building. 3 disappointment or baffle. 4 shame or disgrace. 5 prejudice or damage.	BALK, *Een brok lands daar de ploeg niet overgegaan is, de opgeworpene aarde tusschen twee vooren, – een balk.* He has had a sat [?=sad] balk, *Hy heeft een lelyk ongeluk gehad.* Balk (shame, or disgrace), *Schande.*

Here we see how Buys follows the order of Martin's definitions, sometimes inserts the English definition as well as the Dutch one, and fills out Martin where he can by an illustrative phrase. The choice, and the method of work, are enlightened: Martin was the most orderly of the octavo English dictionaries that had been published, but it was sadly lacking in illustration, and that was in any case what the foreign users would need.

Symbols Used When we turn to the purely critical side of this dictionary, we find again that Buys is discerning, and ready to learn from his predecessors. Sewel first used marks to condemn some 150 words in the second edition (1708); by the fifth edition in 1754, immediately before Buys took over, this had crept up to a total of about 275; Buys at once increases it to 1500. A number of different symbols are used to designate various classes of words in the dictionary, including Law Terms, Proverbial Expressions and 'Adulterated Dutch Words'. The ones we are here concerned with are the double-barred dagger (‡) to mark 'an Obsolete and Dubious Word, *or* Expression', and the single dagger (†) for 'A mean *or* vulgar Word *or* Expression, as also Words and Expressions of Humour and Burlesque'. This last one occurs also with an inverted dagger beside it where a 'mean Word, *or* Expression' is used in a figurative sense.

Categories of English Words Marked These are all taken over by Buys, but his use produces a rather different pattern of verbal criticism from that in Sewel. Almost half the words marked by Buys are colloquialisms of one kind or another (in Sewel it was about a quarter). These include a good number of eighteenth-century ephemera such as *bam*, *to careen a wig* ('an Expression used among the Beaux'), and *popper* ('a pistol'); others such as *fun* and *nizy* (here marked as obsolete) were dismissed by Dr Johnson as low words, and items such as *to bouse (=* booze*), elbow-grease* and *to sheer off* have probably always belonged to colloquial speech.

To chime with one ('Ja en Amen spelen') places in the eighteenth century an expression first quoted in the OED from Dickens. Similarly we find antedating of OED in such items as *to titter-totter, a very coot* ('Een gek in folio'; there are American examples from 1794). *I care not a fiddlestick for it, random-shot* ('Een onbedagte daad, een bedryf zonder oogmerk'; the earliest quotation in a figurative sense is from Burns in 1785). *The wherry-go nimble*, here given as a mean word, seems not to have been recorded before 1904 (Partridge 1938). It is entries such as these which must convince us of the general trustworthiness of Buys's observations, and lend authority to the vast body of words and idioms marked by him as colloquial, and apparently not recorded at all in modern reference books. Some instances are: *His brimstone majesty* ('Den Duivel'), *Who made you an examiner?* ('speaking to an inquisitive person'), *fob-doddle* ('een zotskap, sul'), *To fun one up, Guiny-pepper* ('Goud'), *To pack off* ('to die'), *To do a thing with a powder* ('in great

EGL. EGO. EGR. EGY. &c.

Egging, *Aanlokking, ingeeving.*

EGL.

EGLANTINE, *een Egelantier.*

EGLOGUE, *Een Herdersdicht, Veldgedicht*, zie Eclogue.

EGO.

EGOTIZING, *Geduurig het woord ik gebruikende*, of *van zig zelven ſpreekende, zig veel aanmatigen.*

EGOTISM, *Het ſpreeken van zig zelven, eigen lof.*

EGR.

EGREGIOUS, *Treffelyk, braaf, heerlyk.*

Egregious, (ſignal, taken in an ill ſenſe) *Befaamd, berucht, aanmerkelyk*, in een kwaaden zin.

An egregious knave, *Een beruchte boef.*

Egregiouſly, *Treffelyk.*

☞ Men egregiouſly disaffected to the government, *Menſchen die de Regeering merkelyk haaten.*

EGRESS *or* Egreſſion, *Een uitgang.*

To have free egreſs and regreſs, *Een vryen toegang hebben.*

EGRET, (a kind of heron) *Een kleine witte Reiger.*

to EGROTE, (to conterfeit being ſick) *Zich ziek houden.*

EGY.

EGYPT, *Egipte.*

Egyptian, *een Egiptenaar.*

A counterfeit egyptian, *een Heiden, landlooper*, zie Gipſy.

EJA.

EJACULATION, *Een uitſchieting, uitboezeming van een kort gebed, ſchiet-gebédeken.*

☞ A prayer full of pious ejaculations, *Een gebed vol van Godvruchtige uitboezemingen.*

Ejaculatory, *Uitſchietende.*

Ejaculatory veſſels, (a term of anatomy) *Uitſchietende vaatjes.*

to EJECT, *Uitwerpen, uitſchieten, braaken.*

Ejected, *Uitgeworpen, gebraakt.*

EJECTION, *Uitwerping, uitſchieting.*

EIE, *Een oog*, zie Eye.

EIG.

EIGHT, *Agt.*

Eight-times, *Agtmaal.*

Eight-hundred, *Agthonderd.*

Eight-fold, *Agtvoudig.*

Eighteen, *Agttien.*

I. Deel.

EIG. EIL. EIR. EIS. EIT. &c.

Eighteenth, *De agtiende.*

Eighth, *De agtſte.*

Eightieth, *De tagtigſte, tagtentigſte.*

Eightly, *Ten agtſten.*

Eighty, (*or* fourſcore) *Tagtig.*

EIL.

EILET-HOLE, *Een met zyde geboord gaatje.*

EIR.

EIRE, *Een zéker Gerechtshof*, zie Eyre.

EIS.

‡ EISIL, (an old *Engliſch* word for vinegar) *Azyn.*

EIT.

EITHER, *Een van beide, welk van beide gy wilt.*

I am not ſo tall as either of you, *Ik ben zo lang niet als één van u beide.*

☞ On either ſide, *Aan alle beide de zyden.*

If either of them will, *Als zy één van allen willen.*

In either of the jaws there are two ſharp eye-teeth, *In ieder kinnebak zyn twee ſcherpe oogtanden.*

EITHER, *Of.*

He muſt either go forward or backward, *Hy moet of agteruit of voor uit gaan.*

Either two or none, *Of twee of geen.*

Either one thing or other, *Of 't een of 't ander.*

An excerciſe either of the body or the mind, *Een oeffening van het Lichaam of van den Geeſt.*

‡ Either he is a wiſe man, or a fool, *Hy is een van beiden wys of gek.*

Theſe things will either profit or delight, *Deeze dingen zullen voordeelig of vermaakelyk zyn.*

'T is more than either you, or I could have done, *Het is meer als gy of ik gedaan konden hebben.*

EJU.

†EJULATION, *Gehuil, gekryt.*

EKE.

†EKE, *Ook, als méde, daarenboven.*

to EKE, (*or* to augment) *Vermeerderen.*

to EKE out, *Vergrooten, doen uitdygen, uitzetten.*

☞ All ekes, (*or* helps) *Alles helpt.*

Ee

ELA. ELB. ELD. 217

ELA.

ELABORATE, *Bearbeid, bewerkt, bewrocht.*

An elaborate diſcourſe, *Een bewrocht vertoog.*

An elaborate piece of work, *Een keurlyk werk.*

An elaborate period, *Een doorwrochte periode.*

Elaborately, *Op een bearbeide wyze.*

ELABORATORY, *Stookhuis, werkhuis*, zie Laboratory.

ELAPSED, *Verloopen* (*als de tyd.*)

ELASTICITY, *Veerkragt.*

ELASTICK, *Veerkragtig.*

ELATE *or* Elated, *Hoogmoedig, verwaand, opgeblaazen.*

to ELATE, (to puff up, to tranſport) *Opblaazen, trots maaken.*

To elate one's ſelf, *Zich zelf verheffen.*

A man of an elate mind, *Een Man van een verhéven geeſt.*

ELB.

ELBOW, *De elleboog.*

She leaned on her elbow, *Zy leunde op haare elleboog.*

☞ To be always at one's elbow, *Iemand altoos op zy hangen.*

My coat is out at the elbow, *Myn kleed is aan de elleboog uitgeſléten.*

Elbow of land, of a wall, &c. *Bogt van een Rivier, van een muur*, enz.

Elbow-room, *Vrye handen*, in de figuurlyke en eigentlyke zin.

To have elbow-room, *Zyn handen vry of ruim hebben.*

‡ † Elbow-greaſe, (*or* pains) *Zwaar werk.*

An elbow-chair, *Een leuning ſtoel.*

to ELBOW, *Met den elleboog ſtooten.*

to ELBOW OUT, (to drive out) *Uitdryven.*

The *Phœnicians*, who were the old inhabitants of *Canaan*, were elbowed out by the *Hebrews*, into a ſmall ſlip of land on the ſea-coaſt, *De* Pheniciers, *die de oude inwoonders van* Kanaän *waren, wierden 'er door de* Hebreen *uitgedréven, naar een kleine ſtrook Lands aan den Oever der Zee.*

ELD.

ELDAR *or* Elder, *Vlier.*

Dwarf-elder, *Wilde vlier, hadig.*

Elder-

FIG. 4. Cautioning foreigners on English usage: a page from the 1766 revision by Egbert Buys of Sewel's *Compleat Dictionary English and Dutch.*

haste'; the word *powder* 'to rush' occurs from 1632), *to rogue one off* ('to scold at him severely'), *I am your true tarpawling* ('Ik ben uw onderdanigste voetveeger'), *He is not worth a token* (Ben Jonson has 'a token-worth'), *I have no wash* ('I have no silver').

The next largest group of marked items is the obsolete words, which account for about a quarter of the whole. In Sewel it was about two-fifths, and there is the further difference that the words Sewel marks as old are for the most part the usual obvious Saxonisms (*barn* or *bearn*, *to nil, to ween*, etc.) Buys seems to be more critical, and marks with a double cross many words and idioms which were only just going out in his time. Such are *helvetick* (OED quotes instances only from the eighteenth century), *onslaught* ('een verouderd woord'; it was later revived by Scott), *overfraighting, to quail* (another word later revived by Scott), *to fox* ('Dronken maken'), *I am with child to know* ('Ik ben belust om te weeten').

Buys paid more attention to learned words than Sewel did, and it is very striking that he marks a greater number of them (e.g. *hebetation, incruentous, inspissate, opifice*) with the same mark as the old words. Some may be thought of as merely 'dubious' but the fact is that by this time, in 1766, the problem of the renaissance 'hard words' was settling itself in English. A great number of such words which had probably never enjoyed any vigorous currency were by then becoming obsolete anyway. In treating them in this way, Buys shows perhaps more discernment than many English lexicographers; it may also be that his insight was quickened by the observation of what had already happened in his own language.

He also marks some dialect or 'country' words, as the English lexicographers do (*bid-ale*, 'A western word', *litten, mauther, yate*, etc). He marks some 'poetic' words, as Martin does (*baleful, hy* 'an old word still used in poetry for to go', *welkin*). Like Bailey, he condemns *thereafter*, but adds to it *furthermore, other while, whereto, whereunto*. He seems to dislike conversions (*to dialogue, to journey, to opinion, to vermilion*), and he shares with many eighteenth-century grammarians a special dislike of reduplications (*gibble-gabble, griff-graff, hoity-toity, pintle-pantle, ribble-rabble, riff-raff*).

These details will give some idea of the range of verbal criticism, and show how Buys both confirms and supplements what we learn from the monolingual dictionaries of his English predecessors. The dictionary is, like the English ones, often inconsistent and at times clearly mistaken, but there is much that deserves the attention of the student of eighteenth-century English.

Words marked in the Dutch-English Half No special attention has been paid here to the marks by which Dutch idioms are similarly classified in the second (Dutch-English) volume, where style-markers are also at times extended to the English phrases used in definition (e.g. *Zich in de ëchte staat begeeven*, To marry, † to commit matrimony). De Vooys has pointed out the value of such verbal comments even though (like the English ones) they may not always be reliable (1934, 267-8). A full study of Buys would need to take these into account, relating them to the Dutch as well as the English tradition of lexicography. Buys makes use of Martin; but he gets the idea of marking words from Sewel, and Sewel gets it from Halma (not, as De Vooys supposes, the other way round, since it was only in the second edition of 1708, after he had been working with Halma, that Sewel started marking words). Halma, in turn, gets it from a Frenchman: about 90 per cent of all the words marked in the French-Dutch volume of his dictionary are simply lifted from the dictionary of Richelet originally published in 1680, and more than half of them had been similarly marked by Richelet as being appropriate only to 'le stile simple, dans le Comique, le Burlesque ou le Satirique'.

The European Tradition There is then a European tradition in proscriptive lexicography, and this article can touch only on one small part of it. Such a tradition merits study as a whole: the testimony of the early foreign lexicographers may prove as helpful to the student of words as the testimony of early foreign phoneticians is to the student of phonology. But first we need a fuller knowledge of the sources and relationships of the early bilingual dictionaries, and of the lexicographical traditions in the different countries, so that we may assess the value of each dictionary as a linguistic document. For this, scholarly co-operation between different countries will be needed—a co-operation of the kind which Professor Zandvoort, as editor of *English Studies*, has done so much to foster for so long.

END NOTE

Published in 1964 in English Studies Presented to R.W. Zandvoort on the occasion of his Seventieth Birthday *[A Supplement to* English Studies *Vol. 45, pages 14-20], and reprinted here by courtesy of Swets Publishing Service, Lisse. The original title was 'Early bilingual dictionaries as evidence for the status of words in English'. A detailed study of the Sewel Dutch and English dictionaries is to be found in Osselton 1973, chapters 4 and 5. Bray (1990) has described a system of usage symbols used by Richelet (1680), which has much in common with that of Sewel. Related problems in monolingual French dictionaries are discussed by Corbin and other writers in Glatigny (1990). Werner (1991) provides a useful analysis of the general principles involved in the use of labels in bilingual dictionaries. In an article concerned with the role of dictionaries in the development of standards, Zgusta (1989) gives a list of fourteen graphic devices used by Campe to qualify words entered in his* Wörterbuch der Deutsche Sprache *published in 1807.*

9

Fixing the Spelling: *Errour* and *Honor* in Johnson and Bailey

[1963]

The convention for spelling the *error* – *honour* class of words in English has attracted a good deal of attention, perhaps especially because it forms one of the most immediately obvious distinctions between present-day British and American English in print. This troublesome detail of British English spelling came to be generally settled in its present form in the course of the eighteenth century, and the lion's share of the blame for our present convention has often been put upon Dr Johnson. Mencken (1923, 235) pronounced thus:

> It was Johnson himself who established the position of the *u* in the *-our* words. Bailey, Dyche and the other lexicographers before him were divided and uncertain; Johnson declared for the *u*, and though his reasons were very shaky, and he often neglected his own precept, his authority was sufficient to set up a usage which still defies attack in England.

Before Mencken's time his fellow-countryman Lounsbury, in the most extensive discussion of this class of words known to me, had not only pinned upon Johnson the blame for individual spellings (e.g. *candour*, of which he says 'it was Johnson's adoption of the ending *our* for the word which fixed this erroneous spelling upon the English people'), but had also pronounced of the Dictionary as a whole that 'there is no question that his words did more to prevent the universal adoption of the spelling *or* than any other single agency' (Lounsbury 1909, 213-14). Johnson's own inconsistency and illogicality with these words (*anteriour – posterior* is the classic example) are explained by the statement that he 'preferred the spelling, as do we all, which he himself was wont to use'.

A great deal of this is revealed to be little more than hopeful and inaccurate guesswork when it is tested against Johnson's actual habits of spelling in his letters, and when these are compared with the successive editions of his Dictionary, with the recommendations of the other contemporary dictionary compilers, and with the conventions of the printers of his time.

The Letters and the Dictionary A study of Johnson's letters in the Chapman 1952 edition shows that he was himself far from having any uniform system of spelling for these words, and that where he did keep to one spelling in private correspondence it is not always the spelling recommended in the Dictionary. Johnson's practice in letters as printed by Chapman from MS may be summarized best in three lists of words:

A Words in which Johnson's spelling is uniform, and agrees with modern English usage in having *-our: ardour, behaviour, candour, clamour, colour, endeavour, favour, flavour, harbour, honour, humour, labour, neighbour (neighborhood* occurs, however, alongside *neighbourhood), parlour, rumour, saviour, succour, tumour, vapour, vigour.*

B Words always spelled *-our* by Johnson, but with *-or* in modern English: *emperour, mirrour, posteriour, servitour, superiour, tenour.*

C Words spelled both ways by Johnson (here given in the modern spelling): (i) *error, governor* (*governer* occurs as a third spelling), *horror, inferior, splendour, terror;* (ii) *author, languor* (the other form is *langour*), *liquor, tutor.*

Words spelled consistently with *-or* by Johnson and surviving with that spelling in modern English (such as *ancestor*, *senior* and most agent nouns) are very numerous, and need not be listed here. No instance was found of Johnson spelling consistently with *-or* where modern English has *-our*.

If we now turn to the Dictionary of 1755 we find that the treatment of these words varies with the different groups. The words listed under A are all given the *-our* spelling in the Dictionary: there was no question about these words, for which the printers' spelling habits seem to have been well enough fixed before the period we are considering.

Of the words listed under B, where in his letters Johnson consistently uses the now obsolete *-our* spelling, half are given one way in the Dictionary (*emperour, superiour, tenour*), and half the other, with *-or* as in modern English. Among the words under B, both *tenour* and *superiour* provide good illustrations of Johnson's stated intention of 'leaving to every author his own practice unmolested, that the reader ... may judge between us' (Preface): all fourteen quotations illustrating the senses of *tenour* have the spelling *tenor*. Here the 'reader' has judged between them, and has ignored Johnson.

For the words under C, which Johnson spelled both ways in his letters, we might reasonably expect to find alternative spellings in the Dictionary, but none are given: six of the words have *-our* (*errour, governour, horrour, inferiour, splendour, terrour*) and the other four are given only with the spelling *-or*. It is also remarkable that for these words Johnson has often chosen for the Dictionary spelling the one he less frequently uses himself: the word *author* is one that naturally occurs very frequently in his letters, and though there are a few examples of the spelling *author* (as given in the Dictionary) it is nearly always *authour*. On the other hand, *horror* outnumbers *horrour* by five to one in the letters studied, but the Dictionary has *horrour*.

The many words spelled consistently with *-or* by Johnson in his letters and surviving with that spelling in English today usually appear with *-or* in the Dictionary; but we may notice that *possessor* and *successor*, always spelled that way in the letters, are both given *-our* in the Dictionary.

Printers' Spelling Johnson was thus with these words very far from merely preferring the spellings which 'he himself was wont to use'. It is equally certain that the etymological distinction Johnson makes in his Preface—of *-or* for words of Latin derivation, *-our* for words from the French—could never have been carried through consistently, and can easily be refuted from his actual preferences in the Dictionary. A third possible explanation of the selection of forms given by him in the Dictionary is that he was merely recommending the spelling of the printers of the time. This is a commonly stated view of Johnson's position as an orthographer. The older opinion that Johnson 'fixed' English spelling can still be found, expressed with a greater or less degree of assurance, in handbooks such as those of Wrenn (1949, 99) and

Sheard (1954, 309); a recent and more cautious view of the part he played in the history of English spelling is offered by Sledd and Kolb when they observe in the bicentenary volume:

> in spelling, though the familiar claim that Johnson had 'fixed the external form of the language' will not bear precise scrutiny, his authority was even more generally recognized than it was in matters of diction

and, in another passage, where they say that Johnson enjoyed high orthographic authority 'as the codifier of a spelling already pretty well established by the printers' (Sledd and Kolb 1955, 137, 33).

Even this modest claim seems to be only partly true of the *-or*, *-our* words: Johnson was no doubt in part 'codifying' a recognized spelling, but his treatment differs in certain definable ways from the practice of the printers of his day. In order to test Johnson's preferences against actual printers' usage, examples of these words were noted from forty passages of uniform length selected from publications during the period 1660-1800, spaced out in groups at twenty-year intervals. Five different printers were included in each group, the passages were taken only from first editions by London printers, and they included books and pamphlets of widely varying subject, size, and care of printing. A total of over 3300 examples were thus noted, and while a survey of so limited a size must leave many details unrecorded, the results may be taken as generally representative of London printers' habits for the period, and an analysis of them throws interesting light on Johnson's practice.

Of the twenty words listed under A, where Johnson's letters and his Dictionary were found to agree in *-our*, only two isolated *-or* spellings (*rumor* in 1660, *vigor* in 1700) were found among nearly 250 instances noted. For these words, printers' usage was thus to all intents and purposes fixed nearly a hundred years before the publication of the Dictionary, and Johnson was merely recording a settled spelling convention.

The same may be said of the words listed under C (ii): here, though Johnson himself uses both *-or* and *-our* spellings in his letters, the spelling he gives in the Dictionary, with *-or*, is the only one occurring in the study of printers' usage. With the words listed under C (i), however, where Johnson also uses both spellings in his letters, but gives *-our* as his preference in the Dictionary, both forms are found in the printed documents but nearly all the *-our* forms occur before 1740. *Governor* is a typical example of this group; instances were found as follows:

governour	1680	1700	1720	1740		
governor			1720	1740	1760	1780.

Only with *splendour* were examples of both forms found throughout the period, and *splendour* is the only word of this group which has survived with *-our* in modern English. With *governour* and the others Johnson was, it seems, giving preference to a form not current in 1755, but to a then obsolescent form which was generally current in his youth.

This is also true of the words listed under B, which Johnson himself always spelled *-our* and gave in the Dictionary in that form (no examples occurred of *tenour*):

emperour	1660	1680					
emperor				1720		1760	1780	1800
superiour	1660	1680	1700					
superior		1680		1720	1740	1760	1780	1800

Johnson's insertions of *-our*, *-or* spellings in his Dictionary is thus seen to be selective. In private correspondence he had in general a marked preference for the *-our* form, though there were many words which he spelled indifferently either way. When it came to opting for one form or the other in the Dictionary he often chose a form in conflict with his own preferred practice (*author* is perhaps the most striking example), but his choice, when he did this, was determined by the printers' usage of forty years before. If the evidence from these words is typical, it would be misleading to talk of Johnson setting his stamp of approval on the spelling of the printers—Johnson's recommendations differ from current printers' practice, and where they differ they have no effect whatever. Further investigations might well show that in other details of spelling Johnson was also looking back to the usage of his youth. Words such as *classick*, *Gothick*, etc. provide one instance: my investigations show that the general changeover by printers from *-ick* to *-ic* is a steady process during the period 1720 to 1780. Thus, when Johnson learned to spell, *-ick* forms were pretty universal, but by 1755 they were well on their way out. Johnson gives *-ick* consistently in the Dictionary; there are occasional *-ic* spellings in his letters, but with these words, as with those in *-or*, *-our*, I have not found evidence of any change in spelling habits in the course of his life.

Other Dictionaries Another possible influence on Johnson's selection of *-or*, *-our* spellings might well have been the 1736 edition of Bailey's *Dictionarium Britannicum*, an interleaved copy of which is said to have been used by him. In fact, a comparison of the spellings given in the two works does not yield any evidence to show that Johnson paid any heed to Bailey's choice. Bailey gives alternative spellings in many instances, attempting sometimes a distinction between technical and non-technical use: thus he has, for instance, entries for *Aqueous Humor*, *Crystalline Humor*, etc., but the general sense of the word ('Moisture, Juice; also Temper of Mind; also Fancy, Whim') is given the spelling *humour*; sometimes, as in the case of *inferior*, the adjective is given with *-or*, the noun with *-our*. These distinctions were not taken over by Johnson, and for the *-or*, *-our* words as a whole Bailey has tended to favour more 'modern' spellings than Johnson (*emperor, superior* are examples).

Much the same can be said of the other dictionary which immediately precedes Johnson's work of 1755, Martin's *Lingua Britannica Reformata* (1749). Indeed, Mencken's picture of Johnson's predecessors being 'divided and uncertain', and waiting for the clear declaration of usage which Johnson gave, is manifestly untrue. For these words at least, if we wish to have a clearer account of actual printers' usage in the eighteenth century, we can turn with greater assurance to minor works than to Johnson.

Bailey's *Universal Etymological English Dictionary* provides a good illustration. It was the most popular of all the eighteenth-century English dictionaries and went through thirty editions between 1721 and 1802. The treatment of the spelling may best be represented in tabular form for the list of *-or,-our* words given in the lists B and C above (i.e., those about which usage was uncertain). Seventeen of the thirty editions of Bailey have been checked; only those which are relevant are included in the table, and in each case only the preferred spelling is given (Bailey sometimes brackets two forms, presumably putting the preferred form first (e.g. *clamour* is given above *clamor*):

Spelling as in	**Spelling given in Bailey's UEED**						
Johnson's Dict.	**1721**	**1724**	**1737**	**1753**	**1764**	**1775**	**1783**
author	-or						
inferiour	-or						
liquor	-or						
posterior, n.	-or						
tenor	-or						
tutor	-or						
languor	-our	-or					
governour	-our	-our	-or				
horrour	-our	-our	-or				
splendour	-our	-our	-our	-or			
errour	-our	-our	-our	-or			
emperour	-our	-our	-our	-our	-or		
mirror	-our	-our	-our	-our	-or		
posterior, adj.	-our	-our	-our	-our	-or		
servitor	-our	-our	-our	-our	-our	-or	
terrour	-our	-our	-our	-our	-our	-our	-or

The table shows the steady erosion of *-our* spellings in Bailey's dictionary as the century wears on. He starts in 1721 with a spelling rather more conservative than Johnson's; by 1753, immediately before the publication of Johnson's work, it was closer to actual usage than Johnson's, and by the 25th edition in 1783 all these words with the single exception of *splendor* were given in the form in which we know them today; these silent emendations in the successive editions of Bailey produced a pattern of spelling which approximated ever more and more to modern British usage. Compare this with Johnson's Dictionary: there, the pattern of spelling given for these words in 1755 stayed the same throughout the four editions Johnson himself lived to see, and indeed even after the turn of the century in the 9th edition (1805) only one solitary alteration (*possessour* is changed to *possessor*) occurs among the 74 words of this class which have been examined in the successive editions of the Dictionary. The abridged version, abstracted from the folio, is little better. The 6th edition of this (1778—the last to come out before Johnson's death) repeats exactly the spellings in the 1755 Dictionary. In the 12th edition of it, 1807, only *possessour* and *successour* have been changed.

The reason for this is not far to seek. Bailey died in 1742; in each edition before his death he made, or allowed, spelling alterations, and after 1742 new editions and reprintings followed with bewildering rapidity from a succession of different printers, and the dictionary went through a process of more or less continuous emendation, excision and addition. Under these conditions of publication it is not surprising to find that the recommendations for spelling should go hand in hand with the printers' usage.

Johnson was far more conscious than Bailey of his duties as an arbiter of the English language; when he decided between one spelling and another his decision was meant to be final, and even if it was a wrong decision he saw no reason to alter it. Even in the face of criticism (as with *anteriour-posterior*) Johnson made no concessions to usage in the editions that appeared before his death, and it is hardly surprising that the printers risked none after it. They were thus vainly preserving a pattern of *-or*, *-our* spellings which belonged to the years of Johnson's youth until it was some hundred years out of date, and incidentally demonstrating how little influence Johnson's choice really had on the later usage of printers.

Private Spelling If we are to judge from the evidence afforded by these words, then, the dictionaries of the eighteenth century followed the printers with a certain time-lag, and exercised no influence on the printers' practice. The only sense in which we can perhaps speak of influence is on the habits of spelling in private correspondence. There is evidence enough, in dictionary prefaces and elsewhere, that in the eighteenth century dictionaries were sold and used for the correction of private spelling, whether of the educated or of more ignorant men and women.

Lord Chesterfield speaks (in *The World*, 1754) of 'two very different orthographies, the pedantic, and the polite' which were current at the time, and it seems to me that the history of English spelling in that period must take account of this double standard which both existed and was recognized to exist. Dr Johnson's letters are full of all kinds of spellings which he would never have countenanced in his Dictionary, such as *companiable* (=companionable), *enervaiting*, *Fryday*, *obviateing*, *occurences*, *peny*, *pouns* (=pounds), *stiched*, and he will often use more than one spelling of a word in a single letter—for example *chappel* – *chapel*, *dinner* – *diner*, *does* – *dos*, *dos* – *do's*. So are the letters of other educated men. The recognition of this double standard of spelling explains the disparity with the *-or*, *-our* words between Johnson's own private usage in his letters, and his public recommendations in the Dictionary, and suggests that Johnson would himself not have found any embarrassment in the inconsistency. It also enables us to see the fallacy behind the suggestion of Lounsbury that Johnson, more than anyone else, prevented the English from adopting the universal *-or* spelling in the latter half of the eighteenth century. He refers especially to the words *honor* and *favor*, common on cards of invitation in England at the time, and condemned by John Wesley as 'fashionable improprieties'; Lounsbury argues that there was a definite movement towards uniformity at the time, and quotes Walker 'we hardly even find these words with this vowel (i.e. the letter *u*) but in dictionaries'.

If, however, a clear distinction is made between the printers' and the private spelling, it will be found that though *honor* and *favor*, etc. are common enough in the letters of the time (e.g., of Gibbon, Coleridge, Wordsworth), they occur only spasmodically in the printed documents, where the general pattern already established was never really disturbed. *Honor*, *favor*, etc., were in fact current British English informal spellings during the period 1760-1800, but were never really accepted in formal spelling. Here again, Bailey provides us with a truer picture than Johnson: his UEED gives us, as has been shown, a gradually decreasing incidence of *-our* spellings, until his list corresponds with modern British English usage; with the sole exception of *splendor* (about which the printers were divided in the eighteenth century) it never goes any further than modern usage in accepting *-or* spellings. But in the 25th edition (1783) the UEED lists a number of the remaining *-our* words with alternative forms in *-or* marked as 'Mod. Sp.', (e.g., *favor, honor, humor, labor, savior, valor, vapor, vigor*); these alternative 'modern' spellings are still given in the same way in the last (30th) edition in 1802, and were thus never fully accepted in Bailey's dictionary. They remained, in fact 'fashionable improprieties' of informal spelling which never seriously impinged upon the pattern of formal printers' spelling, and there is no need to summon up Dr Johnson as a kind of bogey man to explain why the British did not do what the Americans did.

At the same time, the judicious appraisal and selection of *-or*, *-our* forms in the 25th edition of Bailey gives us a vivid illustration of how the dictionary really functioned in the history of eighteenth-century spelling: as a means of bringing and keeping together the conventions of formal and informal spelling.

END NOTE

Originally published under the title 'Formal and Informal Spelling in the Eighteenth Century. Errour, Honor *and Related Words' in* English Studies *44 (1963) 267-75, and reprinted here by courtesy of Swets Publishing Service, Lisse. A further study, especially of the later history of this group of words, is to be found in Anson 1990. Johnson's private spelling habits and the preferred forms in the Dictionary are further discussed with reference to the word* despatch/dispatch *in Osselton 1994. For a general discussion of the treatment of spelling in dictionaries, see the recent article by Nina Catach (1989), who complains of laxness on the part of compilers in setting out the principles upon which they have worked.*

10

Phrasal Verbs: Dr Johnson's Use of Bilingual Sources

[1984]

The year 1747, when Dr Johnson published his *Plan of a Dictionary of the English Language*, may be taken as the starting point for the science of lexicography, in England at least. Naturally, many of the more practical problems confronting dictionary makers had already been addressed by his predecessors, and a body of customary procedures had become established. It had been, for instance, quite common in dictionaries before Johnson's time to include a fair scatter of dialect words. Johnson, for reasons which are not hard for us to imagine, decided against substantial inclusions of dialect; and, in doing so, pushed the tradition in a particular direction. So also with proper names. There is, as we all know, a case for including proper names in dictionaries, and a case for excluding them. For two centuries (until recently) the British—though not the Americans—have striven manfully to keep them out. In doing so we have been following Johnson's reaction against earlier dictionaries such as Phillips, Coles and Bailey, which had put them in. Likewise, there is the matter of proscribing words. Despite the very firm disclaimer in his Preface ('[I] do not form, but register the language,' he says), Dr Johnson is of course well known for expressing his disapproval of some of the words which he chose nevertheless to include (Allen 1940). Yet a number of his predecessors such as Kersey, Bailey and Martin had introduced quite elaborate proscriptive systems of their own (Osselton 1958). So here, too, Johnson must be seen to have been working from a base of already existing lexicographical principles. For dialect, for proper names, for cautionary labels and in many other ways, then, useful workaday practices for the lexicographer had come into being before 1747.

There is, however, one area in which the monolingual dictionary had hardly even started to evolve a technique before Johnson's time: the treatment of phrasal verbs. The entries for *to come* in Bailey and in Johnson will serve to illustrate the point. In Nathan Bailey's *Universal Etymological English Dictionary* of 1721 the verb *to come* appears as follows:

> TO COME [coman, *Sax*. **Komen**, *Du*. **Kommen**, *Teut*.] to draw nigh, to approach.

Bailey may be regarded as the nearest thing the eighteenth century had to a standard concise dictionary of English, but the users of the 1721 volume or of any of the twenty-seven editions down to the end of the century had to be content with this meagre two-synonym, five-word explanation. In Dr Johnson *to come* is also in a single entry, but it is an entry with fifty-nine sub-sections, including illustrations of *to come* with twenty-one different particles or particle combinations: *come about, come by, come in, come into, come near, come off, come off from, come over, come up to,* and so on.

The modern omnibus lemma, so well known to us from later dictionaries, had thus been born. And from a survey of the historical evidence, it appears to have been Dr Johnson's invention.

Johnson's main source was not the smaller Bailey dictionary, but the second edition of the *Dictionarium Britannicum* (1736). But even in this substantial work, which we may suppose Dr Johnson to have had before him, the entry for *to come* remains woefully inadequate:

> TO COME *Irr[egular] V[erb]* [**coman**, *Sax*. **komme**, *Dan*. **komma**, *Su*. **komen**, *Du*. **kommen**, *G*.] to draw nigh, to approach; to attain to, to accost, to amount to, to end, to be the consequence of, to succeed, to agree to

—and that is really all, though he adds two proverbs, including *first come, first served* with French and Italian equivalents. There was little in this for Johnson to work with. And for the kind of entry we are here concerned with—*put down, take in, throw over,* etc.—none of the other monolingual dictionaries of the eighteenth century was any better. There was no technique for dealing with the complexities of the phrasal verbs before Johnson turned his attention to them.

The following account seeks to show how Johnson set to work in building up his major entries for such verbs (the biggest one being *to take*, with 133 definitions and over 65 distinct collocations); and to indicate what his main sources for the material were. He is to be seen not only as a dictionary maker getting on with the job, but as the self-critical scholar who was clearly aware of the peculiar difficulties caused by this class of entry. In methodology at least, Johnson's sheer boldness as a lexicographer is perhaps better measured by his treatment of the phrasal verbs than by any other feature in the dictionary.

The Preface to Johnson's Dictionary of 1755 is devoted largely to a setting out of the problems encountered during the compilation of the work, and to a statement of how they were overcome. Or rather, partially overcome, since for Johnson there is no ideal dictionary: lexicography, like any other human activity, is subject to the imperfections of all sublunary nature. Nevertheless, he gives firm decisions on etymology, spelling, choice of authors, and other matters.

There are, however, two highly interesting and—so far as I know—hitherto little regarded passages in which he turns to what he calls certain 'loose and general' verbs such as *give, get* and *put*, which he felt to be something of a blemish on the English language, and saw as posing special difficulties for him as a dictionary maker (as of course they still do for us). These are his words:

> My labour [i.e., in making the dictionary] has likewise been much increased by a class of verbs too frequent in the *English* language, of which the signification is so loose and general, the use so vague and indeterminate, and the senses distorted so widely from the first idea, that it is hard to trace them through the maze of variation, to catch them on the brink of utter inanity, to circumscribe them by any limitations, or interpret them by any words of distinct or settled meaning; such are *bear, break, come, cast, fall, get, give, do, put, set, go, run, make, take, turn, throw* (Johnson 1755, sig. B2[r]).

Johnson, here echoing a complaint made by Bishop Wilkins nearly a hundred years before (Wilkins 1668, 17-18), sees these words as both time-consuming and difficult to handle; and he confesses with characteristic honesty that neither his nor any other man's treatment of them is ever going to be entirely satisfactory. With a fine poetic touch, he declares that their meanings 'can no more be ascertained in a dictionary, than a grove, in the agitation of a storm, can be accurately delineated from its picture in the water'.

He takes the matter further in discussing the same group of verbs (*come, fall, get,* etc.) when they are combined with particles. Here are Johnson's words on phrasal verbs—the very first discussion of the matter by an English lexicographer:

> There is another kind of composition more frequent in our language than perhaps any other, from which arises to foreigners the greatest difficulty. We modify the signification of many verbs by a particle subjoined; as to *come off*, to escape by a fetch; to *fall on*, to attack; to *fall off*, to apostatize; to *break off*, to stop abruptly; to *bear out*, to justify; to *fall in*, to comply; to *give over*, to cease; to *set off*, to embellish; to *set in*, to begin a continual tenour; to *set out*, to begin a course or journey; to *take off*, to copy; with innumerable expressions of the same kind, of which some appear wildly irregular, being so far distant from the sense of the simple words, that no sagacity will be able to trace the steps by which they arrived at the present use. These I have noted with great care; and though I cannot flatter myself that the collection is complete, I have perhaps so far assisted the students of our language, that this kind of phraseology will be no longer insuperable; and the combinations of verbs and particles, by chance omitted, will be easily explained by comparison with those that may be found (Johnson 1755, sig. B1^{v}).

It is a remarkable passage, in which he identifies unerringly some of the crucial points lexicographers are here concerned with. First, the fact that their idiomatic nature makes them perplexing to a foreign learner. Secondly, that many of them are semantically unpredictable: why should *give over* and *give up* both mean 'abandon'? why should *set out* and *set off* both mean 'embellish'? Such randomness is not pleasing to the lexicographer's orderly mind, and as Johnson elsewhere observes (in the *Plan* 1747, 9), such particles seem to be 'originally assigned by chance'. Thirdly, Johnson states very clearly the selectional problem involved: you can't put them all in your dictionary, and you don't need to anyway, because many of them are self-explanatory. There are no grounds for including *give away*, if *give* means 'give' and *away* means 'away'. But somewhere between boringly predictable items such as this and highly idiomatic ones such as *give in*, meaning 'surrender', there is a grey area in which lexicographers have been floundering ever since.

This passage from the preface is, however, not the only comment on the problem of phrasal verbs in the Dictionary: in later editions the subject is addressed also in some of the entries themselves. Out of the sixteen 'loose and general' verbs complained about in the preface, thirteen have notes appended to them in the 9th edition (1805) expressing the compiler's near-despair at the problem of coping with them. In the article on *make*, for instance, after listing sixty meanings with sixteen different collocations he adds an article No. 61, which reads simply:

> This is one of the words so frequently occurring, and used with so much latitude, that its whole extent is not easily comprehended, nor are its attenuated and fugitive meanings easily caught and restrained,

and at the end of *run* we read:

> This is one of the words which serves for use when other words are wanted, and has therefore obtained a great multiplicity of relations and intentions.

'When other words are wanted': it may seem a strange notion to suggest that the English language, lacking other words to express the ideas, had to use these tiresome phrasal verbs instead. But, of course, it makes rather better sense if one has Latin in mind. If we consider, for instance, a group of Latin derivational verbs formed on the base *curro*:

curro	run
decurro	run down
intercurro	run between
percurro	run through
praecurro	run before
recurro	run back, etc.

then the English language may indeed seem deficient in tidy separate lexemes for each idea such as Latin has. It is then quite understandable that the early lexicographer should regret finding himself stranded with a mass of material which is very hard to sort out because it doesn't lend itself (as Latin does) to single-run alphabetical ordering.

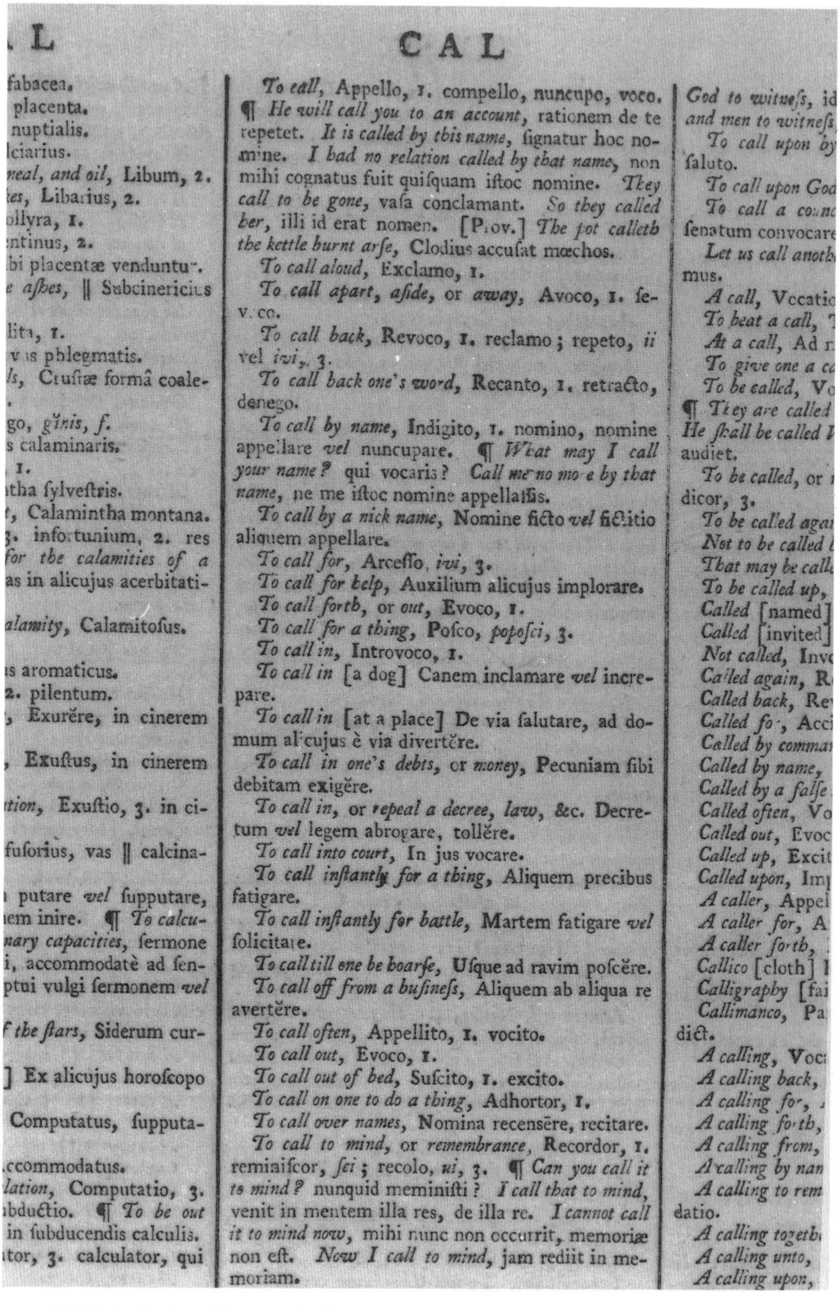

CAL

To call, Appello, 1. compello, nuncupo, voco. ¶ *He will call you to an account*, rationem de te repetet. *It is called by this name*, ſignatur hoc nomine. *I had no relation called by that name*, non mihi cognatus fuit quiſquam iſtoc nomine. *They call to be gone*, vaſa conclamant. *So they called her*, illi id erat nomen. [Prov.] *The pot calleth the kettle burnt arſe*, Clodius accuſat mœchos.

To call aloud, Exclamo, 1.

To call apart, aſide, or *away*, Avoco, 1. ſevoco.

To call back, Revoco, 1. reclamo; repeto, *ii* vel *ivi*, 3.

To call back one's word, Recanto, 1. retracto, denego.

To call by name, Indigito, 1. nomino, nomine appellare *vel* nuncupare. ¶ *What may I call your name?* qui vocaris? *Call me no more by that name*, ne me iſtoc nomine appellaſſis.

To call by a nick name, Nomine ficto *vel* fictitio aliquem appellare.

To call for, Arceſſo, *ivi*, 3.

To call for help, Auxilium alicujus implorare.

To call forth, or *out*, Evoco, 1.

To call for a thing, Poſco, *popoſci*, 3.

To call in, Introvoco, 1.

To call in [a dog] Canem inclamare *vel* increpare.

To call in [at a place] De via ſalutare, ad domum alicujus è via divertĕre.

To call in one's debts, or *money*, Pecuniam ſibi debitam exigĕre.

To call in, or *repeal a decree, law*, &c. Decretum *vel* legem abrogare, tollĕre.

To call into court, In jus vocare.

To call inſtantly for a thing, Aliquem precibus fatigare.

To call inſtantly for battle, Martem fatigare *vel* ſolicitare.

To call till one be hoarſe, Uſque ad ravim poſcĕre.

To call off from a buſineſs, Aliquem ab aliqua re avertĕre.

To call often, Appellito, 1. vocito.

To call out, Evoco, 1.

To call out of bed, Suſcito, 1. excito.

To call on one to do a thing, Adhortor, 1.

To call over names, Nomina recenſēre, recitare.

To call to mind, or *remembrance*, Recordor, 1. reminiſcor, *ſci*; recolo, *ui*, 3. ¶ *Can you call it to mind?* nunquid meminiſti? *I call that to mind*, venit in mentem illa res, de illa re. *I cannot call it to mind now*, mihi nunc non occurrit, memoriæ non eſt. *Now I call to mind*, jam rediit in memoriam.

FIG. 5. Robert Ainsworth, *Thesaurus Linguae Latinae Compendiarius* (2nd edn 1746): the opening entries for the verb *to call.*

It is a revealing complaint (though not one we should make today) because it has to do not only with the structure of the English verb system but also with the way in which dictionaries evolved historically. Examination of the earliest dictionaries with an English alphabetical list (such as the *Promptorium Parvulorum* in the fifteenth century) makes it very clear that such phrasal verbs as do occur are often there because they correspond to single Latin lexemes: original Latin-English entries have become reversed to give English-Latin ones, with little or no regard to the question of whether they have earned a place in an English list. This is a curious fact of lexicographical history which cannot be explored further in the present context. But it seems at least very likely that the choice of phrasal verbs for entry in dictionaries was skewed from the start, because of the Latin.

The question remains, however, of where Johnson got his phrasal verbs from, since they were clearly not in Bailey. Even at this late stage in lexicographical development, in the mid-eighteenth century, the monolingual dictionary of the vernacular was still in essence a hard-word book, devoted for the greater part to the explicitly scholarly vocabulary of English. Around 1700 the process had got under way by which common words came to be included as well. But (as any lexicographer will know) you cannot simply sit down and dream up the words you want: you need another list. And when John Kersey, the first to include common words systematically, set about the business of doing that, he turned to the bilingual dictionaries to find them (see chapter 3 above). Foreign learners, and learners of Latin, had long needed them, though native speakers of English had not.

In the passage quoted above from Dr Johnson's preface he refers to the great inconvenience caused to foreigners by these verbs. In the light of this, it seems worth investigating the relationship between the complex entries Johnson devised for such verbs and the material that would have been available on them in the bilingual dictionaries. A further reason for doing this is that we know from the sale catalogue of Johnson's library after his death that he did indeed possess a number of large bilingual dictionaries, notably Willem Sewel for Dutch and English, Abel Boyer for French and English, and the Latin-English dictionary of Robert Ainsworth. There is then a presumptive reason to suppose that Johnson might have used any or all of them.

Even the most cursory look at any of these bilingual works shows that they do indeed provide immeasurably better coverage of the phrasal verbs than any monolingual dictionary had ever done. In Boyer, for instance, there are over seventy entries for the verb *break*, including

break down	break off
break forth	break open
break in	break through
break into	break up

and so on. It is also striking that in Johnson's Dictionary only nine of the sixty-four meanings given for *break* are unsupported by quotations: but that eight of these nine correspond to entries in Boyer. The significance of this will be clear. If Johnson enters a word and provides a quotation this may (though it need not necessarily) mean that he is working from private memory of actual usage, or is basing the entry on quotation from some literary work laid under contribution. But if he enters a word and either cannot or does not provide a quotation, it is at least likely that he is getting it from another man's list.

Because of the complicated patterns of interrelationships between the European bilingual dictionaries of the period, it will probably remain impossible to prove which one Johnson is using at any given moment. The Ainsworth Latin dictionary already referred to is, however, very likely to have been among his sources. To illustrate the structure of Johnson's lemma for *call* I have taken for the purposes of comparison the latest edition of Ainsworth's dictionary (that of 1746) which could have been available to him when he started work.

In turning to Ainsworth, Johnson would have been confronted by a jumble of fifty-one lemmata for *call* (see Figure 5). These include straight definitions of the simplex word, phrasal verbs, purely idiomatic phrases such as *to call to mind*, and some more improbable items such as *to call by a nick name* or *to call till one be hoarse*. Here is a sample group of consecutive entries from the fifty-one items in Ainsworth:

To call in a rash word
To call together
To call unto
To call up

To call up spirits
To call one up [in the morning]
To call as a partridge
To call upon
To call upon for help
To call upon often
To call upon for a witness
To call to witness
To call upon by the way.

The Latin 'definitions' have been omitted here; in some cases, such as *cacabo* for 'To call as a partridge', they leave us with little doubt that we have to do here with an inverted entry from earlier Latin-English lists such as have been mentioned above.

All this Dr Johnson has formed into two main sections, one for the transitive verb, the other for the intransitive, as the following skeleton of his entry for *call* will show:

TO CALL. v.a. [calo *Lat.* kalder, *Danish*]

1. To name; to denominate ... (Genesis)
2. To summon or invite, to or from any place, thing or person. It is often used with local particles, as *up, down, in, out, off* ... (Shakespeare, Milton, etc.)
3. To convoke ... (Shakespeare, Clarendon)
4. To summon judicially ... (Clarendon, Watts)
5. To summon by command ... (Isaiah)
6. In the theological sense ... (Romans)
7. To invoke ... (2 Cor.)
8. To appeal to ... (Clarendon)
9. To proclaim ... (Gay)
10. To excite ... (Cowley, Pope)
11. To stigmatize ... (Swift)
12. *To call back*. To revoke ... (Isaiah)
13. *To call for*. To demand ... (Shakespeare, Milton, Dryden, Rogers)
14. *To call in.* To resume money ... (Addison)
15. *To call in.* To resume anything that is in other hands ... (Locke, Swift)

16. *To call in.* To summon together ... (Shakespeare, Denham)
17. *To call over.* To read aloud a list or a muster-roll (No quotations)
18. *To call out.* To challenge ... (Dryden)

TO CALL. v.n.

1. To stop without intention of staying ...; it is now used with great latitude. This sense is well enough preserved by the particles *on* or *at*; but is forgotten, and the expression is barbarous, by *in*.
2. To make a short visit ... (Jonson, Temple, Addison)
3. *To call on.* To solicit a favour ... (Shakespeare)
4. *To call on.* To repeat solemnly ... (Dryden, Broome)
5. *To call upon.* To implore ... (Psalms).

It will be clear from this that Johnson has simply cut out idiomatic locutions which were felt to be inappropriate to the monolingual dictionary. As for the verb-particle combinations, the sixteen that he would have found in Ainsworth are reduced to seven:

call back	call for	call in	
call on	call out	call over	call upon.

For items such as *call for* ('demand') there was evidently sufficient semantic justification for inclusion. But under the main entry of the verb *call*, he notes that 'it is often used with local particles, as *up, down, in, out, off*'; that is, he provides a blanket acknowledgement of the capacity of the verb to enter into all kinds of free combinations which (unlike set locutions such as *call for*) scarcely merit separate entry.

It is all very orderly, and reveals that a vast amount of careful thought went into imposing some system on the mass of material that was available to him: and the pattern which Johnson produces is very much like what we are used to today.

There remains, however, the matter of quotations. The seven phrasal verbs involving *call* to which Johnson accords separate entry are all in Ainsworth with the same meaning, and it seems very likely that he got them from there, even though he provides illustrations for six of them from the Bible (*call back*, *call upon*) and from major authors such as Shakespeare, Milton, Dryden and Locke. It seems reasonable to suggest that the list of entries in Ainsworth served as a kind of catalyst for his literary memory: '*call for*, arcesso' in Ainsworth touched off appropriate quotations from Shakespeare, Milton and Dryden, and was therefore included. On the other hand, the verb *call down* in the sense of 'denounce, decry' was not in Ainsworth, and sure enough it does not appear in Johnson, even though he might have illustrated it from Bacon and other writers of the time. Then, what about *call together*, which is in Ainsworth, and which Johnson might have illustrated from the Bible? Did he simply not remember the appropriate passage? Or did he consider it to be one of those verbs merely self-explanatory? It is hard for us to know. But clearly there was room then, as now, for a personal judgement to enter into the matter.

This leads to a final point, which has to do with coverage. How reliable and how full a record is Dr Johnson's Dictionary of the usage of his age? That will, in the end, be much harder to tell with the phrasal verbs than for most lexical items. But maybe we owe it to Johnson in this bicentenary year of his death to do for the Dictionary of 1755 what Jürgen Schäfer (1980) has done for the OED. The concordances of Bacon, Shakespeare, Milton, Dryden, Pope—all the writers most favoured by Johnson—are there for us to use. If the argument here is accepted, namely that Johnson was for those verbs using a bilingual dictionary as a catalyst for literary memory, then further work on his 'authorial reliability rate' might tell us much about the man as well as the procedures he adopted in the book.

But however full or inadequate the coverage is, there can be little doubt that, in terms of technique and of lexicographical method, Johnson was in all this highly innovative, and very successful. He was the first English dictionary maker to make anything like a real job of the phrasal verbs.

END NOTE

Originally delivered as a lecture at the First Fulbright Colloquium, held in London from 13 to 16 September 1984, and published thereafter in Ilson 1986, 7-16 with the title 'Dr Johnson and the English phrasal verb'. Now reprinted here by courtesy of the Fulbright Commission, London. Recent works referring to Johnson's compiling procedures include DeMaria 1986 and Reddick 1990.

11

A Dictionary Compiler at Work in the Sixteenth Century

[1986]

Little is directly known about the practical working methods of early dictionary makers. Dr Johnson is traditionally supposed to have used an interleaved copy of Bailey's *Dictionarium Britannicum*, and we can deduce something from his marking-up of books which were to be laid under contribution (McCracken 1969, Clifford 1979, 46-51). We know that Benjamin Martin instructed his amanuenses to place Ainsworth's Latin dictionary in front of them so as to force upon themselves the different senses that English words could bear (Starnes and Noyes 1946, 152). For visual evidence of early practices, we have an elegant engraving dating from 1727 showing the Dutch lexicographer Willem Sewel in his library, pen in hand, with reference books propped up all around him (Osselton 1973, frontispiece). But such incidental bits of direct evidence are few, and any general impression of how the first compilers set to work must be gained by inference from their completed works. Historical study of the early English dictionaries has produced fairly detailed conclusions about sources: for instance, we know that Phillips used Bullokar, Cockeram and Blount, and threw in items from Cowell too (Starnes and Noyes 1946, 48-54); but his actual procedures for marrying up the word lists remain obscure.

The chance survival in Bodl. MS Rawlinson Poet.108 of an early and evidently abortive attempt at starting off a monolingual English dictionary (henceforward 'the Rawlinson dictionary') is therefore of interest. The more so since, as I shall show, it is a very tentative effort, a mere initial draft for a dictionary text, with the false starts, gaps, corrections and duplications which are to be expected when a compiler is feeling his way in a hitherto unattempted mode.

The MS is of additional interest because of its date: the collection in which it occurs is dated by the Bodleian to c.1570, and so the text may well antedate the earliest known English-English dictionary—that of Cawdrey—by some decades. But we cannot be sure about this. The dictionary entries have been added on blank pages of an already-existing MS some time after the original compilation it contains. Evidence for dating from handwriting will probably remain inconclusive, and no firm *terminus ante quem* can plausibly be established. Nevertheless, nothing has been found in the dictionary which would militate against a date in the last quarter of the sixteenth century. We know also that once monolingual English dictionaries do begin to be published, successive compilers habitually draw upon their predecessors' efforts. If the Rawlinson compiler had set to work after Cawdrey and Cockeram, he would in all likelihood have used Cawdrey and Cockeram. But there is no evidence of his having done so, and there are therefore grounds for believing that this abruptly terminated alphabetical list represents the earliest known attempt at making a monolingual English dictionary. It is a text which therefore invites comparison with the first such dictionary ever to be published, Cawdrey's *Table Alphabeticall* (1604), and points of similarity and contrast between the two will be offered in this preliminary report on its contents.

Compiling Procedures The author of the Rawlinson dictionary drew up his text on sheets already prepared by another hand for the compilation of a book-index. The dictionary entries occur on the first three pages (each divided into four columns) out of 35 which had been left blank for the insertion of the index at the end of a manuscript medical treatise. These 35 pages had previously been marked up in alphabetical blocks with the headings *Ab-*, *Ac-*, etc., ready to receive the entries for the foregoing text. Some medical items had been put in with their page references; thus we find under *Ba-* (in a different hand from that of the dictionary entries) references such as 'Balsom 49.95.123', and under *Be-* 'Belly great and hard 145' and '(Belly) ache 184'. But there are very few of these. The medical indexer had evidently quickly given up, leaving most of the page surface blank.

The intending lexicographer thus found here a convenient receptacle for arranging his dictionary entries as he collected them: a complete series of alphabetical slots or boxes already in some measure proportioned to his needs. *Be-*, for instance, has been allocated about 20 column inches, as against 9 for *Ap-*, and only 3 for *Aw-*. But by using these sheets the compiler of the Rawlinson dictionary was accepting what may seem to us a surprising constraint upon his activities: he was content to work within an alphabetical framework set up by another man for an entirely different purpose. This meant that he simply had to get everything in on the sheet in front of him—all the words from *abandon* to *amphibology* on the first page, those from *analogy* to *azure* on the next, and so on. I know of no other evidence for such constraints on length accepted by or imposed upon early lexicographers, though doubtless they will then (as now) have had to accede to limits imposed by publishers.

The compiler's actual procedure may be illustrated from the MS entries under *Ab-*. These begin with a list of twenty entries (mainly verbs):

abandon - forsake
abaleanate -
Abase - humble
abash
abate - diminish
abbreviate }
} - abstract
abbridge }
abhomination - offence
abhorre - loath
abide - tarry
abide - suffer
abiect - forsake
abiure - forsweare
able - power
abolish - destroy
abound - plenty
abrogate - destroy
absolue - pardon
absolutnesse - perfection
absurdity - foolishnesse.

Below the entry for *absurdity* a single ink line has been drawn across the whole column. There then follows a supplementary alphabetical list of nine entries, this time consisting chiefly of nouns, with no definitions and again with a terminal line:

abbot
abbey
ablatiue case
abortiue
abricot appl
absence
abstinence
abstract
abuse.

This total of 29 entries fills up about three-quarters of the space that was available for words beginning with *Ab*-, and the rest is left blank, except that to the right and immediately above the section for *Ac*-, the single word *abstract* has been scribbled in.

All this gives the impression of a compiler who is casting about for an appropriate scale of entry, and a balance between word types. The first trial list of twenty words fell short, so he had a second alphabetical run, this time incorporating more nouns. At some stage *abstract* has been jotted in for inclusion, and it duly appears in the second list. The column-to-column line after *absurdity* would presumably serve to warn a reviser or printer that a supplementary list was being started, and that alphabetical incorporation was therefore needed (though a division of verbs and nouns into two lists had been an established tradition at least as early as the *Promptorium Parvulorum* c. 1440). Evidently the compiler was content with the total of 29 entries for *Ab*- (Cawdrey, we may note, has 27) because the remaining space of about one and a half inches is left blank. But he did not (or did not yet) go back to provide definitions for the nine extra entries.

Under *Ac*- the same procedure is followed, with 21 items in the first list, and only 5 in the second (he seems to be getting better at it). This time there are five additional jottings at the end of the section (*accuse, acorne, acte, actiuity, action*). Since they correspond (more or less) to entries among the first 21, it is likely that the compiler was putting down useful items before even starting on the alphabetical list proper.

The *Ac-* items nicely fill the half column available for them, and the dictionary maker must have decided at this point that he had now got the scale about right; at any rate from then on there are no more double alphabetical lists.

The rest of the letter A is completed in the same manner and seemingly with a roughly similar coverage of the vocabulary, giving an effective total of 337 lemmata for the whole letter. Some of the ready-prepared spaces on the pages remained partly unfilled—there are only three entries for *Aw-*, for instance, though there would have been room for about eighteen. In the section for words beginning with *Ar-*, however, the author overshoots badly: with the word *arsnick* he reached the bottom of the page, with no room for any more. He therefore continued his alphabetical series of *Ar-* words with *Art*, *Artechoke*, etc., written upside down above the beginning of the section in a space which happened to have been left unused at the end of *Ap-* (see Figure 6). The device of finishing the entries upside down would presumably have been intended to deter any unheeding printer from setting them in the wrong place.

Only 81 consecutive entries have been filled in under the letter B, and there, with the word *baskett*, the manuscript dictionary unfortunately comes to an end. A few jottings further on in the alphabet (*besom, flattery, height*) serve to indicate at least that he had plans to proceed further.

Projected Length The Rawlinson dictionary contains 337 entries for the letter A, as against 286 in Cawdrey, a difference of 18%. Projection of these figures might lead us to believe that had it been completed the dictionary would have had some 3000 entries, as against the 2543 in Cawdrey. This total may however be misleading, because Cawdrey's dictionary is noticeably skewed in its uptake of words through the letters of the alphabet, with about 11.5% of all entries falling under the letter A, as against a normal expectation for an English word-list of about 6.5%. A calculation based on 6.5% for the letter A would give the Rawlinson dictionary a projected total of 5184 entries, making it comparable in size with Bullokar's *English Expositor* of 1616.

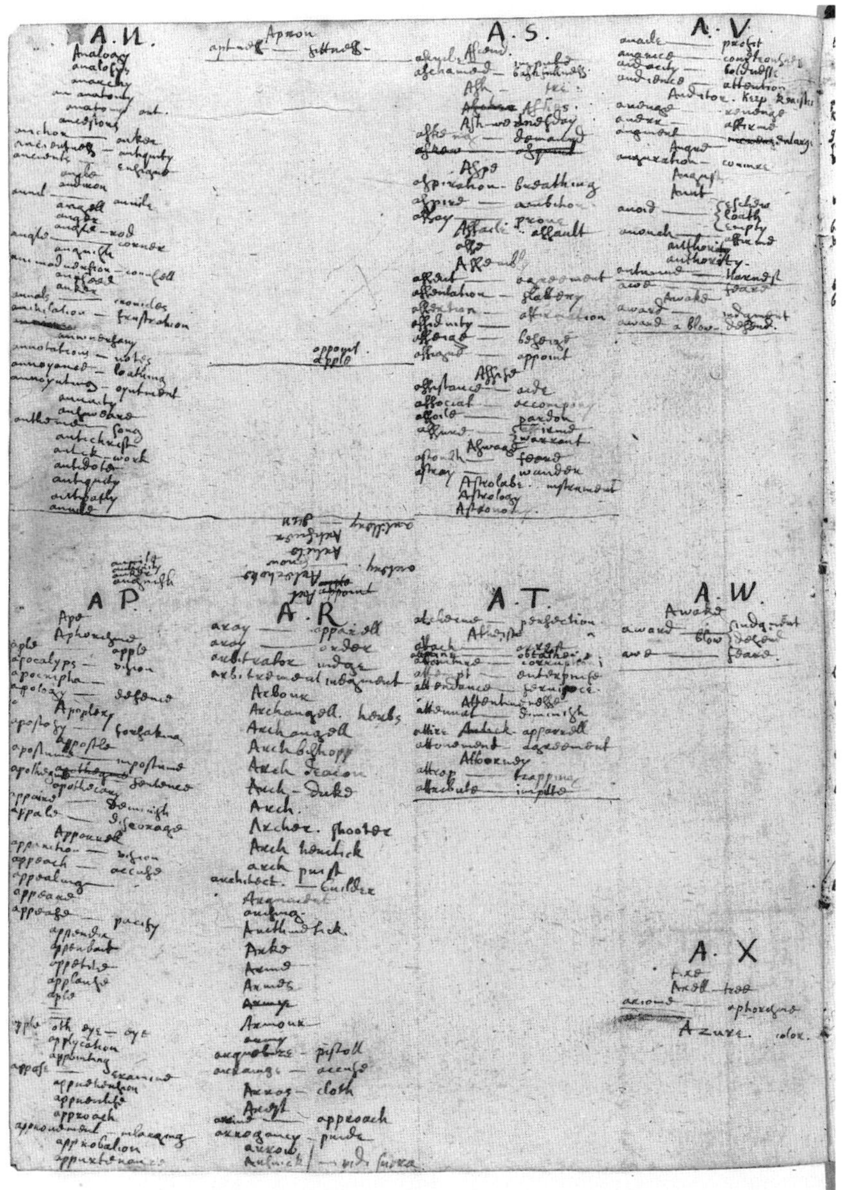

FIG. 6. Draft list of words from *analogy* to *azure* for an early monolingual English dictionary (Bodl. Rawlinson MS Poet.108).

Definitions Definitions or explanations have been provided for about half of all the words entered under the letter A. There is however a noticeable tailing off, as though the compiler was already wearying of his task. Under the initial list of *Ab-*, 18 out of the 20 words have explanations, but under *An-* only 12 out of 34; and for the letter B, not more than about one in six can be said to have anything that can be called a definition.

In general, one-word explanations are given (*abandon* forsake, *aduantage* gaine), though occasionally the compiler permits himself a brace with multiple senses

assure { affirme
warrant

or gives successive entries for homographs (*aray* apparell, *aray* order). Some definitions (such as those for *alembick, ambiguity* and *artillery*) appear to have been added in another hand.

One puzzling feature of the Rawlinson dictionary is that those entries for which no definition has been provided are in general (though not always) centred in the column. Yet it does not seem likely that the compiler was envisaging a dictionary where (as happens sometimes in spelling-books) explanations are given only of selected entries. As the following successive entries may show, some centred entries do have definitions, and it is by no means the case that only 'easy' words are left unexplained:

Amesse - robe
Amity - friendship
Amphitheatre
amphibology.

The Rawlinson compiler is in general much inferior to Cawdrey in the matter of defining. Sometimes their entries correspond exactly (both give 'breathing' for *aspiration*) but Cawdrey normally provides fuller explanations or lists of synonyms, having for instance 'cast away, or yeelde vp, to leaue, or forsake' where Rawlinson gives just the one word 'forsake' for the meaning of *abandon*. In addition to this, and to the many gaps in his list of entries (though one may assume that the intention was to go back and fill these in), the Rawlinson compiler shows himself to be less consistent in method. There are entries where the 'explanation' is in fact a mere indication of the context of usage ('ace – dice', 'Badger. for corne', 'barre where ye plead'); other items are given in the *X or Y* formula ('bar – or bolt'); and with some there is a failure to match word-class between entry and definition ('aspire – ambition', 'aschamed – bashfulness'). In some cases, such as 'anihilation – frustration', he shows a rather alarming ignorance about the words he was putting in.

Deletions and Corrections There are as we might expect a number of deletions and corrections in the MS. Mostly these are of no significance (repeated entries, items out of alphabetical sequence, etc.). But there is some evidence of the author having second thoughts about including an item he had initially selected, as with the deletion of *adioyning* and *askew* ('asqint'). There are also changes in the definitions: 'decree' has been crossed out and replaced by 'statute' for the explanation of *act*, and 'chance' is deleted in favour of 'fortune' as an equivalent for *aduenture*. On the whole, however, the MS evidence suggests that the compiler proceeded with remarkably little hesitation in making his selection of words.

Word Selection The difference between the Rawlinson dictionary and Cawdrey in their approach to the selection of words for entry may perhaps best be illustrated by setting alongside each other the complete list of entries for the words beginning *Ag-* and *Ai-* (erratic alphabetization has been adjusted):

Rawlinson	**Cawdrey**
age	
agent	agent
	agglutinate
agrauate	aggrauate
agility	agilitie
	agitate
aglet	
agnaile	
agnition	agnition
agony	agony

Rawlinson	Cawdrey
agreement	
ague	
aide	
	aigre
aime	
aire.	

It is a well-known fact that the first monolingual dictionaries of English (Cawdrey, Bullokar, Cockeram and their successors) were 'hard-word' books, concentrating on the newly-acquired and unfamiliar Latinate vocabulary of renaissance English, and that it is not until the eighteenth century with the work of John Kersey (see chapter 3 in this volume) that any systematic and serious attempt is made to cover the ordinary or everyday words of the language. But it will be clear even from the short selection given above that the Rawlinson dictionary, had it ever been completed and published, would in this matter have been radically different from the other dictionaries of its time. The compiler does not ignore the learned words (*agrauate, agility, agnition*) though—despite his longer list—he takes in fewer of them than Cawdrey does. But in his decision to include common words such as *age, aime* and *aire* (as well as, elsewhere, *alehouse, apple, apron, arm, axe, barber, barly* and many others) he shows himself to be a century ahead of his time in his view of what the monolingual dictionary should contain.

Source Given that the Rawlinson text (however defective it may be) represents the first known attempt at putting together a monolingual English dictionary, the question of what source the compiler used is of considerable interest. Even a cursory inspection of his vocabulary suggests that it must have been a Latin one. We find, for instance, an entry which reads *band of souldiers*. Now it is sensible enough to have an entry for *band* (under B) and to have one for *souldiers* (under S). But *band of souldiers* seems rather pointless, and its presence is hard to explain until we note that the English noun phrase corresponds to a simplex lexical item in Latin, namely *cohors*. So also with 'bag and baggage' (that is, *impedimenta*), 'bay for shipps to be in' (*statio*) and many others which point to some hidden Latin source. Among them is an interesting group of phrasal verbs all listed under *back*:

put back - repulse
keep back - reteine
giue backe - recoile
goe backe - returne.

These four suggest an original finding-place under *re-* in a Latin source (e.g. *repello, retineo, recedo, regredior*). One would in any case hardly expect the items to turn up in English under the letter B. For further discussion of phrasal verbs in early dictionaries, see chapter 10 below.

By the time when the Rawlinson compiler set to work, a number of English-Latin dictionaries had been produced (Starnes 1954, Parts I and II), and any of these could have provided a basic alphabetical list of English words upon which the innovator of a monolingual dictionary might build. If (as in this case seems likely) he were working in the last decade of the sixteenth century the obvious choice among such dictionaries would have been John Rider's *Bibliotheca Scholastica* (1589). This went through numerous editions and revisions during the next eighty years (Starnes 1954, 218-71).

A comparison of the Rawlinson text with the first edition of the Rider dictionary shows that this could very well have been the main source of the English word-list. At least three-quarters of the hundred items from *almes* to *aptness* occur in Rider. For many of his entries, such as *ambiguity* 'doubtfulnes', or *appaire* 'diminish', the compiler would have been able to find his definition there too. Like many English-Latin dictionaries of the time, Rider frequently gives an English synonym before the Latin equivalent, so as to help out with polysemous words. Where (as under *Ab-* and *Ac-*) the Rawlinson compiler took a second cull of words to extend his list, these too appear to have come from Rider.

The Rider dictionary was able to provide learned as well as common words (*apostume, ancle*), and the Rawlinson compiler has added his own in both kinds (*amphibology, applause*), though he has been very selective in the common words taken over—omitting, for instance, *alone, already, am* and *amorous* (all of which are in Rider) and preferring in general to keep to nouns and verbs. Comparison of the entries under the letter A suggests that he used Rider simply as some kind of a browsing ground, picking up any suggestions for words which suited his purpose at that point in the alphabet. *Ambushment*, for instance, is not given an entry in Rider, but happens to occur in the entry for *ambush*; Rider has *An angling rodde* but Rawlinson prefers *angle-rod*; *ambrey*, in Rider, is merely a cross-reference item ('*vide* cupboard'), but the reference 'cupboard' becomes the explanation for *ambrey* in the Rawlinson list.

It is of course almost impossible to prove a lexicographical source, but the correspondences between the two works are sufficiently close for us to infer that Rider was used, and we can in any case be certain that the Rawlinson dictionary was heavily indebted to one or another of the many dictionaries of English and Latin.

The Rawlinson MS Dictionary and English Lexicographical Tradition

This manuscript dictionary is unfortunately only a fragment, though it is a fragment big enough for us to know that the work, had it been finished, would have been appreciably bigger than Cawdrey—perhaps even twice the size. We must also regret that the author never really advanced beyond the vocabulary-selection stage, to tidy up entries, and supply the definitions for the many items which now stand as a single word. Indeed, given the curiously haphazard and illogical nature of some of his entries ('able – power', 'abound – plenty', 'accomplish – perfection') one may even wonder whether he did not give up because he saw that the task was too much for him.

The fact that this MS dictionary is located at the end of a medical treatise provides a nice though somewhat fortuitous confirmation for the view (Schäfer 1984) that historians of the early English dictionary need to pay greater regard to all kinds of glossaries appended to learned and technical books published in the vernacular. More important than this are the limitations resulting from the use of index pages. The acceptance of pre-defined blocks for the insertion of dictionary entries, with only so many inches per letter combination, gives us a unique insight into what is (so far as I know) a hitherto undocumented compiling method. The decision to press into service the unfilled index pages may have been merely opportunistic; but on the other hand what was felt to be an acceptable method for compiling a glossary might well have seemed a serviceable technique for lexicographers too.

It is hard to know whether the compiling techniques indicated by this manuscript were widely used or not. One curious but striking piece of evidence that they probably do reflect common practice was unknowingly provided by Sledd some fifty years ago in his unpublished thesis on Baret's *Alvearie* (1573). Baret's dictionary belongs to the schoolroom, and its compiler explains how materials for inclusion were collected by diligent pupils and then cast into dictionary entries by him: an unusual example of team-work in early dictionary compiling. Sledd points out that the alphabetization in Baret is imperfect, and as an example refers to the group of words beginning with *an-*. These have *aniuersarie* and *answer* tacked on at the end, 'although the preceding entries, from *ancher* to *any*, are properly arranged' (Sledd 1947, 20). This detail of lexicographical arrangement surviving in the printed text of Baret corresponds exactly to what we find in the Rawlinson MS, and it suggests that the *A ante N* type of heading which is so familiar a feature on the pages of early dictionaries may have functioned not only as a help to the user's eye, but as a unit for the collection of data as well.

The use of an English-Latin dictionary as a main source of material is striking. The first English hard-word dictionaries have been shown to derive their word-lists in large measure from Latin-English (not English-Latin) dictionaries, by a process of wholesale anglicization of Latin items. By turning to an English-Latin source the Rawlinson compiler provided himself with a much wider range of lexical material to draw on. His decision to include 'ordinary' words (which goes with the choice of source) was entirely at variance with contemporary practice. Cawdrey has long been associated with the establishment of the 'hard-word' tradition, and has even been blamed for it (Noyes 1943). Even from the fragmentary text now found in the Rawlinson MS we can see that Cawdrey's choice was not a self-evident one at the time: the English dictionary might very well have been more balanced in its vocabulary even from the start.

END NOTE

This study was included in The History of Lexicography, *edited by R.R.K. Hartmann. John Benjamins Publishing Company. Amsterdam/ Philadelphia, 1986, 175-84, and is reprinted here by kind permission of the publishers. The illustration from the MS has now been added, and the text above is a slightly expanded version of a paper delivered at the Dictionary Research Centre Seminar in Exeter in March 1986, under the title 'The first English dictionary? A sixteenth-century compiler at work'.*

Further information on Cawdrey's predecessors is available in Stein (1985a). On the early glossaries see Schäfer (1989).

12

Alphabetization in Early Dictionaries of English

[1989]

The first monolingual English dictionary was called a *Table Alphabeticall*. But just how alphabetical was it? and how alphabetical was it even intended to be? The problems of *dégroupement* and *regroupement* begin early in the history of dictionary making, and it is instructive to study the practices of pioneer English lexicographers and their printers.

In the medieval glossary tradition, listing of words in AB order was widespread—that is, according to only the first two letters of any item in the list. Such rudimentary alphabetization will no doubt have done very well where lists were not too long. But the reader used to modern dictionaries may blench at finding no more than an AB order operating in quite substantial compilations such as the fifteenth-century *Catholicon Anglicum*, containing some 8000 English entries with Latin explanations. Here is how the *ne-* words begin:

N ante E
to Nee as a horse
a Nebbe
a Negligence
Negligent
a Neddyr
a Nede.

Words 1 2 3 4 5 6 are here in the order 4 1 5 6 2 3; not a good score, though there are sections (e.g., *G ante R*, with 96 entries) where ABC order is maintained rigorously, and even ABCD in part. In general, however, nothing like the modern alphabetization obtained in the English bilingual dictionaries before Cawdrey (Stein 1985a). In partial justification one might say that in an age when the spellings of so many words were still unsettled, or even a matter of personal taste, precisianism in alphabetical matters would have been pretty pointless anyway.

The very choice of the title *A Table Alphabeticall* is also more significant than it might seem, since other ways of listing words (e.g., according to grammatical classes, or semantic categories such as 'the parts of the body') had long been current in educational and reference works. Furthermore, there is evidence enough that when Cawdrey launched his dictionary in the early seventeenth century his public still needed educating in this. In his front matter (Cawdrey 1604, A4^{v} *To the Reader*) he tells them how to use the alphabet:

> If thou be desirous (gentle Reader) rightly and readily to vnderstand, and to profit by this Table, and such like, then thou must learne the Alphabet, to wit, the order of the Letters as they stand, perfect[l]y without booke, and where euery Letter standeth: as (b) neere the beginning, (n) about the middest, and (t) toward the end. Nowe if the word, which thou art desirous to finde, begin with (a) then looke in the beginning of this Table, but if with (v) looke towards the end. Againe, if thy word beginne with (ca) looke in the beginning of the letter (c) but if with (cu) then looke toward the end of that letter. And so of all the rest. &c.

Cawdrey took this passage expounding AB order almost unchanged from Coote's *English Schoole-maister* (1596, 73), one of the source-books he used for his word-list. Coote had presented a more specific challenge of ABCD order to his users by saying at the end 'and if thou obseruest the same for the third and fourth letters, thou shalt finde thy word presently', but his general heading 'Directions for the vnskilfull' suggested very effectively where the problems really lay.

A random sample of ten pages (218 entries) in Cawdrey yielded 26 words placed out of strict alphabetical sequence, with a maximum of five on any one page (about a quarter) and a total average of just under 12%. This is perhaps a better result than the tentativeness of his prefatory matter might have led us to expect, and it is possible also to discern several different types of deviance that occur.

Random Deviance Incorrect sequences at ABCD level are commonest (*canopie – capitall – capable – capitulation*) but these usually involve displacement by only one or two entry-words. *Demoniacke* (placed between *deacon* and *deambulation*) is exceptionally separated from its proper neighbour *demonstrate* by 43 entries (two pages) and would therefore not easily be found. But in general, even when the system has gone into a muddle, as in the following sequence, there will have been no great reference problems:

> **donatiue,** a gift, in money or other things
> **dulcimur,** } (k) instrument
> **dulcimar,** }
> **duarchy,** the equall raigne of two princes together.
> **driblets,** small debts
> **dulcifie,** sweeten.

Here, there is disturbance even at AB level, but since the nomenclature of the dictionary is so small (Cawdrey has only 2543 entries; Schäfer 1989, 51) the reader's eye will have taken it all in easily enough. There are also some items (e.g. *assent*) which have been wrongly placed, and are then repeated in the right sequence later.

Printer's Preferential Forms The entry for *impacience* occurs after (not before) *impart*. This suggests that Cawdrey's intention was *impatience*, but that his printer put in a form more familiar to him without adjusting the alphabetical sequence. Both spellings were perfectly current in the early seventeenth century. Other instances are *tiranize* between *turbulent* and *type*, and *ariue/ariuall* between *arride* and *arrogate*. Such cases provide a nice illustration of an early lexicographer unable to control his printer.

Derived Forms The placement of derived forms is still a problem today, some dictionaries preferring to give them main entry status, in strict alphabetical sequence, while others will regroup them under a base form. It is important to remember that Cawdrey was operating with only two founts, roman for entry-words and black letter for everything else. Typographically highlighted derivations within a main lemma were therefore not practicable. But with sequences such as the following it looks very much as if he is sacrificing alphabetical order in the interests of getting the base form in first:

assigne, appoint, ordaine
assignation, appointment

captiue, prisoner
captiuate, make subject, or a prisoner.

Cawdrey had thus like many of his successors sensed the need for this, and if his solution would not satisfy us today, that is because of our more rigorous demands in the matter of alphabetizing entry-words.

Bracketed Morphological Variants There are some sixty instances in Cawdrey of bracketed entries such as:

criminous, **criminall,**	} faultie, that wherein is some fault

extemporall, **extempore,** **extemporarie,**	} suddaine, without premeditation, or studie

vnitie, **vnion,**	} peace, or concord.

Here, morphologically related words of the same meaning (in Cawdrey's view at least) are bracketed together in incorrect alphabetical sequence. Presumably we may take it that in such cases the item given first is the preferred one. It would be hard to see any other reason for breaking order, and the phenomenon is of some interest to the historical linguist. This again seems a sensible technique (given the small scale of the dictionary) for coping with the presentation of vocabulary features now commonly dealt with by means of main and sub-entries.

Bracketed Spelling Variants The word *engine* appears in Cawdrey only under the letter I, where it is bracketed with *ingine*:

> **ingine,** } an instrument to doo
> **engine,** } any thing with.

This is hardly good lexicographical practice, since the user looking under the letter E will draw a blank. In the parallel case of *embark/imbark* he does rather better with

> § **embark,** } to ship a thing, or
> **imbark,** } load a ship

since at more or less the right point under the letter I there is a further entry for *imbarge/imbarke* with a reference to the spelling *embarke*.

There are other bracketed non-alphabetical spelling variants such as *dulcimur/dulcimar* (quoted above) which stand well enough on their own. The use of brackets in this way would I suppose not be tolerated today, but we might say in its favour that it is economical in definition, and enables both forms to be given main entry status.

Though Cawdrey, the very first monolingual English lexicographer, thus sins against the alphabet, it is often possible to see why he sins, and it is clear that we still share some of the problems which made him do so.

Cawdrey's Successors The immediate successors to Cawdrey in the seventeenth century stayed remarkably close to the pattern which he had set. Deviation from alphabetical order generally runs at about 6 to 8% (Blount 1656 rather less, at 4.5%; Coles 1676 rather more, at 11%).

Random errors of alphabetization diminish in number through the century, but are still to be found even in Johnson (1755) with, for instance, *hodmadod* before *hodge-podge*. Disturbance caused by printers' preferences seems to peter out early, though in Bullokar (1616) I have noticed the Spenserian *forewelked* placed between *fortitude* and *foster*, where the more historical spelling *forwelked* would have fitted in. The urge to place a base form first, regardless of the alphabet, seems always to be there, so that we get *odour* – *odoriferous, penurie* – *penurious*, in that order in Bullokar, and *flatuous* – *flatuosity* in Blount. Brackets for spelling variants or semantic equivalents grouped in non-alphabetical order of the type *loam/lome*, *pigrity/pigritude* were used in Cockeram (1623), Blount (1656) and Bailey (1721, 1730), though not in Bullokar.

Phillips (1658) appears to be the first of the English monolingual lexicographers to adopt the more modern formula of *x or y* for such items, after the following fashion:

> **Indocility**, or **Indocibility,** (lat.) an unaptnesse to be taught or learn.

This saves breaking the alphabetical order of the entry-words, and again the order in which the forms are given presumably indicates the compiler's preference. Where the spellings are far apart (e.g., '*A Hodge-poge*, or *Hotch-pot* ... flesh cut to pieces, and sodden together with Herbs') cross-references are at times provided.

Other innovations occur in Cockeram and Coles. Cockeram's dictionary is in three parts, and in the highly interesting second part containing 'Vulgar' terms glossed by their more learned equivalents, one finds sequences such as this:

> **Pardoning**, Absolution.
> **not to be Pardoned,** Vnremissable.
> **one whose Parents are of sundry Nations,** Hibridan.
> **the Paring of the nayles,** Pesegme.
> **belonging to Parents,** Paternall.
> **a shee Paramour,** Amatrix.
> **an inner Parlour,** Conclaue.
> **Part of a thing,** Particle.

Nouns in Cockeram are thus (where appropriate) preceded by an article (compare *a Mother, the Moon*, with *Neernesse* in Figure 7), and verbs are given the infinitive particle *to* (*to muse, to pair the Nalis*). This is a useful mode of grammatical coding. But it means that the alphabetized word may become displaced to the right, as in the sequence from *Pardoning* given above; the initial capitals were of use here to the compiler because they serve to point up the alphabetical order, and counteract the river-like effect down the page. In this Cockeram is doubtless following the earlier English-Latin dictionaries, where similar problems had arisen (Stein 1985a, 278). But the capitalization of entry

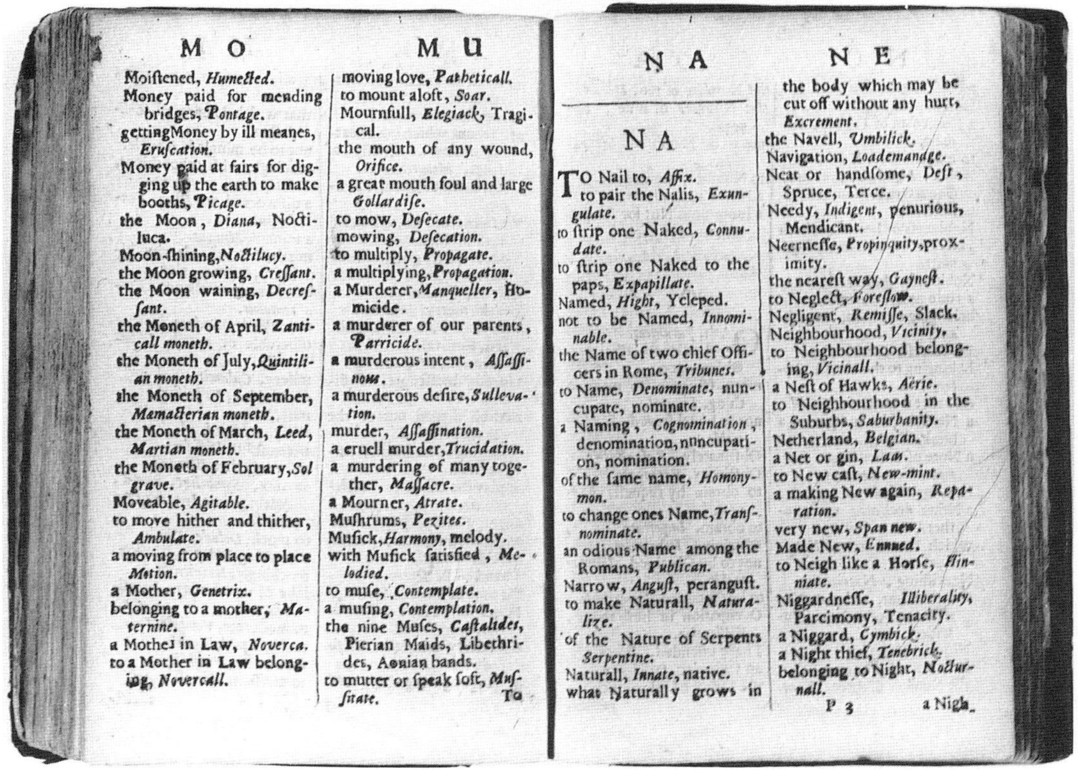

MO MU

Moiſtened, *Humected.*
Money paid for mending bridges, *Pontage.*
gettingMoney by ill meanes, *Eruſcation.*
Money paid at fairs for digging up the earth to make booths, *Picage.*
the Moon, *Diana*, Noctiluca.
Moon-ſhining, *Noctilucy.*
the Moon growing, *Creſſant.*
the Moon waining, *Decreſſant.*
the Moneth of April, *Zanticall moneth.*
the Moneth of July, *Quintilian moneth.*
the Moneth of September, *Mamacterian moneth.*
the Moneth of March, *Leed, Martian moneth.*
the Moneth of February, *Sol grave.*
Moveable, *Agitable.*
to move hither and thither, *Ambulate.*
a moving from place to place *Motion.*
a Mother, *Genetrix.*
belonging to a mother, *Maternine.*
a Mother in Law, *Noverca.*
to a Mother in Law belonging, *Novercall.*
moving love, *Patheticall.*
to mount aloft, *Soar.*
Mournfull, *Elegiack*, Tragical.
the mouth of any wound, *Orifice.*
a great mouth foul and large *Gollardiſe.*
to mow, *Deſecate.*
mowing, *Deſecation.*
to multiply, *Propagate.*
a multiplying, *Propagation.*
a Murderer, *Manqueller*, Homicide.
a murderer of our parents, *Parricide.*
a murderous intent, *Aſſaſſinous.*
a murderous deſire, *Sullevation.*
murder, *Aſſaſſination.*
a cruell murder, *Trucidation.*
a murdering of many together, *Maſſacre.*
a Mourner, *Atrate.*
Muſhrums, *Pezites.*
Muſick, *Harmony*, melody.
with Muſick ſatisfied, *Melodied.*
to muſe, *Contemplate.*
a muſing, *Contemplation.*
the nine Muſes, *Caſtalides*, Pierian Maids, Libethrides, Aonian bands.
to mutter or ſpeak ſoft, *Muſſitate.* To

NA NE

NA

TO Nail to, *Affix.*
to pair the Nails, *Exungulate.*
to ſtrip one Naked, *Connudate.*
to ſtrip one Naked to the paps, *Expapillate.*
Named, *Hight*, Ycleped.
not to be Named, *Innominable.*
the Name of two chief Officers in Rome, *Tribunes.*
to Name, *Denominate*, nuncupate, nominate.
a Naming, *Cognomination*, denomination, nuncupation, nomination.
of the ſame name, *Homonymon.*
to change ones Name, *Transnominate.*
an odious Name among the Romans, *Publican.*
Narrow, *Anguſt*, peranguſt.
to make Naturall, *Naturalize.*
of the Nature of Serpents *Serpentine.*
Naturall, *Innate*, native.
what Naturally grows in the body which may be cut off without any hurt, *Excrement.*
the Navell, *Umbilick.*
Navigation, *Loademandge.*
Neat or handſome, *Deſt*, Spruce, Terce.
Needy, *Indigent*, penurious, Mendicant.
Neerneſſe, *Propinquity*, proximity.
the neareſt way, *Gayneſt.*
to Neglect, *Foreſlow.*
Negligent, *Remiſſe*, Slack.
Neighbourhood, *Vicinity.*
to Neighbourhood belonging, *Vicinall.*
a Neſt of Hawks, *Aërie.*
to Neighbourhood in the Suburbs, *Saburbanity.*
Netherland, *Belgian.*
a Net or gin, *Lam.*
to New caſt, *New-mint.*
a making New again, *Reparation.*
very new, *Span new.*
Made New, *Ennued.*
to Neigh like a Horſe, *Hinniate.*
Niggardneſſe, *Illiberality*, Parcimony, Tenacity.
a Niggard, *Cymbick.*
a Night thief, *Tenebrick.*
belonging to Night, *Nocturnall.*
P 3 a Nigh-

FIG. 7. Ordering and capitalizing entry-words: from the Second Part of Cockeram's *English Dictionarie* (11th edn 1658).

words was imperfectly executed from the start, and the two pages in Figure 7 show that it had deteriorated badly by the 11th edition in 1658. It is likely that Cockeram would have experienced great difficulty with his printers in seeking to impose systematic capitalization. One reason for this would be the growing practice in the seventeenth century of giving an initial capital to all nouns and to other 'weighty' words in the sentence (Osselton 1985).

Coles was unusual in seeking a different solution to the problem of presenting derivationally-related clusters of words in English. There are in his dictionary very frequent entries with cross-lemma definitions of the following type:

> **Evade,** *l.* to make an
> **Evasion,** an escape, shift.

The practice occurs also in spelling-books of the time, and it is here innocent enough, causing no disturbance to the alphabetical order. But that is not always the case, as with *obliquation – obliquity – oblique*, where the sequence is 1 3 2, and the base-word has dropped to final position (at a time when most contemporaries were rather desperately shunting it up to the top).

A very extreme example of the Coles technique running across five lemmata occurs with the Machiavelli words:

> **Machevalize,** the same as
> **Machiavelianize,** to play the
> **Machiavelian, -villian,** he that
> practiseth or studieth
> **Machiavelianism,** State-policy,
> the Doctrine of *Nicholas*
> **Machiavel,** a famous Historian
> and Recorder of *Florence*, whose
> politicks have poison'd almost
> all *Europe*.

The proper alphabetical sequence would be 1 5 3 4 2. Such virtuoso concatenations could hardly last, though the practice of linked entries occurs also in Kersey (1702).

The arrangement of entries in Johnson's Dictionary is highly organized, as might be expected, though as we have already seen this does not mean that it is strictly alphabetical. The important technical innovation lies in the use of large and small capitals for the entry-words.

In the early eighteenth century the original practice of *black letter* + *roman* (Cawdrey, Blount, Kersey-Phillips 1706) or *italic* + *roman* (Phillips, Coles) gave way to the general use of *capitals* + *roman* (Bailey, Martin), leaving italic for giving etymologies, etc. Bold-face type, so widely used now in dictionaries, was not invented until the nineteenth century (Bray 1986, 47). Johnson (or his printers at least) thus employed capitals for entry-words, but added a further refinement in distinguishing type size in the main word list, which therefore no longer needed to be strictly alphabetical. The following sequence from *cow* to *cowl* in Johnson will illustrate the point:

COW ...	COWARDICE
COW-HERD	COWARDLINESS ...
COW-LEECH	COWER
COW-WEED	COWISH
COW-WHEAT	COWKEEPER
COWARD	**COWL** ...

There are here three main entry-words in large capitals, namely *cow, coward* and *cowl*, and the system of arrangement is that derivations and hyphenated compounds follow immediately upon their base-word (e.g., *cow-herd, cowardice,*). But the reader who wants to find *cow-keeper* and might reasonably expect it to be between *cow-herd* and *cow-leech* will find it (if he finds it at all) more than a column away. Can he know beforehand that *cow-herd* is to have a hyphen, but *cowkeeper* will not? Hyphenation is always a pretty uncertain principle for arranging entries in English dictionaries, and Johnson's alphabetical system often seems pretty opaque anyway: why should the two items

EARED *adj*. [from *ear*] Having ears ...
EARLESS *adj*. [from *ear*] Without any ears ...

be separated by eight entries including *earwax* and *earwig*? The distinction of one of them as being verbal and the other as nominal appears to be the answer, but it is asking quite a lot of the user to expect him to see this.

In the first century and a half of monolingual English dictionary compiling there was then a general tightening up of the rather approximative systems of alphabetization inherited from the mediaeval word-lists. From the start, the pattern of deviation from alphabetical order shows lexicographers struggling especially with the problems of spelling variants and derived forms. These are still a matter of methodological uncertainty today. From this age of experimentation not all the techniques which were tried have survived, and the efforts of the early lexicographers were certainly hampered by the lack of typographical sophistication in their time.

END NOTE

Originally published in James (1989, 165-73). The general principles and problems of alphabetization in dictionaries are set out by Wiegand (1989). Catach (1989) deals with the problems of alphabetization in French dictionaries, offering the useful distinction between mots graphiques *and* mots linguistiques.

13

An Eighteenth-Century Bilingualized Learners' Dictionary

[1994]

Learners' Dictionaries and Bilingualized Learners' Dictionaries The evolution of bilingualized learners' dictionaries is a recent phenomenon which is now beginning to receive critical commentary and analysis (Zöfgen 1991; Hartmann 1994; James 1994). The remarkable growth of the language-learning industry since the Second World War saw the establishment of the *learners' dictionary* as one of the major lexicographical genres of our age. It is an area where great commercial success has gone with intense experimentation. Such well-established works as the OALD, LDOCE and COBUILD are monolingual, *English-English* dictionaries devised specifically for the foreign learner—*any* foreign learner—as an alternative to the conventional bilingual dictionary; in these new works, great ingenuity has gone into presenting the material so as to enable more advanced learners to absorb the information they need while retaining all the benefits of using a reference book wholly in the target-language.

The *bilingualized learners' dictionary* has now taken the process a stage further by adding foreign-language glosses to the explanations of word-meaning provided by the normal learners' dictionary. Thus for instance in the *Oxford Advanced Learners' Dictionary of Current English. English-English-Korean*, the originally monolingual OALD is bilingualized by the addition of the Korean words. To illustrate what a bilingualized learners' dictionary entry looks like on the page, I give here the entry for *earthworm* and an extract from the word *earth* from the

Password English Dictionary for Speakers of French (1989) as quoted by Hartmann 1994:

> **earthworm** *noun* (usually **worm**) a kind of small animal with a ringed body and no backbone, living in damp earth. □ **ver de terre**
>
> **earth** 4 dry land; the ground: *the earth, sea and sky.* □ **terre** 5 a burrow or hole of an animal, *especially* of a fox. □ **tanière**.

In entries such as these the gloss gives the foreign learner a rapid identification tag for the term he is concerned with (or the initial assurance that he has pitched on the sense that he wants) before he takes in the more detailed information provided in the monolingual text.

An Eighteenth-Century Precursor The needs of people learning foreign languages will not have changed much over the centuries, and it is therefore of interest to find a learners' dictionary in the eighteenth century employing similar techniques. The *Orthographical Dictionary*, printed as the second part of Nathan Bailey's so-called *Volume II* (1727), contains entries such as the following:

> *ABA'FT, those Parts of a Ship towards the Stern. *La poupe*, F. *Puppis*, L.
> *A'NSWERABLE, accountable, obliged to answer to or for. *Responsable*, F. *Obligatus*, L.
> **Answerable**, conformable. *Conformé*, F. *Consonus*, L.
> *DA'LLIANCE, Toying, Wantonness. *humeur folâtre*, F. *lascivia*, *petulantia*, L.
> *To REMA'RK, to take notice of, &c. *Remarquer*, F. *Notare*, L.

Here too the policy has been to give the meaning of the word in English first in simple terms, and then to back this up by foreign glosses.

The choice of language for bilingualization (or rather trilingualization) is entirely appropriate to the age. Bailey explains (*Introduction* A2^{v}) that he has acted on the supposition 'that the generality of Gentlemen-travellers are accomplish'd with the knowledge either of the Latin or French Languages'. This makes good sense at the time, and there need be no doubt that the presence of French and Latin glosses will have made his dictionary generally accessible to educated users throughout Europe, whatever their mother tongue might have been. The usefulness of Latin as an international language of scholarship had been realized by earlier lexicographers: Latin tags were for instance used for the purposes of meaning discrimination as early as 1591 in Percyvall's dictionary of Spanish and English (Steiner 1991). With the decline of Latin, modern editors of bilingualized dictionaries are alas constrained to be more local in their choice of language for the glosses.

For Bailey, trilingualization with Latin and French conferred the further advantage of lexical overlap: for items such as *declamation* or *original*, where the French is the same as the English, and both are derived from the Latin 'differing from it only in a letter or two', undue repetition is avoided by use of the note *F[rench] of L[atin]*. The English definition is then omitted, since foreigners familiar with the French *déclamation* or the Latin *declamatio* would hardly stand in need of further explanation.

Varieties of Dictionary Adaptation Bailey was not alone in his lexicographical inventiveness. In the formative years of early European lexicography compilers exploited the possibilities of cross-category experimentation in many ways:

- converting monolingual into bilingual dictionaries;
- using a bilingual dictionary word-list as a basis for a monolingual dictionary;
- building up ever more comprehensive polyglot dictionaries from a bilingual start;
- creating a bilingual dictionary for a new combination of languages by drawing on existing bilingual dictionaries: for instance, a two-way dictionary of languages A and B (A-B, B-A) arrived at by drawing on A-C and B-D, the text of languages C and D being then converted into languages B and A respectively.

Some instances of this common market in lexicographical goods (going back as far as Calepinus 1502) are given in a list of 'translated dictionaries' in Hartmann (1994). James (1994) offers a highly interesting taxonomy of such bilingualized works.

The one which comes nearest to Bailey in date (and is referred to by both Hartmann and James) is François Halma's *Grand Dictionaire*

François et Flamend (1717). This is, as James observes, largely a bilingualization of the monolingual (French-French) dictionary of Richelet. But Halma differs quite radically from Bailey in the set-up and purpose of his dictionary. Here are his entries for *banque*, *ocasion* and *raisonneur*:

> BANQUE, *s.f.* Lieu où on met son argent en depôt. *De bank,* of *wisselbank, een plaats daar men zyn geldt in verzeekering,* of *bewaring geeft.*
> OCASION, *ou* OCCASION, *s.f.* Heureux moment, *ou* temps pour faire, *ou* pour tenter quelque chose. *Gelegenheit, de rechte tydt om iets te doen,* of *te onderneemen.*
> RAISONNEUR, *s.m.* Celui qui réplique trop à une personne à laquelle il doit du respect. *Redeneerder, kakelaar, keffer, snateraar, snaterbek. Een die te veel snaps heeft tegen dien die hij eerbiedigheit schuldig is.*

These typical entries will make it quite clear that though Halma's work may rightly be called a *translated dictionary*, and the compiler has certainly produced a combination of monolingual (French-French) and bilingual (French-Dutch), the added bilingualizing component (in Dutch) is far from being a mere gloss: French and Dutch explanations of the words are pretty much co-extensive. Since precisely the same techniques are employed in the Dutch-French half (*Woordenboek der Nederduitsche en Fransche Taalen*) Halma's work can perhaps best be characterized as a mono-bilingual dictionary aimed equally at Dutch and French speakers in an area of the world where these languages needed to coexist on equal terms. It is then no accident that the preface ('Avis au lecteur/Berecht aan den Lezer') is printed in parallel columns in the two languages.

Halma's two handsome volumes provide us then with a fine example of an early translated dictionary giving full treatment in both languages of the vocabulary items taken up in it. What the compiler is doing is thus a far cry from Bailey's practical, low-level tagging of words and meanings in Latin and in French.

Bailey's *Volume II* has received little scholarly attention, and has indeed been dismissed by Starnes and Noyes (1946, 108) as a bookseller's freak. But it is a highly interesting freak, not only for its bilingualization, but because of other innovative lexicographical techniques that were adopted for the benefit of learners. The following account will show that the compiler (bookseller, Bailey, or whoever he was) deserves more credit than he is usually given.

B A

rus manualis, L.

* To BA'RTER, to exchange. *troquer*, F. *merces commutare*, L.

* BA'RTERING. *troc*, F. *permutatio*, L.

† A BA'RTON, a Coup for Poultry. *poulalier*, F *cavea*, L.

* BASE, low, mean, vile, &c. *bas, mepriſable*, F. *abjectus, nullius pretii, vilis, ſordidus*, &c. L.

* A BASE, a Foundation, F. *baſis*, L.

* BASE, knaviſh. *honteux*, F. *pravus*, L.

* BASE } in Muſick. *la baſſe*, F. *baſ-*
BASS } *ſus*. L.

* BASE, counterfeit. *de bas aloy*, F. *adulterinus*, L.

* BA'SELY, meanly, cowardly, vilely, knaviſhly. *baſſement, ſachement, villainement*, &c. F. *turpiter*, L.

* BA'SENESS, unfairneſs, knaviſhneſs. *baſeſſe, honteuſe*, F. *turpitudo*, L.

* BA'SHFUL, ſhamefaced. *qui a de la pudeur*, F. *verecundus*, L.

* BA'SHFULLY, modeſtly. *avec pudeur*, F. *verecundé*, L.

* BA'SHFULNESS. *honnête honte*, F. *verecundia*, L.

* BA'SILISK, a kind of Serpent. *baſilic*, F *baſiliſcus*, L.

* To BA'SK, to lie in the Sun, &c. *ſe chauffer*, F. *apricari ad ſolem*, L.

* BA'SKET. *une corbeille*, F. *calathus*,

* BA'SON. *un baſſin*, F. *pelvis*, L.

* BASS, a Straw Cuſhion. *un lit d'joncs*, F. *ſcirpea*, L.

* BA'SSET, a Game. *baſſette*, F.

* BASSO'ON, a muſical Inſtrument. *baſſon*, F.

* BA'ST, Ropes made of Bark of Trees. *nates de tilleu*, F.

* BA'STARD, a baſe born Child, &c. *batârd*, F. *nothus*, L.

* BA'STARD, counterfeit. *faux*, F. *ſpurius*, L.

* To BA'STARDISE, to make or declare to be a Baſtard. *abatardir*, F. *nothum pronuntiare*, L.

* BA'STARDY, the Condition of a Baſtard. *batardiſe*, F. *ortus infamis*, L.

* To BASTE Meat in roaſting. *arroſer le roti*, F. *deguttare*, L.

* To BASTE, to ſow ſlightly. *baguer*, F. *filo conſuere*, L.

* To BASTE, to beat ſoundly. *battre*, F. *fuſtigare*, L.

* BASTINA'DO, a beating with a Cudgel. *coups de baton*, F. *fuſtigatio*, L.

* To BASTINA'DO, *baſtonner*, F. *fuſtigare*, L.

* BA'STION [in *Fortification*] a Maſs of Earth raiſed on the Angles of the Polygon. *un baſtion*, F.

* BA'T, a Fowl. *une chauve ſouris*, F. *veſpertilio*, L.

B A

* BAT, a Club to play at ball. *croſſe* F. *fuſtis*, L.

* BATCH of Bread, what is baked at once. *une fournée*, F. *panis coctura*, L.

† To BATE, to abate, *i. e.* to take leſs. *baiſſer, diminuer*, F. *de ſumma remittere*,

† BATE, Strife. *debat*, F. *contentio*, L.

* BATH, a Place to bathe in. *bain*, F. *balneum*, L.

* To BATHE, to waſh, &c. *baigner*, F. *lavare*, L.

* BATO'ON, a ſhort Staff. *un baton groſs & court*, F. *bacillum*, L.

* BATTA'LIA, Order of battle. *ordre de bataille*, F. *acies inſtructa*, L.

* BATTA'LION, a Body of Foot Soldiers. *bataillon*, F. *agmen*, L.

To BA'TTEL } to wallow in Mire,
To BA'TTEN } &c. *ſe veautrer*, F. *fimo volutari*, L.

To BA'TTEL } to grow fat. *ſe engra-*
* To BA'TTEN } *iſſer*, F. *pingueſcere*.

* To BATTER, to demoliſh. *battre*, &c. F. *pulſare. demolire*, L.

* To BA'TTER, to beat. *battre*, F. *tundere*, L.

* BA'TTER for Pancakes, &c. *farine detrempée*, &c. F.

* BA'TTERY, in Fortification. *batterie*, F. *agger*, L.

* BA'TTERY, a beating and bruiſing. *batterie*, F. *verberatio*, L.

* BA'TTLE, a Fight. *bataille*, F. *prælium*, L.

* BA'TTLEDORE, to play at Shuttlecock. *un battoir*, F. *pala repercuſſoria*, L.

* BA'TTLEMENTS, Turrets of Houſes built flat, &c. *creneaux*, F. *minæ murorum*, L.

* To BA'TTLE at a College. *victus debita & impenſus in nomina referre*, L.

* A BA'TTLER, *batalarius*, L.

† BAUBE'E, a Farthing. *un liard*, F. *quadrans*, L.

* BA'UBLE, a play Thing, a Triffle. *babiole, bagatelle*, F. *tricæ*, L.

* BA'VIN, a bundle of Fire Wood. *un bourée*, F. *faſcis*, L.

* BA'UD } a Procureſs. *une maqua-*
* BAWD } *relle*, F. *lena*, L.

* BA'UDY } [the Practice] *maque-*
* BAW'DRY } *rellage*, F. *lenocinium*,

* BAU'DY } obſcene Words. *obſcenité*,
* BAW'DY } F. *obſcænitas*, L.

* BA'UDY } (adj.) filthy, lewd. *obſcene*,
* BAW'DY } *ſale*, F. *obſcænus, turpis*,

* BAU'DINESS } the being bawdy.
* BAW'DINESS }

* To BA'WL, to cry out or ſpeak aloud. *criailler, clabauder*, F. *vociferari*, L.

* BA'WLING. *criaillerie, clabauderie*, F. *vociferatio*, L.

† BA'WSIN, a Badger. *un blereau*, F. *meles*,

FIG. 8. A monolingual learners' dictionary with French and Latin glosses: *barter* to *bawsin* in Bailey's 'Vol. II' (1727).

The Volume II and Bailey's Other Dictionaries Bailey is the most famous eighteenth-century English lexicographer after Johnson. His *Universal Etymological English Dictionary* (UEED), with its twenty-eight editions between 1721 and 1800, and some 40,000 or more entries, may be regarded as the standard middle-sized English dictionary of the eighteenth century, and his *Dictionarium Britannicum* (1730) was the most substantial folio dictionary of English before Johnson.

Rather curiously, only six years after the launch of the highly successful UEED (already into its third edition), the similar-sized *Volume II* was put on the market. The title-page sets out in part the ways in which it differs from the parent volume:

> **The Universal Etymological English Dictionary: In Two Parts:** Containing, **I**. An Additional Collection ... Of some thousands of Words not in the former Volume ... **II**. An Orthographical Dictionary, showing both the Orthography and the Orthoepia of the English Tongue ...
> A Work useful for such as would understand what they read and hear; speak what they mean in a proper and pure Diction; and write true *English* ...
> **Vol.II. By N. Bailey.**

Though it is clearly billed as a supplementary volume and has an identical title, the book had a quite separate publishing history from the UEED proper (Alston 1974, Vol. V, items 127-35), and it disappeared from the scene after its seventh edition in 1776.

The first part of the volume has 568 pages and contains (according to the preface) both material that had newly come to hand from 'Persons of generous and communicative Dispositions' and items which the compiler would have put in before if he had had room for them. There is in particular a new focus on classical and heathen antiquity, technical terms and proper names, and there are many entries for additional past-participle meanings and compound phrases. A full discussion of contents and sources is to be found in Starnes and Noyes (1946, chapter 15).

The second part has separate pagination (rather shorter, at 424 pages) and an additional title-page of its own as follows:

> **An Orthographical Dictionary**, Shewing both the Orthography and the Orthoepia of the *English* Tongue, by
> I ACCENTS placed on each Word, directing to their true Pronunciation.
> II ASTERISMS, distinguishing those Words of approv'd Authority from those that are not.

III THEIR various Senses and Significations, in *English*, and also in *French* and *Latin*, for the sake of Foreigners, who desire an Acquaintance with the *English* Tongue.
IV THE Idiom, Phrases, and proverbial Sentences belonging to it.
A WORK useful for such as would speak what they mean in a proper and pure Diction; and write true *English*.
Vol. II. By N. Bailey.

'For the sake of Foreigners, who desire an Acquaintance with the *English* Tongue': this is the phrase (under III) which marks it out as primarily a learners' dictionary. A similar claim to serve the purposes of foreigners had been made on the title-pages of a good number of ordinary monolingual dictionaries in the early period, and this must clearly have been a selling point. But in the case of Bailey's *Volume II* the claim is backed up by the contents of the book.

Creating a Learners' Dictionary by Adaptation The bilingualized learners' dictionary in Bailey's *Volume II* is to be seen as an offshoot of the earlier UEED. It is worth quoting here the entries from the UEED corresponding to those quoted at the beginning of this chapter, to show how his original and more conventional dictionary was adapted:

ABAFT or AFT, those parts of the Ship which are towards the Stern. *S.T.*
ANSWERABLE, that is obliged to Answer to a Thing, accountable; also Proportionable, that has some Relation to a Thing.
DALLIANCE, Toying, Wantonness.
To REMARK, [*remarquer*, F.] to observe, to take Notice of.

A number of changes have been carried out here in addition to the crucial one of adding the foreign equivalents. The label *S[ea] T[erm]* is removed from *abaft* (the definition leaves little doubt about the matter anyway); the two senses of *answerable* are presented in separate entries; the single French phrase *humeur folâtre* will do for *dalliance*, but two Latin key-words are given and these are presumably intended (despite their sequence) to capture the respective meanings conveyed by 'toying' and 'wantonness'; what was in UEED presented as an etymology for *to remark* is now transferred to become the French key-word for it in *Volume II*.

Other Lexicographical Innovations Bailey's adaptation goes further than this: not only does he add the French and Latin key-words (clearly not intended in any way for the English users) but he enhances the usefulness of his text to the learner in two other ways, each of them equally revolutionary in his time.

The first (alluded to under I on the title-page) is the marking of word-stress throughout the dictionary. In the introduction, Bailey is quite explicit about the need for this:

> the *English* and *Foreigners*, especially the *French*, differ as to placing the Accent, or laying a particular stress or force of Sound upon Syllables, the *English* most commonly place the Accent far from the last Syllable, and the *French* nearer; and this difference in Accentuation makes the Pronunciation of *English*, according to the custom of Foreigners, sound uncouthly to *English* Ears.

Bailey's *Volume II* is the very first English dictionary to indicate stress (or indeed to do anything about pronunciation at all) thus initiating what was to become a normal feature in lexicographical practice (Bronstein 1986). Words are marked by means of an accent placed immediately after the vowel of the stressed syllable (see Figure 8). The task has been carried out conscientiously throughout the alphabet, and details cannot be discussed here, but many interesting records of eighteenth-century pronunciations are to be found (e.g. *anchovy*, *to confiscate*, *decorous*, *to illustrate*, *restoration*, *shampinion* 'a mushroom' and *tenure,* all stressed on the second syllable).

The second feature for the benefit of foreign learners (also to be seen in Figure 8) is his use of asterisks to mark words which were fully acceptable, 'of approv'd Authority and imitable by the Illiterate' and suitable for use 'on any common Occasion'. These were to be distinguished from other words (marked by a dagger) of more restricted currency —words which the learner would do well to avoid, even though they might fittingly occur 'in the Pen of an accomplish'd Writer, intermix'd with an agreeable Stile'.

Thus *diligence*, *diligent* and *diligently* are all given asterisks, but *diligentness* has a dagger. *Promulgation* and *subsidy* are safe to use, but the learner is advised to keep off *to promulge* and *to subside*, as well as many other items such as *gingerly*, *lazar*, *lugubrious* and *spotty*. The practice of marking items with a cautionary dagger begins (in English) with Edward Phillips's *New World of English Words* in 1658, and I have given elsewhere a full account of the words thus proscribed in the English monolingual dictionaries down to Johnson (Osselton 1958). Bailey, in his *Volume II*, differs in the operation of this device from his fellow lexicographers Phillips, Kersey and Martin: here, *every* item in the dictionary has been assessed and is given either an asterisk (as fully acceptable), or a dagger, or—in a small minority of cases—is left unmarked because the compiler felt that he could not determine for or against them. It may be a somewhat crude lexicographical device, but it is one that recognizes the need for giving that extra guidance on usage which is so marked a feature of learners' dictionaries today.

Later History The bilingualized dictionary in Bailey's *Volume II* can thus be seen to incorporate new and important features for learners—help with pronunciation, extra guidance on usage—as well as providing the French and Latin glosses. It is no accident that a work so specifically aimed at foreign learners should have been dedicated to the German-born children of George II (including Carolina Elizabeth, then 14 years old) with the expressed hope that it might contribute at least something to their studies of the English language ('aliquid saltem adminiculi studiis vestris Anglicanis adferre posse sperans').

Yet this innovative dictionary was dropped from the second edition of Bailey's *Volume II* in 1731 and did not reappear in any of the later editions. One reason may be that the compiler had never been able to carry through his design consistently. The distinctive pattern of monolingual explanation plus foreign equivalent wears thinner and thinner as he progresses through the alphabet: only a quarter of the first hundred entries under the letter W have explanations (e.g. '*a Ward*, a minor') or other indications of meaning (e.g. '*Wambling*, in the stomach') alongside the French and Latin equivalents. All too many (such as '*Waggon*, Chariot, F. Vehiculum, L.') are left simply in the form of the conventional multilingual dictionary. There is a passage in the introduction which suggests that Bailey's intentions in the matter may have been thwarted by the publisher: 'finding the Work to swell under my hands, and about to exceed the number of Sheets convenient for a Volume, [I] was oblig'd to retrench it'. His rather half-hearted conclusion that nevertheless 'it may answer indifferently well to the End propos'd' is not the stuff that best-sellers are made of.

Bailey's highly original learners' dictionary of English—dedicated to the young Hanoverian princes, and the first ever to adopt the device of bilingualizing entries for the benefit of foreigners—was then clearly not a commercial success. Perhaps it did not deserve to be. But this does not detract from the interest of it as the earliest example of a type of dictionary which we have now been busy reinventing for our own age.

14

Secondary Documentation in Historical Lexicography

[1989]

It is generally the intention of a historical dictionary to give an objective record of verbal usage in the target language during a specified period. In major works it has been the practice to incorporate original quotations which are themselves the evidence for the linguistic record presented. Great attention has rightly been given to the selection of texts laid under contribution, so as to achieve a proper chronological spread of representative quotations from primary sources, though (Schäfer 1980) practice often falls short of the ideal.

Given such aims, one might expect a strong resistance to the inclusion of secondary material. By secondary material I mean other dictionaries, glosses, glossaries, etc.: all kinds of word-lists in which propositions are made about words, but which do not (or do not necessarily) constitute reliable evidence for the currency of those words at that time. In an ideal world, where an abundance of original quotations is available, there would clearly be no absolute need to call upon any secondary documentation. Yet in the OED, by my calculation, between 7 and 8% of all citations are from secondary sources. In the light of this, it seems worth while to consider the lexicographical principles involved in their use, and to inquire into actual practices.

THE NATURE OF SECONDARY DICTIONARY MATERIAL

Entry Words There is an analogy to be made between the way in which a historical dictionary compiler draws (or should draw) upon earlier lexicographical works and the tactics employed by the sociolinguist in dealing with informants. The interview as a means of eliciting information about the language always carries with it the risk of some distortion.

So also with other men's dictionaries. When in 1646 Sir Thomas Browne employs the word *paleous* (meaning 'full of chaff'), this constitutes a linguistic fact, a piece of usage, evidence for the actual existence of a word which no one else has ever used the since his time. Even once should be enough for the historical linguist. But when ten years later the lexicographer Thomas Blount enters the word *palatical* ('pertaining to ... the palate') in his dictionary (Blount 1656) and again there is no record of the word elsewhere, this does *not* constitute firm evidence for the word's existence: it is merely a statement of belief about language, to be treated with a reserve similar to that which a researcher would use for words elicited by questioning dialect speakers about what they call a horse-fly. The evidence from early dictionary entries differs radically from the evidence of early texts.

Dictionary Metalanguage Another type of evidence from early dictionaries lies in the metalanguage of definition. The word *frivolously* is first recorded in actual usage in the OED in 1712 (Steele); but that can be antedated by more than a century if we take account of the dictionary of Randle Cotgrave, who gives the English *frivolously* as the equivalent of the French *vainement* (Cotgrave 1611). Does this really count? The context is of a man driven into finding an equivalent for a foreign word, and this makes for anything but spontaneous usage. We might more safely say that the occurrence of *frivolously* in Cotgrave illustrates a derivational possibility belonging to Shakespeare's time, than that it is a genuine antedating by 101 years. A different problem arises with *adonize* 'To make an Adonis of; to adorn; to dandify' (also from Cotgrave, who has to *adonize it* 'to resemble Adonis'): this time, the first known textual instance recorded by the OED is from Smollett in 1761, and the dictionary beats him to it by 150 years. But since the word in Cotgrave occurs in the entry for the French *adoniser*, we have to do here with a minimal translational adaptation, and the case for arguing continuity of usage is very slight indeed. I should be inclined to regard Smollett's use of it as a re-invention. With *accowardize*, we have a similar case, though not of antedating but postdating. Caxton used the word in the fifteenth century, and the OED records this, adding only the instance from Cotgrave. Can the word be said to survive into the seventeenth century or not? Since it is provided as an equivalent of the French *acouhardir*, probably not. But one might equally suppose that the French model has triggered off the memory of a thoroughly obsolescent item.

Such examples show that great caution is needed by the historical lexicographer in taking up material from the metalanguage of other dictionaries, and that the users will even then need to treat it with some reserve.

Successive Editions A further methodological difference in the use of secondary documentation lies in the significance of re-issues and new editions. If you are giving a quotation from *Paradise Lost*, this will normally be from the first edition of 1667. There is simply no point (indeed it would be regarded as misleading) to quote from an eighteenth-century edition of Milton's poem as evidence for the currency of the word at that time. So also with all other literary texts, except where there may be significant reading variants between early and late editions, as for instance between the quartos and folios of Shakespeare.

But with dictionaries it is otherwise. If a word occurring in the first edition of Bullokar (1616) is still there in the 19th edition in 1775, this is a significant linguistic fact, worthy of our attention as a part of the historical record. Such a word might of course be there through simple neglect, because no one has thought of throwing it out. Nevertheless, we know that many of the early dictionaries did undergo revision, they purport at least to represent current usage, and there is a clear need for the historical lexicographer to have a policy on the use of successive editions.

Edward Phillips's dictionary (1658) will serve to illustrate the inconsistencies which arise from the casual use of later editions. It contains *malacy* 'a longing of Women with Child' (a word apparently never used), and the OED rightly records it in all five of the editions of Phillips between 1658 and 1696. But for the similar ghost-word *spatiation* 'a walking at length' it gives only the first edition of 1658, even though the word occurs in the later ones. For *ducape*, a kind of silk, the first quotation given is from the fourth edition (1678), though the third (1671) contains it as well. Many thousands of such instances could be given, especially from late seventeenth and early eighteenth-century dictionaries (Blount 1656, Coles 1676, Bailey 1721), of where later (or earlier) editions provide evidence of currency additional to that given in the OED. Schäfer (1989) has now provided copious illustration of the same phenomenon from dictionaries before 1640.

Naturally one cannot expect within the historical dictionary a full record of all editions for every word. But where documentation from other dictionaries is being quoted, some systematic check of early and late editions is needed if distortions are to be avoided.

CATEGORIES OF SECONDARY MATERIAL

I distinguish below six categories of material drawn on by historical lexicographers from earlier dictionaries, each of which entails its own technical problems. In considering these I take the term 'dictionary' in the sense 'general dictionary of language', to the exclusion of dialect, legal, and other specialized word-lists, and glossaries to individual books. But I include bilingual general dictionaries whether of Latin or the vernacular, though these of course call for careful handling because of possible interference from the second language.

The Dictionary as Sole Evidence for the Existence of a Word The strongest case for the historical lexicographer to make use of secondary material is when a word occurs in early dictionaries, and nowhere else. This would apply *a fortiori* to the glosses of Old English, which are so important a source for the earliest stage in the history of the English vocabulary that it would be simply perverse for the lexicographer to ignore them. But even at later stages when an extensive printed corpus can be exploited, other men's lists of words deserve attention.

Blount's *Glossographia* (1656), for instance, contains many hundreds of English words which have never been found outside dictionaries. Should these be regarded as part of the historical record of English? Most of them are thinly disguised Latinisms such as *regifical* for 'royal', or *monticulous* 'full of hills'. We know from the way in which the monolingual dictionaries came into being that compilers often felt impelled to fabricate English equivalents for Latin words where none existed (Starnes and Noyes 1946, Osselton 1958, Schäfer 1970). This may be an argument for saying that the historical lexicographer can safely ignore such 'dictionary' words. On the other hand, though some (such as *metient* 'measuring', *obundation* 'a flowing against') died stillborn with Blount's dictionary, others (such as *mollitude* ('softness'), or *epulosity* 'great banqueting') survived through later dictionaries, sometimes right down to our own day. For the latter there has thus been some kind of historical consensus about what ought to exist, or may exist, in English, and one might consider this an interesting linguistic fact in itself, worth recording in a historical dictionary.

The record of such items in the OED is patchy and highly unpredictable: *pascuous, pastilicate, patration* and *pavidity* are entered there, but *pacator, papaverean, plantigerous* and *platanine* are not. It would be hard to discover any principles of selection in this. I would question anyway whether it is the business of the lexicographer to select. The only proper procedure is surely to enter them all, or to leave them all out: to put some in, and to omit others is to distort the historical record. One strong argument for inclusion is that such dictionary entries very frequently antedate known usage, sometimes by centuries: if the compilers thus got it right so often, then they may be said to deserve the benefit of the doubt when the records are incomplete. I have taken Blount as my example, but it is well known that this category of word proliferates through most of the English dictionaries of the seventeenth and eighteenth centuries. It is a great misfortune that we have no single reliable record of them, though the recent volumes of Schäfer have provided a start for the early seventeenth-century works (Schäfer 1989).

In addition to the thousands of Latinisms, the early dictionaries are also the sole source of evidence for other items, especially derivations and compounds: *rurality* is well-established in English, but *ruralness* is recorded only by Bailey (1730), and it is hard to believe that he simply made it up; *Mercury-woman* ('a seller of newspapers') is recorded in the early eighteenth-century *New English Dictionary* (J.K. 1702) and there is no reason to doubt the testimony of the compiler with such terms of everyday life (though the OED does not enter this one). Bilingual dictionaries have also been shown to be a valuable source for everyday terms and idioms not recorded elsewhere (see chapter 3 above, also Osselton 1973; Bately 1983).

The Dictionary as Evidence for Particular Meanings What credence should one give to statements about meanings in early dictionaries? Their usefulness to us is limited partly because satisfactory defining techniques were slow to evolve and were still in a very unrefined state before the middle of the eighteenth century.

In some instances early dictionaries may be deemed to be reliable because of their circumstantial detail. *Frondosity* is a general word meaning 'leafiness', but the OED rightly admits it also as an architectural term ('a flourishing with green leaves, being just under the architrave') solely on the evidence of Phillips (1658). From Bailey there is a memorable account of what the word *text-book* meant in 1730: '*Text Book* (in Universities) is a Classick Author written very wide by the students, to give Room for an Interpretation dictated by the Master &c, to be inserted in the Interlines.' There can be no doubt about the genuineness of that. Such detailed items may be few, but a habitual user of Bailey will often come upon senses which have escaped the OED: *fashioner* 'one who affects following the fashion', *nombril* 'navel', *rudity* 'ignorance', *wearish* 'boggy'. Clearly a more careful trawl of the eighteenth-century dictionaries would add usefully to the semantic record.

The ultimate compliment to a predecessor is openly to adopt his definition because it cannot be bettered. It is Dr Johnson who is most often honoured in this way in the OED (e.g. *flap* 'anything that hangs broad and loose, fastened only by one side'), though the editors will also at times adopt the *ipsissima verba* of Blount (*fraudation*), Bailey (*falsific*) and others.

The Dictionary Record Predates Known Literary or General Use There is also a strong argument for including secondary material from dictionaries where this will provide earlier datings, even though continuity of usage in such cases may be problematical.

Many hundreds of words in English dictionaries of the seventeenth century are not recorded in actual use until the nineteenth: for instance Cockeram's dictionary of 1623 records *pregust* (1824), *to tumulate* (1866); Blount, published in 1656*, has nival* (1894), *rubid* (1858). The dates of earliest recorded use are appended in brackets. With such items, where we may have to reckon with the probability of words being re-created, the secondary documentation is of limited value for the historical record.

The other extreme may be represented by Miège's inclusion of the English word *dustman* for the French *boueur* in 1688 just 19 years before the historical record begins (see chapter 3 above): here, the secondary evidence may be held to be very nearly as good as the primary.

The case for including *all* dictionary antedatings seems to me to be unanswerable. Though the policy of the OED seems to have been to do that, there can have been no systematic survey. Bailey's UEED (1721), a standard work drawn on extensively in the OED, will (if anyone cares to look) provide many striking antedatings such as the verb *to ruff* (at the game of bridge) by 40 years, and *nymphomania* by 80. As we have noticed in the case of Phillips, where this kind of secondary material is taken up, it is often handled inconsistently.

Dictionary Entries Postdate Known Usage It must seem very questionable whether the historical lexicographer should seek to record the survival of words in early dictionaries beyond their natural currency. Early dictionaries are known to have proceeded by a process of plagiarism, and those often reprinted tend not to have been pruned effectively in later editions. There is therefore in general much dead wood in them.

Nevertheless, I would argue that the inclusion or retention of a word can sometimes tell us something about currency, despite any natural delay in discarding the obsolete: it represents a kind of judgement (even if a passive one) about what belongs to a language.

The French word *papelard* meaning 'hypocrite' is for instance used in Middle English, and occurs down to 1491, not being recorded after Caxton. But it is in the Blount dictionaries down to 1681, and that is surely worth knowing, since there are after all very many other words from Middle English which he does *not* include. *Nolition*, meaning 'unwillingness' occurs in English from 1653 to 1683 (less successful than the companion word *volition*). It is however in the 25th edition of Bailey's UEED in 1783, a hundred years later. Since the word is not in the earlier editions of Bailey (at least, not down to 1757), this implies a deliberate insertion at a late date and therefore constitutes quite strong evidence for currency at the time.

There is, in the OED, some recognition of the value of dictionary postdatings, but very little consistency in presenting them. We often find the general note 'Hence in mod. dicts.' But for *tenebrosity* 'darkness' (known to have been used from 1490 to 1603) the editors only add Blount (1656), even though the word occurs in many seventeenth and eighteenth-century works and is indeed still to be found today (Chambers 1988). Hundreds of other examples could be given, and in general it seems that little effort has been made to provide any systematic coverage of the evidence for word survival. Given the current active interest in the phenomenon of word death (Schäfer 1983), this seems to me to be a major omission.

Dictionary as Evidence for Continuity of Usage It seems to me to be an undesirable thing in a historical dictionary to have dictionary citations simply thrown in among the actual quotations illustrating usage. Mixing primary and secondary documentation will perhaps not confuse the cautious and informed user, but it can give a skewed look to the record of a word.

One circumstance under which such references to dictionaries may legitimately be made is where there has been a dearth of quotations. A good instance is the English word *carnage* meaning 'a great slaughter'. The OED provides examples from Shakespeare's contemporary Philemon Holland in 1600 and 1601, then Phillips's dictionary in 1696, then Gibbon in 1776 and so on to later quotations; and the editor adds the comment 'Frequent in Holland, then rare till late in the 18th c.' Here the secondary citation from Phillips serves effectively to illustrate the presumed continuity.

But with others the reason is not so clear, and I think it would have been better to desist. Why record Cockeram (1623) for *antagonist* when he is neatly bracketed by quotations from Ben Jonson (1599) and Milton (1667)? Like instances will be found under *fragility*, *sagacity* and in many other places.

The Dictionary as Evidence for Lexical Status Early dictionaries abound in usage comments. Those of Dr Johnson are the most famous (Allen 1940), but there are useful gleanings elsewhere too. The word *fare* meant 'voyage' in Old English (*faru*), and dies out (if we are to believe the record) soon after 1600. But it is entered in the later editions of Blount (e.g. in 1681) with the striking statement 'a word still in use among Watermen'. Such side-comments may add usefully to our word histories, though one might argue that they are at best an optional extra for the historical lexicographer. There are however other circumstances where the status implications of secondary material cannot be ignored.

Examples of this are where the early compilers use daggers or other marks to register unacceptability (Osselton 1958; McAdam 1970; see also Figure 4 in chapter 8 and Figure 8 in chapter 13 above).

The basic argument for taking cognizance of secondary documentation at all in our historical dictionaries is that an entry—any entry—in any of the early general dictionaries of the language bears worthwhile witness to a currency at that time. But the use of daggers or other stylistic labels shows us that not all entries are equal. Some indicate full currency, others imply a kind of half currency; and any failure to distinguish this fact inevitably leads to distortions. Thus, the word *finance* was formerly used to mean 'termination, ending', and the last reference to it in that sense in the OED is from Bullokar (1616); but this gives a false impression because no mention is made of the fact that Bullokar put an asterisk against it to show that it was obsolete for him too. The daggers used so extensively by Phillips, Kersey (1708) and others to indicate the doubtful acceptability of certain words are largely ignored by the editors of the OED, with the result that equal status is accorded to unlike items. So far as I have observed, no heed is ever paid to the fact that some compilers such as Benjamin Martin (1749) distinguished foreign or unassimilated words entered in the dictionary by putting them into italics.

THE PRESENTATION OF SECONDARY MATERIAL

In each of these six categories the treatment of the material in the OED appears to be defective. I do not refer to mere incompleteness—for no historical dictionary can ever be complete—but to the patchy and misleading way in which early dictionaries have been used.

Secondary documentation in historical dictionaries must be recognized as being quite different, and in need of more structured treatment than does the listing of the basic documentation consisting of quotations from authors. One strategy for the historical lexicographer (as I have said) might be to ignore secondary material completely: merely to record usage, as seems to have been done in Littré's *Dictionnaire de la langue française* (1863). But if secondary material is to be used at all, then it seems to me that certain principles need to be observed. These are:

i. there should be a defined corpus of representative dictionaries, to include both early and late editions of major works;

ii. these should be surveyed systematically (not consulted incidentally);

iii. all entry words within the secondary corpus should in principle be held to merit inclusion in the historical dictionary even where no primary source exists;

iv. antedating and postdating of primary material should be recorded consistently;

v. citations from dictionaries should show marginalized lexical status (e.g. obsolescence) where this is relevant.

Throughout the above I have sought to show the distinctive character of secondary lexicographical material. Because it is so different, it seems to me that it should be kept physically and typographically separate from the chronological lists of quotations within the lemma. Much of the imprecision within the OED in this matter arises from the casual way in which the dictionary citations are interlaced with quotations from primary sources.

It is instructive to look at the procedures of other major historical dictionaries in dealing with such material. In the *Deutsches Wörterbuch* of Grimm (1854-1960) much fuller reference to occurrences in early dictionaries (especially bilingual ones) is generally provided, and this is given in a separate statement. For instance, for the word *nördlich (nordlich)* some ten seventeenth- and eighteenth-century dictionaries are listed (German-French, German-Swedish, etc.) together with a note of its absence from some of the major German-Latin dictionaries of the period.

The first volumes of the historical dictionary of Dutch—the *Woordenboek der Nederlandsche Taal* (De Vries 1864)—seldom make any reference to early dictionaries of the language; but in the volumes published from round about 1960 this has been done fairly consistently, so that we find for instance under the word *vorstendom* references to its appearance in Plantin (Dutch-French-Latin), Hannot-Van Hoogstraten (Dutch-Latin) and Mellema (Dutch-French) in a brief survey before the literary examples begin.

Perhaps the fullest treatment of such sources is to be found in the *Trésor de la langue française* (Imbs 1971) in the articles placed within the lemma under the heading 'HIST[oire]'. Thus, for *abominer* the historical comments include the very helpful information that the word was 'donné unanimement comme inusité ou presque aux xviie et xviiie siècles par les lexicographes qui l'ont recensé. Nicot 1606, Cotgrave 1611, Furetière 1690, 1701, Trévoux 1704, 1752, 1771 ...'.

So magnificent an array of facts reflects, I suppose, a contemporary interest in sociolinguistic features which is far greater than could have existed in the heyday of comparative-historical linguistics, when Murray began his work. But since it is known that the Oxford University Press is embarking on a new OED—a work very different from the old in both conception and execution—we may hope that secondary documentation will now receive there the rigorous and systematic treatment which it deserves.

END NOTE

Originally presented at a symposium in Essen in 1989 with the title 'Distorting the Linguistic Record: Secondary Documentation in the Oxford English Dictionary*', and published in Hüllen 1990, 183-93. Now reprinted by courtesy of Nodus Publikationen, Münster. The use of secondary data in historical dictionaries is further discussed by Reichmann (1990).*

15

Dictionary Criticism: Three Historical Dictionaries

[1989]

It has for long been the fate of dictionary compilers to be criticized more extensively on matters which they would regard as being trivial than on the substance and method of their work (Murray 1977, 234-5). With certain noteworthy exceptions such as Johnson 1747, Trench 1857 and Littré 1897, until recently few systematic statements of lexicographical principles have been offered outside the prefaces of the dictionaries themselves. Criticism has thus been impoverished because the slow methodological evolution of the great historical dictionaries took place without real dialogue between the dictionary makers on the one hand and the philologists and linguists on the other (Quemada 1967, 16-17; Quemada 1972, 433). This lack of depth in critical appraisal is the more remarkable because the major works to be considered here—Johnson's *Dictionary of the English Language* (1755), the *Deutsches Wörterbuch* (1854-1960) of the Grimm brothers (DWB), the *Woordenboek der Nederlandsche Taal* begun in 1864 and still unfinished (WNT) and the *Oxford English Dictionary* published between 1884 and 1928 (OED)—all bear indelible marks of the linguistic ideals of their time.

The Pre-Critical Period and Johnson Dictionaries did not escape comment even in the pre-critical period before Johnson. Charges of plagiarism and erroneous definition occur in the seventeenth century (Starnes and Noyes 1946, 51-3) and the supposed redundancies and deficiencies in the word-lists of rival dictionary makers became the staple of self-advertisement in eighteenth-century prefaces (Starnes and Noyes 1946, 71, 82, 100). Even Johnson, it has been said, received little intelligent criticism in the reviews and so must be counted 'his own best critic' (Noyes 1954, 191). The truth of this last remark is clear enough from a reading of the preface, since Johnson there effectively forestalls most of the objections which could even conceivably be made to his performance. But the extensive collections of contemporary criticism in Rypins 1925, Noyes 1954, and Congleton and Congleton 1984 show how many of the now familiar themes of dictionary criticism had by then become established, even though this often happened in an *ad hoc* manner: Johnson was berated by Withers in 1788 for his circular definitions such as *long* 'not short', *short* 'not long', by the *Critical Review* in 1783 for defining common words by means of erudite ones as in *twisted* 'contorted', by Webster in 1807 for the lack of order in his definitions, and in particular by De Rivarol in 1797 for placing figurative meanings before the literal; in the view of the *Gentleman's Magazine* in 1788 he indulged too much in learned 'dictionary' words such as *morigerous* and *tenebrosity*, he was blamed for excluding (and also for including) archaic and dialectal words by Maxwell in 1755 and Croft in 1788, as well as for his neglect of synonymy (by Adam Smith in 1755); further, Maxwell, Adelung c. 1780 and Webster 1807 all referred to his failures in etymology which became best known to posterity from Macaulay's unkind comment that he was 'a wretched etymologist'.

In the matter of his use of quotations Johnson's critics were divided. There was praise, especially for the preference given by him to authors who (as Boswell put it) showed no tendency to hurt sound religion and morality. But he was condemned by the *Gentleman's Magazine* for making use of 'the least reputable of our modern authors' and by Webster for making 'injudicious choices' such as Sir Roger L'Estrange. Johnson was acknowledged by Adelung to be strong on the written, literary language, but weaker in his coverage of common usage, idioms, phraseology, etc., and it was of course for the latter that he needed to turn especially to non-literary sources. He was thus both criticized for including words unsupported by quotations—by Callender in 1782—and blamed for an overkill of literary evidence on the commonest words (six citations for *finger* 'the flexible member of the hand by which men catch and hold'). The problem of covering everyday usage in large scholarly dictionaries had come to stay.

Trench on Dictionary Deficiencies The older tradition of dictionary making was effectively demolished by Trench in his papers read to the Philological Society of London (Trench 1857), which constitute one of the most sustained pieces of dictionary criticism in the nineteenth century. Trench condemns wholeheartedly the prescriptive principle, which he associates with the dictionary of the *Académie française*, and refers to the 'constant confusion' which exists in men's minds about the real function of the dictionary. For Trench, a dictionary 'according to that idea of it which seems to me to be alone capable of being logically maintained, is an inventory of the language', and the dictionary maker has no concern with the *delectus verborum*: he is the historian of a language, not a critic. The matter has seldom been expressed so forcibly or so clearly, and most of Trench's strictures on the dictionaries before his time proceed from this firm and committed view. He considers Webster to be 'deprived of all value' because of its lack of illustrative quotations, and expresses his strongest disapproval of those who 'make our Dictionaries the representation merely of what the language now is, and not also of what it has been'. In Trench's view, as in that of many of his contemporaries, the study of language gave as ready an access to the cultural heritage of the past as did that of history, of laws, or of literature. His dismissal of merely synchronic dictionaries clearly reflects this belief, as do the high demands he placed on the historical dictionary as the treasure-house of the nation's linguistic past: it must contain not only all the words of the language ('good or bad'), but must give the first (as well as the last) recorded instances of a word's use—Johnson, he says, has never even tried to do this; it must present senses in strict chronological sequence (Johnson again falls short here) and must record faithfully the older forms and spellings of words (in this Richardson 1836-7 is found wanting) and give a full record of all the derivations, which are, he says, far more numerous than existing dictionaries would lead us to believe. At the same time Trench criticizes earlier works for a superfluity of technical terms (though Richardson is praised for excluding them) and self-explanatory compounds (especially in Webster). He also rejects utterly the 'strange medley' of encyclopaedic matter which had crept into them—'they are gazetteers, mythologies, scientific encyclopaedias, and a hundred things more'.

Trench's powerful criticism was to act as a catalyst for work on the OED, which has indeed remained largely true to the ideals implied in it; though it is striking to find modern critics still exercised by some of them—e.g. Burchfield 1973 on the matter of names, and Stein 1983 on that of prescriptive editorial comments.

The Critical Reception of the Deutsches Wörterbuch Not surprisingly, the critics of the first parts of the great German historical dictionary by the

Grimm brothers took up many of the same topics (the Grimms were honorary members of the Philological Society), and Trench himself praised the DWB for its treatment of synonymy (Trench 1857, 47; Aarsleff 1967, 257). Trench was proposing full coverage of the older stages of the language, but in 1852 Sanders was already taking Grimm to task for the over-representation of earlier periods to the neglect of the modern (for this and further references, see Kirkness 1980). On the other hand he was rebuked by Wurm for the lack of legal, medical and other technical terms such as Trench had warned against. He was criticized also for having no rational plan for the selection of compounds and derivations. There was praise for the leaving out of foreign loan-words, but puzzlement over the seemingly arbitrary entries which had been made (why *Anekdotenjäger*, but not *Anekdote*?).

The fully documented objections of Grimm's reviewers also covered topics such as alphabetization, spelling, syntax and morphology (gender, pluralization, verb forms). The general tone of the criticism was hostile, and there were also charges of protestant bias both in the selection and definition of religious words, and the inevitable disputed etymologies. In the selection and use of illustrative quotations modern German authors were said to have been neglected (Jacob Grimm was later to accept this point) and quotations were said to be unevenly distributed and inadequately identified. One of the more substantial criticisms provided both by Sanders and Wurm has to do with inconsistencies in the techniques adopted for the explanation of words in the DWB. Some had been left wholly unexplained (*Abendspaziergang*), sometimes a French synonym would be given (*Allheit* 'totalité') and often the compilers had resorted to Latin (*Achtpfünder* 'tormentum octo librarum globos emittens'). Such a gratuitous use of bookish explanations leads Sanders to conclude that the dictionary is rendered unusable for the unlatined ('especially for women'): 'Heiliger Gott', he exclaims, 'muss man denn wirklich, um Deutsch zu verstehen, nothwendig Lateinisch kennen?'. The complaint is reminiscent of criticisms made of Johnson's contorted and polysyllabic definitions of words such as *network*. Johnson, admittedly, could do it all in the vernacular language, but the odium of *ignotum per ignotius* still clings to many of our dictionaries today.

It is of interest to record the spirited defence provided by the Grimms. Their argument that the use of Latin for the explanation of word meanings gave the dictionary an air of permanency smacks rather of eighteenth than nineteenth-century beliefs. Their justification of Latin because it helped foreigners and would in any case be understood by two-thirds of the population is of course a historically conditioned one. They note its usefulness in dealing with obscenities (this was to last till the twentieth century) and strike a curiously modern note in saying that where illustrative quotations are provided a definition is not strictly necessary anyway.

Did all this remarkably detailed criticism achieve any results? It appears that the Grimms never came to an effective dialogue with their critics Sanders and Wurm (Kirkness 1980, 207), and that such improvements as were made in going along probably owed more to their increased lexicographical experience than to any process of feedback from their detractors.

The Woordenboek der Nederlandsche Taal and Problems of Long-Term Lexicographical Projects Publication of the DWB took over a hundred years; it was completed only in 1960. The corresponding historical dictionary of the Dutch language (WNT) was begun in 1864 and is still not finished, though as things are now going it should be completed by the end of this century. Such protracted work on a single scholarly project imposes strains on those who carry it out: Quemada has argued that unity of conception and method can be sustained at the most for 25 or 30 years (Quemada 1972, 430). Whether we accept that figure or not, it is striking that in the case of the WNT much of the academic criticism has centred on the inconsistencies and blemishes which were the unhappy and almost inevitable outcome of delay in execution (on this, and other details of criticism, see Van Sterkenburg 1984). Even in 1883 Van Vloten was saying that the dictionary could never be completed on the scale envisaged: at that time, after thirty years' endeavour, no single letter of the alphabet was finished, though four letters had been started. Van Vloten's criticism was marred by being intemperate and personal, but it had an uneasy ring of prophecy about it: as recently as 1971 the editor Kruyskamp was himself pessimistic about the chances of completion. Cosijn, who had worked on the dictionary for some years, also found the plans of the editor Matthias de Vries too grandiose and idealistic, arguing in 1892 that not all words entered in the dictionary merited the extensive treatment they had been given—why supply the meaning of the common ones anyway? There was also an unnecessary ballast of hypothetically existing words supported only by fictitious illustrations.

The unfortunate decision to leave the editor of each letter to tackle it in his own way led to what De Tollenaere has since called a methodological shambles. In the early volumes the editor De Vries had excerpted mainly nineteenth-century texts, taking even from major writers of the seventeenth and eighteenth century only what could still be counted as current in his own day. He eschewed technical terms and strictly excluded Gallicisms and Germanicisms. But his successors decided to upgrade the WNT to a historical inventory of the language, shunted the *terminus a quo* back to 1500, and adopted a more liberal admissions policy, with the result that in the later volumes the non-literary language and foreign loans became fully represented. In 1882 De Vries had announced that the collection of material for the whole alphabet was complete; but successive additions of newer material were made at later stages, and it was not until 1972 that the year 1921 was finally fixed on as the definitive *terminus ad quem*. Van der Voort van der Kleij could thus justifiably say in 1976 that it was simply impossible for the dictionary to be internally consistent in character or quality, since no permanent principle for collecting the material had ever existed. Van Sterkenburg characterizes the WNT as 'hybrid' (1984, 88) and the major criticisms which have been made of it—many virtues though individual volumes may possess—have arisen not only from the lack of editorial control over a long period, but from the problem of combining the synchronic description of a major cultural language with a large-scale historical account of it: Van Sterkenburg points out that 'contemporary Dutch' meant the period from 1852-84 for Part I (*A - ajuin*), but it meant 1957-71 for part XXI (*ves-vluwe*), and argues that as a research tool the dictionary must remain flawed if for that reason alone.

The Oxford English Dictionary and the Historical Principle Early reactions to the publication of the OED tended to be commendatory, descriptive and critical only of incidental details (Bivens 1980-81). The sheer scale of the work may have daunted reviewers. The OED is more inclusive, and covers a longer period of language history, than Littré, Grimm or the WNT. But the decision to do this seems to have been accepted without question, and once the work was under way there appear to have been few doubts about the viability of the whole project such as those which arose with the WNT. Perhaps because of the proclaimed aim of comprehensiveness, critics tended to batten upon omissions which they had discovered; even as early as 1889 the American scholar Lounsbury was offering antedatings, thus giving rise to the enthusiastic if somewhat nit-picking scholarly industry which flourished (especially in the columns of *Notes & Queries*) until well into the second half of the twentieth century.

The inclusion of nonce-words caused a certain uneasiness from the start, and it is a category still being recognized as 'controversial' by Burchfield in 1973. Much the same can be said of scientific and technical terms: Trench had cautioned against including too many of them, Grimm had been rebuked for neglecting them in the DWB, the WNT had switched its policy on them, and we find that modern reviewers of the OED Supplement (Potter 1973, Samuels 1983) have severally rediscovered the same problem.

Some early references are to be found to the need for avoiding 'inferior' authors (echoing criticism of Johnson a century before). It is a complaint which goes with the rejection in the *Edinburgh Review* in 1859 of the descriptivist approach, and a call in the same journal thirty years later (as well as by Lounsbury in 1886) for more 'authoritative' quotations by which 'the best' usage might be established.

The superficiality of much of the early criticism contrasts sharply with the impressive reviews published by Henry Bradley in *The Academy* (Bradley 1884), which 'marked him out as one of the few who were competent to appreciate the Dictionary at its proper value, or to offer helpful criticism' (OED, Vol. I, General Introduction, xvii). Bradley offered specific comparisons with Littré and Grimm, pointing out that the OED went much further back than either of these, giving us in effect a dictionary of Middle English and Old English as well. It was also superior in the number and precision of its citations and the fullest in its vocabulary (he criticized Grimm for a 'Teutonic purism' which misled him into excluding many words known to all Germans). On the other hand he saw the OED as falling short of Littré in the coverage of idiomatic phrases, and accorded it the 'middle rank' between Littré and Grimm in regard to its definitions (though Littré had at times fallen into 'an over-refinement which is rather confusing than helpful'—for instance in its 23 numbered senses for the word *eau*).

Bradley was able to offer expert comment on etymologies, finding the OED in general 'all but faultless' in that department, and he was quickly rewarded for his criticism by being recruited on to the editorial team. It is easy to see why. Alone among the critics his comments were informed by a sense of the practical needs of the dictionary user. For instance, he deals with typography, praising the great variety of types in the OED, which 'abridge the labour of consulting the Dictionary' (whereas Littré, he says, was a typographical chaos), and praises the phonetic notation not as ideal but as striking a balance between precision and facility.

In particular Bradley reveals a sensitive understanding of the problem of ordering the different senses of a word in the historical dictionary. He shows that Murray does not keep rigorously to a single system (such as Trench would have approved of) with the original or etymological meaning first, but argues rightly that there are good reasons for not doing so in the case of foreign loans. This is creative criticism at its best, and Bradley seems, even in 1884, to have sensed what was later to be identified as a major methodological problem in historical dictionaries: the distortion introduced by including material from the few years immediately preceding publication, which savours too much of 'bringing the work down to the latest date'. For earlier periods the editor is dealing with a 'lexicographically closed' vocabulary (Burchfield, 1980), but among recent items it is hard for him to decide what is ephemeral, so that coverage of contemporary usage must be an interim exercise; though, as Bradley concedes, such material will retain its value for students of the history of the language. Is it possible to cover the whole of the recorded language in a single work? Bradley had seen that synchrony and diachrony made unhappy bedfellows, and it is a view which would find support in more recent lexicographical writings. Quemada (1972, 436) proposed 500 years as the maximum period for inclusion in a historical dictionary, and many of the more modern projects (such as the *Trésor de la langue française*) have taken a tranche far slimmer than that.

Dictionary Criticism and Dictionary Research In the range and perceptiveness of his criticism Bradley must be counted exceptional among the OED critics. For the most part the criticism of all these great historical dictionaries reveals a surprising lack of interest in general principles, with incidental sniping taking the place of any real exploration of the intentions with which the works being criticized had been set up. Omissions are lamented and superfluities condemned, but the whole basis for determining the nomenclature remains largely undiscussed. The near-total absence of concern for the semantic principles of definition is specially striking, and the topic of lemmatization is seldom raised. User-convenience is hardly an issue. Even the reviews of the Supplements to the OED published from 1972 onwards have tended to content themselves with well-worn topics such as casual omissions, unassimilated terms, etc., trundled out in the familiar way.

But dictionary criticism, like literary criticism, is now in the process of becoming professionalized. The publication of Schäfer 1980 has marked for the OED at least a turning-point at which the dictionary ceases to be merely the subject of criticism but becomes also the object of research. With full statistical paraphernalia Schäfer shows retrospectively the extent to which the OED is flawed in historical coverage because of the excerption methods used. Such a demonstration is of course beyond the capability of the instant reviewer, but with the computerization of texts the insights provided by such research will doubtless in time become the common coin of criticism. Meantime the first of a series of Round Table Conferences on Historical Lexicography had been held at Florence in 1971. With the current quickening of scholarly interest in lexicographical theory, and the practice of getting out progress reports on major projects (such as the *Toronto Dictionary of Old English* in Bammesberger 1985) we may hope for more settled and purposive canons of dictionary criticism in the future.

END NOTE

Originally published in Hausmann et al. 1989-91, Vol. I, 225-30, with the title 'The History of Academic Dictionary Criticism with Reference to Major Dictionaries', and reprinted here by courtesy of Walter de Gruyter & Co., Berlin. Further information on the relationship of Grimm and the OED is to be found in Zgusta (1989a).

16

Bilingual Dictionaries with Dutch: a Case Study in European Lexicography

[1991]

Bilingual lexicography with Dutch or Flemish (no further distinction between the terms is offered here) has developed to a high degree during the past four and a half centuries. The production of dictionaries involving Dutch and other languages can be seen to reflect the needs of a minor-language community which has at the same time always been a major trading nation with strong international ties, both cultural and political. The following selective list, based on Claes 1980, of dates for the earliest known bilingual dictionaries involving Dutch with other languages, shows that geographical contiguity was far from being the main factor in determining the repertoire of foreign languages with which Dutch was combined:

Dutch with:

French	1546	Danish	1826
Malaysian	1612	Javanese	1827
Spanish	1617	Japanese	1855
English	1647	Sranan	1855
Yiddish	1710	Chinese	1882
Italian	1710	Swedish	1907
Portuguese	1714	Turkish	1971
German	1719	Polish	1971.
Russian	1813		

The early take-up of exotic languages is noteworthy. Claes records five items for Malaysian in the seventeenth century. Despite the long land frontier and all the language contacts this must entail, German is relatively late in the list—after Italian, and a century and a half later than French. The appearance only in 1971 of the first bilingual dictionary for Turkish and Dutch reflects new contacts resulting from the reverse flow from east to west of the twentieth-century migrant workers.

The Early Dictionaries: Sources and Methods of Compilation The first bilingual dictionaries with Dutch, like those with other European languages, derived much in both form and content from the well-established tradition of bilingual works combining Latin with a vernacular which go back to the Middle Ages; they also drew directly or indirectly on the very substantial renaissance polyglot compilations such as the Plantin *Thesaurus* (1573) and Kilianus (1599) with its 40,000 entries (Osselton 1973, 49; Claes 1977, 210-17). Thus in the earliest French-Flemish dictionary, Meurier (1557, 1563), the word-list is based on a French-Latin compilation of Estienne, while the other half of the combination (Flemish-French) uses a Dutch-Latin version of Dasypodius (Claes 1977, 207-8).

At a later stage the tendency was to take material from combinations of two vernacular languages, as when Hexham for his Dutch-English dictionary (Hexham 1647, 1648) drew on the Dutch-French list of Mellema 1618 (see chapter 7 above). The initial disinclination to use single-language dictionaries as a base-text might seem surprising, though these were often drawn on later for supplementary material, as for instance by Sewel (Osselton 1973, 79-80, 88). In the early stages suitable works were no doubt not often to hand; in many respects the evolution of monolingual dictionaries lagged behind that of bilingual ones, and in any case another man's list incorporating a different foreign language would be more likely to provide a suitable set of items. But the rather opportunistic borrowing that went on from various combinations of foreign languages can be shown to have resulted at times in an initial imbalance between the two halves, from and into the native language (Riemens 1921, 17; Osselton 1973, 44-9).

This complex pattern of sources and interrelationships between the early vernacular dictionaries of Europe (upon which much research still needs to be done) has resulted in striking similarities between the types of word-stock which many of them contain. The Dutch works share fully in this common tradition from the sixteenth century onwards.

Dutch and French Combinations with French dominate the early history of Dutch bilingual lexicography, and not surprisingly the first volumes come from that area of the southern Netherlands where the two languages were (and still are) most forcibly in contact: the Dutch-French *Naembouck* (1546) was published in Ghent, and the dictionaries of Meurier (1557, 1563) and Sasbout (1576, 1579) in Antwerp. It was not until Waesberghe (1599) and the Mellema dictionary of 1618 that the scene shifted to what is now called Holland; the partially regional character of the vocabulary of early Dutch-French dictionaries is a matter of some scholarly interest (De Tollenaere 1977, 222; Van Sterkenburg 1984, 46).

Meurier's dictionary (like that of Cotgrave 1611) contains some neologisms, and he could boast of a certain literary colouring to his vocabulary, with items from Marot and Ronsard (Riemens 1921, 11), but no such claim could ever be made for the productions going under the name of Mellema, which with their numerous editions between 1587 and 1641 may be regarded as the standard practical translation or decoding dictionaries of their time. The 47,000 Dutch entries in the 1636 edition nearly double the number to be found in his predecessors. The entries are commonly single-line items, and little effort has been made to structure lemmata so as to distinguish main entries, derivations, illustrative phrases, etc. Many of the seemingly redundant entries such as '*lam in een been*, Ohie d'vne jambe' are of a type which has been shown to go back to Latin sources, and from which the vernacular dictionaries took centuries to free themselves (Osselton 1973, 49).

Other dictionaries in the seventeenth century continued much in the same tradition. Van den Ende (1654, 1656) has been called 'le premier "dictionnaire phonétique" destiné aux Hollandais' (Riemens 1921, 216), though the compiler was aiming primarily at warning his users against the vagaries of French spelling. The work of d'Arsy (1643, with editions down to 1699) was little more than a reissue of Mellema, and he was also involved in revising Van den Ende (De Tollenaere 1977, 221): the dictionary publishing world was still a small one.

As typical of the eighteenth-century productions we may take Halma (1708, 1710) with its numerous editions down to 1784. With 1023 pages for Dutch-French and 774 pages for French-Dutch it is a very substantial work indeed 'composé sur le modele des Dictionaires de Richelet, Pomey, Tachard, et Danet, Revû & considerablement augmenté sur le Dictionaire & la Grammaire de l'Academie Françoise'. It is typographically much superior to Mellema, and there is by now quite an impressive coverage of technical terms, as the following extract may show:

> DIMINUTIF, *s.m. (Terme de Grammaire.) Een verkleinwoordt, verkleinnaam,* of *verkleining.*
> DIMINUTION, *s.f. Vermindering, verkleining, afneeming.*
> Diminution de crédit. *Vermindering van geloof, van gezagh,* of *aanzien.*
> DIMISSION. (Mot inusité.) *Voyez* Demission.
> DIMISSOIRE, *s.m. (Terme de l'Eglise Romaine.) Zekere Bisschoppelyke brieven, volmagtbrieven.*
> DIMISSORIAL, *adj.* Lettres dimissoriales. *Zekere volmagtbrieven van eenen Bisschop.*
> DINANDERIE, *s.f. Allerhande geel koperwerk.*
> DINDON, *s.m.* Jeune poulet d'Inde. *Een jonge kalkoen.*
> DINDONNEAU, *s.m.* Petit dindon. *Een kieken van een kalkoen.*
> DINE, diner, *s.m. 't Middagmaal, de middagmaaltydt,* (Brabantsch, *De noen, of noenmaaltydt*).

Cautionary guidance is given after the fashion of Richelet on jocular words, archaic words and figurative meanings. The volumes no doubt kept their place in the market despite the rival works of the Frenchman Marin (1701, 1710), particularly on account of the wide range of idiomatic and illustrative phrases (there are for instance 22 for the verb *donner*), though these are by modern standards still somewhat haphazardly arranged.

Marin produced the first *Dictionnaire portatif* (Marin 1696), and up to a quarter of the 21 new Dutch and French dictionaries listed by Claes (1980) as being published in the eighteenth century appear to have been abridged or compact volumes: 'un grand livre est un grand mal' is the selling-point put forward by Des Roches in the interesting 'Observations générales' to his handy volume (1769)—why have fifty phrases to illustrate the meaning of a word when your user may be satisfied with three? All this serves to highlight the dominant characteristic of the early Dutch and French dictionaries: they were of the market place, not of the scholar's study, and served the practical, everyday needs of a partly bilingual society.

Dutch and English Dictionaries combining Dutch with English appear a century later than those with French. They are fewer in number (only three substantial works down to the end of the eighteenth century) and are to be associated with the needs of translators and readers of foreign books rather than with the schoolroom. Henry Hexham, who produced the first one, was, like the author of the first Dutch-Spanish dictionary (Rodriguez 1624), a soldier who fought in the Spanish wars in the Netherlands. Hexham had stayed on in time of peace, and turned his hand to the translation of French, Latin and Dutch works into English. His dictionary is heavily dependent on the sources he chose: an English-Latin dictionary (Rider 1589) for the English-Dutch half, and a Dutch-French one (Mellema 1618) for the Dutch-English half (see chapter 7 above). His dictionary is said to be for 'divines, students and others', but Hexham generally kept clear of over-bookish terms, and added a number of contemporary idiomatic items of his own (Osselton 1973, 44-54). The 35,000 English and 47,000 Dutch entries commonly provide a single equivalent in the target language, and there is a very extensive use of cross-reference ('a Banket, *Siet* banquet') which would no doubt be especially useful at a time when the instability of spelling in both languages could be a problem for the foreign reader. No grammatical information is given in the individual entries, but the Hexham dictionary is notable for its inclusion in all editions of an appended grammar of each language.

Hexham's dictionary was totally replaced at the end of the seventeenth century by the famous and quite independently contrived dictionary of Willem Sewel, the historian of the Quakers, who was also a formidable translator, philologist and literary journalist. Sewel (1691), like Hexham, draws too heavily on a Latin-English dictionary (Coles 1677), and a Dutch-French one (Van den Ende 1654, 1656; revised 1681). It is no bigger than Hexham, but it is generally better thought out, more up-to-date, and has more precise definitions (Osselton 1973, 72). Sewel's philological interests are reflected in his decision to include a treatise on Dutch spelling, and guides to the pronunciation of the two languages as well as grammars of them. He provides also more grammatical information in the text itself, for instance by placing the article before Dutch nouns to indicate gender. The presence of some characteristic items from Sir Thomas Browne *(to supererogate, testaceous)* shows the influence of Sewel's activities as a translator.

Sewel's dictionary was to remain the standard work throughout the eighteenth century. He devoted four years to a revision which appeared in 1708. He turned to an English monolingual dictionary (Kersey-Phillips 1706) for many political, ecclesiastical and technical terms on which Dutch users might need fuller information. With meticulous editorial changes throughout, and a better typography, it is a greatly improved work.

There were further editions in 1727, 1735, 1749 and 1754, but it is in the two volumes of 1766 'more than the half part augmented' that we reach the high point in the cumulative tradition of eighteenth-century bilingual lexicography in Holland. The reviser Egbert Buys had himself produced a technical dictionary and, drawing especially on Boyer's English-French dictionary (Boyer 1764) he incorporated a vast amount of new material to improve the coverage of eighteenth-century usage. The following extract will serve to illustrate the range of idiomatic coverage:

To grow rich, *Ryk worden.*
It grows day, *Het wordt dag.*
It grows towards evening, *Het begint avond te worden, de avond begint te vallen.*
To grow little, (*or* lesser, to grow short,) *Korter worden, inkrimpen.*
The days begin to grow short, *De dagen beginnen te korten.*
To grow stronger and stronger, after a fit of sickness, *Na een ziekte in kragten toeneemen, sterker worden.*
To grow young again, *Wéder jong worden.*
To grow dear, *Duur worden.*
To grow weary of a thing, *Iets moede worden, een afkeer ergens van krygen.*
To grow a scholar, *Een geleerde worden.*
To grow tame, *Tam worden.*
There grew a quarrel upon it, *Daar ontstond een krakeel uit.*
To grow INTO fashion, *In 't gebruik komen, de mode worden.*

There is a total of 48 items under this verb, *to grow*, and these two volumes, each with roughly a thousand pages in triple columns, are still valuable reference works even today for anyone working on eighteenth-century Dutch or English texts.

The dictionary of Holtrop (1789, 1801) is a somewhat condensed version of Sewel, with improvements to the arrangement of material, so that the compiler achieves something approximating to a modern pattern of lemmatization. He gives parts of speech, indicates the stress-pattern of English words, and—rather late in the day—benefits from the Johnson and Bailey dictionaries for some of his new items. For the Dutch-English half he too appears to have turned to the Dutch-French dictionary of Marin (Osselton 1973, 100-107).

Dutch and German It was not until the eighteenth century that the first dictionary of Dutch and German was published, and the late appearance has been plausibly explained (De Tollenaere 1977, 224) on the ground that the two languages were sufficiently close for people to get on without feeling the lack of a lexicographical prop. Whatever the reason, the need for one was evidently felt first by German speakers, for the earliest dictionary combining the two languages (Kramer 1719) was published in Nuremberg. The compiler of this bulky work, Matthias Kramer, was a teacher of languages and a member of the Prussian Academy of Sciences. He was 78 when the dictionary came out, but, revised by others, this work held the market throughout the eighteenth century. Kramer's initial Dutch word-list was based on the Halma Dutch-French dictionary (De Vooys 1947, 266) and at times retains gratuitous French explanations ('*Onder-rok* ... Unter-rock/Unter-röcklein. *gall.* sou-jupe, cotillon'). The Kramer dictionary is unusually strong on grammatical information, and is typographically more inventive than Halma. It was drastically cut down by J.D. Titius for the octavo second edition (Leipzig 1759) but extended again for the third (Leipzig/Amsterdam 1768), in which the spelling was revised and information inserted on gender by the Dutch reviser Adam van Moerbeek. In the Dutch-German half there are some 62,000 entries, and it is clear that much of the added material (including whole illustrative sentences) has simply been lifted from the 1766 edition of Sewel.

The Nineteenth Century and After With the improved communications and expanding world trade of the nineteenth century, production of bilingual dictionaries of all kinds grew explosively. For Dutch, the combinations with the three languages of the nearest neighbours remained dominant. The table given below lists the numbers of new publications for these languages in the seventeenth, eighteenth, nineteenth and twentieth centuries as recorded in Claes (1980). It shows clearly how French was in the lead from the start, and was totally dominant in the nineteenth century, when English lay third to German:

	Dutch and French	*Dutch and English*	*Dutch and German*
1600-99	15	11	-
1700-99	33	14	6
1800-99	111	33	42
1900-	165	142	83

The figures also illustrate the considerable levelling up which has taken place in the twentieth century.

Typical of the new productions of the nineteenth century are the Bomhoff dictionaries. Bomhoff was of humble origins and worked his way up from paper-maker's apprentice to become a well-known translator and writer on spelling, grammar and literature. He first produced a dictionary of Dutch with English (Bomhoff 1822) which went through five editions, then one with French (Bomhoff 1835), and finally a German one (Bomhoff 1846). They are serviceable works, with for instance about 32,000 entries for English-Dutch (in the 1832 edition) and some 67,000 in the companion Dutch-English volume—a discrepancy in bulk which he attributes in part to the need to include so many Dutch compound words. The new thing about them is that there should have been the three dictionaries from the single Bomhoff stable for what in Holland today are still called the 'school languages': English, French and German. Whether Bomhoff himself was personally responsible for all three language combinations might be worth investigating. But the pattern of the triple two-volume series became firmly established: other nineteenth-century examples are those of Calisch and Servaas de Bruin (Claes 1980). Even in the highly commercialized world of twentieth-century bilingual dictionary production it is not hard to trace the same pattern of the basic three combinations of Dutch with the three dominant modern foreign languages. These often go with a monolingual dictionary as the 'flagship' of the series, and it has been shown (Van Sterkenburg 1983) that the bilingual dictionaries of Marin and Halma are the direct forefathers of the authoritative Van Dale monolingual dictionary of present-day Dutch (Van Dale 1984). Disparities between the volumes of such series will always occur. But it is a tradition well-placed to reap the full benefits of normalization which may now be achieved by the use of computerized data-bases.

END NOTE

Originally published in 1991 in Hausmann et al. *1989-91, Vol. III, 3034-39, with the title* Bilingual Lexicography with Dutch, *and reprinted here by courtesy of Walter de Gruyter & Co., Berlin. A companion article by Rasmussen on the history of bilingual lexicography with Danish reveals striking parallels with the above, though in Denmark English was clearly low in status before the nineteenth century, 'étant utilisée surtout par des commerçants et des officiers de marine à des fins pratiques' (Rasmussen 1991, 3055).*

Bibliography

DICTIONARIES AND EARLY WORKS OF REFERENCE

Ainsworth, Robert 1736. *Thesaurus linguae Latinae compendiarius*, London: Printed for J. and P. Knapton (2nd edn 1746)

Arsy, Jan Louis d' 1643. *Le Grand Dictionaire François-Flamen. Het Groote Woorden-Boek vervattende den Schat der Nederlantsche Taele, met een Fransche uit-legghinge*, Utrecht: H. Specht

Bailey, Nathan 1721. *An Universal Etymological English Dictionary*, London: E. Bell (2nd edn 1724; 4th edn 1728; 8th edn 1737; 15th edn 1753; 17th edn 1757; 20th edn 1764; 21st edn 1770, 1775; 25th edn 1783)

— 1727. *The Universal Etymological English Dictionary: In Two Parts ... Vol. II*, London: Printed for T. Cox

— 1730. *Dictionarium Britannicum*, London: Printed for T. Cox (2nd edn 1736)

Barclay, James 1774. *A Complete and Universal English Dictionary on a New Plan*, London: Richardson and Urquhart

Baret, John 1573. *An Alvearie or Triple Dictionarie, in Englishe, Latin, and French*, London: Henry Denham

Berlaimont, Noel de 1637. *The English, Latine, French, Dutch, Schole-Master. Or, an Introduction to teach young Gentlemen and Merchants to travell or trade*, London: A.G. for Michael Sparke

Blount, Thomas 1656. *Glossographia*, London: Printed by T. Newcomb (5th edn 1681)

Bomhoff, Derk 1822. *New Dictionary of the English and Dutch Language. Nieuw Woordenboek der Nederduitsche en Engelsche Taal*, Nijmegen: Thieme

— 1835. *Nouveau dictionnaire français-hollandais et hollandais-français*, Zutphen: Thieme

— 1846. *Vollständiges Deutsch-Holländisches und Holländisch-Deutsches Taschen-Wörterbuch*, 's-Gravenhage: Noordendorp

Boyer, Abel 1699. *The Royal Dictionary. In two Parts. First, French and English, Secondly, English and French*, London: R. Clavel

Browne, Richard 1700. *The English-School Reformed*, London: Printed for A. & J. Churchil

Bruggencate, K. ten 1974, 1978. *Engels Woordenboek. I Engels-Nederlands, II Nederlands-Engels*, Groningen: Wolters (18th edn)

Bullokar, John 1616. *An English Expositor*, London: Printed by John Legatt (19th edn 1775)

Catholicon Anglicum 1483. *Catholicon Anglicum, an English-Latin Wordbook*, ed. S.J.H. Herrtage, London: Early English Text Society, 1881

Cawdrey, Robert 1604. *A Table Alphabeticall*, London: Printed by I. R[oberts]

Chambers Twentieth Century Dictionary 1901. Edinburgh: Chambers (1972, 1983; 1988 with title *Chambers English Dictionary*, Cambridge: Cambridge-Chambers)

Cockeram, Henry 1623. *The English Dictionarie: or, an Interpreter of Hard Words*, London: Printed for Edmund Weaver

Coles, Elisha 1676. *An English Dictionary*, London: Printed for Samuel Crouch

— 1677. *A Dictionary, English-Latin, and Latin-English*, London: Printed by John Richardson

Collins German-English English-German Dictionary 1980. London: Collins

Collins Cobuild English Language Dictionary 1987. London: Collins

Collins Dictionary of the English Language 1979. London: Collins (2nd edn 1986)

The Concise Oxford Dictionary of Current English 1911. Oxford: Clarendon Press (6th edn 1976; 7th edn 1982; 8th edn 1990)

Coote, Edmund 1596. *The English Schoole-maister*, London: Printed by the Widow Orwin

Cotgrave, Randle 1611. *A Dictionarie of the French and English Tongues*, London: Adam Islip

— 1650. *A French-English Dictionary Compil'd by Mr Randle Cotgrave: with another in English and French [by Robert Sherwood]*, London: W.H. for Octavian Pulleyn

Cowell, John 1607. *The Interpreter: or Booke Containing the Signification of Words*, Cambridge: John Legate

Dale, Johan Frederik van 1984. *Groot Woordenboek der Nederlandse Taal*, 's-Gravenhage: Nijhoff (11th edn)

Defoe, B.N. 1735. *A New English Dictionary*, Westminster: John Brindley

Duden 1977. *Das grosse Wörterbuch der Deutschen Sprache*, Mannheim: Duden

Dyche, Thomas and Pardon, William 1735. *A New General English Dictionary*, London: Richard Ware

Elyot, Sir Thomas 1538. *The Dictionary of Syr Thomas Elyot*, London: Thomas Berthelet

Ende, Caspar van den 1654, 1656. *Le gazophylace de la langue Françoise et Flamande. Schatkamer der Nederduytsche en Francoysche tale*, Rotterdam: Jean Naeran (also 1681)

The English Schole-Master, or, Certaine Rules and Helpes 1646. Amsterdam

Estienne, Robert 1549. *Dictionnaire francois-latin*, Paris: Impr. de R. Estienne (also 1564, 1614)

Gazophylacium Anglicanum 1689. London: Printed by E.H. & W.H.

Glossographia Anglicana Nova 1707. London: Dan. Brown

Gouldman, Francis 1664. *A Copious Dictionary in Three Parts*, London: Printed for John Field

Grimm, Jacob and Grimm, Wilhelm 1854-1960. *Deutsches Wörterbuch*, Leipzig: Hirzel

Halma, François 1708, 1710. *Le Grand Dictionaire François & Flamend. Woordenboek der Nederduytsche en Fransche Taalen*, Amsterdam, Utrecht: F. Halma, W. van de Water

Hannot, S. and Hoogstraten, D. van 1771. *Nederduitsch en Latynsch Woordenboek*, Amsterdam: G. de Groot

Harris, John 1704. *Lexicon Technicum: or, An Universal Dictionary of Arts and Sciences*, London: Dan. Brown

Hexham, Henry 1647-8. *A Copious English and Netherduytch Dictionarie ... Het Groot Woorden-Boeck: Gestelt in't Nederduytsch, ende in't Engelsch*, Rotterdam: Aernout Leers (also 1658-60, 1672-78)

Holtrop, John 1789, 1801. *A New English and Dutch Dictionary. Nieuw Nederduitsch en Engelsch Woorden-boek*, Dordrecht, Amsterdam: A. Blussé

Holyoke, Thomas 1677. *A Large Dictionary in Three Parts,* London: Printed by W. Rawlins

Huloet, Richard 1552. *Abcedarium Anglico Latinum,* London: William Riddel

Imbs, Paul 1971. *Trésor de la langue française. Dictionnaire de la langue du XIXe et du XXe siècle (1789-1960)*, Paris: Centre national de la recherche scientifique

Johnson, Samuel 1747. *The Plan of a Dictionary of the English Language*, London: Printed for J. & P. Knapton

— 1755. *A Dictionary of the English Language*, London: W. Strahan (9th octavo edn 1805; abridged edns 1778, 1807)

K[ersey], J[ohn] 1702. *A New English Dictionary,* London: Printed for Henry Bonwicke

Kersey, John 1708. *Dictionarium Anglo-Britannicum: Or, a General English Dictionary*, London: Printed by J. Wilde, for J. Phillips

Kersey-Phillips 1706. *See* Phillips 1658

Kilianus, Cornelius 1599. *Etymologicum Teutonicae Linguae*, Antwerp: Officina Plantiniana

Kramer, Matthias 1719. *Het Koninglyk Neder-Hoog-Duitsch, en Hoog-Neder-Duitsch Dictionnaire. Das Königliche Nider-Hoch-Teutsch, und Hoch-Nider-Teutsch Dictionarium*, Nuremberg: Bey dem autore (2nd edn 1759; 3rd edn 1768)

Latham, Robert Gordon 1866. *A Dictionary of the English Language. Founded on that of S. Johnson as edited by H.J. Todd*, London: Longman

Littleton, Adam 1678. *Linguae Latinae Liber Dictionarius Quadripartitus*, London: Printed for T. Basset

Littré, Emile 1863. *Dictionnaire de la langue française*, Paris: Hachette

Lloyd, William 1668. *An Alphabetical Dictionary, Wherein all English Words ... are either referred to their Places in the Philosophical Tables, Or explained by such Words as are in those Tables*, London: Printed by J.M. for Samuel Gellibrand and John Martin [sig. Aaa1^r - Ttt3^r in Wilkins 1668]

Longman Dictionary of Contemporary English 1978. London: Longman

Longman Dictionary of the English Language 1984. London: Longman

Luython, Glaude 1552. *Dictionaire en Franchois et Flameng ou bas allemant. Dictionaris in Fransoys ende vlaemsch oft neder duytsch*, Antwerp: Gregorius de Bonte

Marin, Pierre 1696. *Dictionnaire portatif Hollandais et Français of Nederduitsch en Fransch woordenboekje,* Amsterdam

— 1701. *Nieuw Nederduits en Frans Woordenboek. Nouveau Dictionaire, Hollandois & François,* Amsterdam: Wed. Gysb. de Groot (also 1717 with title *Compleet Nederduitsch en Fransch Woordenboek*)

— 1710. *Compleet Fransch en Nederduitsch Woordenboek*, Amsterdam: Wed. Gysb. de Groot

Martin, Benjamin 1749. *Lingua Britannica Reformata: or, A New English Dictionary*, London: Printed for J. Hodges (2nd edn 1754)

Mayre, Marten le 1606. *The Dutch Schoole Master*, London: George Elde for Simon Waterson

Mellema, Elcie Edouard Leon 1587. *Dictionaire ou Promptuaire Flameng-Francoys, tres-ample et tres copieux*, Antwerp: Jan van Waesberge

— 1618. *Le Grand Dictionaire francois-flamen ... Den Schat der Duytscher Tale,* Rotterdam: Jan van Waesberge (also 1636)

Meurier, Gabriel 1557, 1563. *Vocabulaire François-Flameng. Dictionaire Flamen-Francois,* Antwerp: Christofle Plantin, Jean Waesberghe

Miège, Guy 1679. *A New Dictionary French and English, with another English and French*, London: Printed for Thomas Basset

— 1688. *The Great French Dictionary. In two Parts*, London: Printed by J. Redmayne for Thomas Basset

— 1701. *The Short French Dictionary*, The Hague: H. van Bulderen (5th edn)

Monboddo, Lord (James Burnet) 1774-92. *Of the Origin and Progress of Language*, Edinburgh: Printed for A. Kincaid

Naembouck van allen naturelicken, ende ongheschuumden vlaemschen woirden 1546. Ghent: Joos Lambrecht

The Oxford Advanced Learner's Dictionary of Current English 1974. London: Oxford University Press

The *Oxford Advanced Learner's Dictionary of Current English. English-English-Korean* 1981. Seoul: Panmun

The Oxford Dictionary of English Proverbs, ed. F.P. Wilson, 1935. Oxford: Clarendon Press (3rd edn 1970)

The Oxford English Dictionary, ed. J.A.H. Murray, H. Bradley, W.A. Craigie and C.T. Onions, 1884-1928. Oxford: Clarendon Press (2nd edn 1989 prepared by J.A. Simpson and E.S.C. Weiner)

Partridge, E. 1938. *A Dictionary of Slang and Unconventional English*, London: Routledge

The Password English Dictionary for Speakers of French 1989. Mont-Royal: Modulo

Phillips, Edward 1658. *The New World of English Words*, London: Printed for J. Phillips (3rd edn 1671; 4th edn 1678; 5th edn 1696; 6th edn 1706 rev. by J.K[ersey] with title *The New World of Words: or, Universal English Dictionary*)

Plantin, Christophorus 1573. *Thesaurus Theutonicae linguae. Schat der Neder-duytscher spraken*, Antwerp: Christophorus Plantinus

A Pocket Dictionary or Complete English Expositor 1753. London: J. Newbery

Promptorium Parvulorum c.1440. *The Promptorium Parvulorum. The first English Dictionary*, ed. A.L. Mayhew, London: Early English Text Society, 1908

Ray, John 1674. *A Collection of English Words not Generally Used*, London: H. Bruges (2nd edn 1691)

Richardson, C. 1836-7. *A New English Dictionary of the English Language*, London: William Pickering

Richelet, César-Pierre 1680. *Dictionnaire françois*, Geneva: Widerhold

Rider, John 1589. *Bibliotheca Scholastica*, Oxford: Printed by Joseph Barnes (also 1633)

— 1640. *Riders Dictionarie, Corrected and Augmented with the addition of many hundred Words ... by Francis Holy-Oke*, London: F. Kingstone, for R. Whitaker

Le Petit Robert. Dictionnaire alphabetique et analogique de la langue française 1986. Paris: Le Robert

Roches, Jean des 1769. *Nieuw Nederduytsch en Fransch Woorden-Boek. Nouveau Dictionnaire François-Flamand*, Antwerp: J. Grangé

Rodriguez, Juan Francisco 1624. *Nieuwen dictionaris om te leeren de Nederlandtsche ende Spaensche talen*, Antwerp: C.I. Trognesius

Roget, Peter Mark 1852. *A Thesaurus of English Words and Phrases*, London: Longman

Sasbout, Mathias 1576, 1579. *Dictionaire Flameng-Francoys, tres-ample et copieux. Dictionaire Francoys-Flameng tres-ample et copieux*, Antwerp: Jean Waesberghe

Scott-Bailey 1755. Scott, Joseph Nicol *A New Universal Etymological English Dictionary ... Originally Compiled by N. Bailey*, London: T. Osborne

Sewel, Willem 1691. *Nieuw Woordenboek der Nederduytsche en Engelsche Taale*, Amsterdam: Bij de Weduwe van Steven Swart (also 1708, 1727, 1735, 1749, 1754)

— 1766. *A Compleat Dictionary English and Dutch ... entirely improved by Egbert Buys*, Amsterdam: Kornelis de Veer

Skinner, Stephen 1671. *Etymologicon linguae Anglicanae*, London: T. Roycroft

Thomas, Thomas 1587. *Dictionarium linguae Latinae et Anglicanae*, London: Richard Boyle (13th edn 1631)

Tilley, M.P. 1950. *Dictionary of the Proverbs in England in the Sixteenth and Seventeenth Centuries*, Ann Arbor: University of Michigan Press

Todd, Henry J. 1818. *A Dictionary of the English Language by Samuel Johnson. With Numerous Corrections and Additions by H.J. Todd*, London: Longman

Vries, Matthias de 1864-. *Woordenboek der Nederlandsche Taal*, The Hague: Nijhoff

Waesberghe, Jean 1599. *Dictionnaire Francois-Flameng, tres ample et copieux*, Rotterdam: Jean Waesberghe

Walker, John 1791. *A Critical Pronouncing Dictionary*, London: G.G.J. and J. Robinson

Wase, Christopher 1662. *Dictionarium Minus: A Compendious Dictionary English-Latin & Latin-English*, London: Printed by D. Maxwell

Wesley, John 1753. *The Complete English Dictionary*, London: W. Strahan

Wilkins, John 1668. *An Essay towards a Real Character and a Philosophical Language*, London: Printed for Samuel Gellibrand

OTHER WORKS

Aa, A.J. van der 1852-78. *Biographisch Woordenboek der Nederlanden*, Haarlem: J.J. van Brederode

Aarsleff, H. 1967. *The Study of Language in England, 1780-1860*, Princeton: Princeton University Press

Algeo, J. 1993. 'Desuetude among new English words', *IJL* 6, 281-93

Allen, H.B. 1940. *Samuel Johnson and the Authoritarian Principle in Linguistic Criticism*. Unpublished dissertation, University of Michigan

Alston, R.C. 1964. 'English Grammars in Dutch and Dutch Grammars in English. A Supplement', *English Studies* 45, 389-94

— ed., 1969. *English Linguistics 1500-1800. Facsimile Edition of A New English Dictionary ... by J.K.*, Menston: Scolar Press

— 1974. *A Bibliography of the English Language from the Invention of Printing to the Year 1800. A Corrected Reprint of Volumes I - X,* Ilkley: Janus

Anson, C.M. 1990. 'Errours and endeavors: a case study in American orthography', *IJL* 3, 35-53

Arn, M-J. and Wirtjes, H., eds, 1985. *Historical and Editorial Studies in Mediaeval and Early Modern English*, Groningen: Wolters-Noordhoff

Ayto, J. 1988. 'Fig. leaves. Metaphor in dictionaries', in Snell-Hornby 1988, 49-54

Bakker, D.M. and Dibbets, G.R.W. 1977. *Geschiedenis van de Nederlandse taalkunde*, 's-Hertogenbosch: Malmberg

Bammesberger, A., ed., 1985. *Problems of Old English Lexicography*, Regensburg: Friedrich Pustet

Barfoot, C.C., Beukema, F.H. and Perryman, J.C., eds, 1980. *Times and Tide. Writings offered to Professor A.G.H. Bachrach*, Leiden: Rijksuniversiteit te Leiden

Bately, J.M. 1967. 'Ray, Worlidge, and Kersey's Revision of the New World of English Words', *Anglia* 85, 1-14

— 1983. 'Miège and the development of the English dictionary', in Stanley 1983, 1-10

Béjoint, H. 1994. *Tradition and Innovation in Modern English Dictionaries*, Oxford: Clarendon Press

Bivens, L. 1980-81. 'Nineteenth-century reactions to the OED: an annotated bibliography, *Dictionaries. Journal of the Dictionary Society of North America* 3, 146-52

Boisson, C., Kirtchuk, P. and Béjoint, H. 1991. 'Aux origines de la lexicographie: les premiers dictionnaires monolingues et bilingues', *IJL* 4, 261-315

Bond, W.H., ed., 1970. *Eighteenth-Century Studies in Honor of Donald F. Hyde*, New York: Grolier Club

Bongaerts, T. 1978. *The Correspondence of Thomas Blount (1618-1679) a Recusant Antiquary*, Amsterdam: APA-Holland Universiteits Pers

Bradley, H. 1884. 'Review of A New English Dictionary ... Edited by James A.H. Murray. Part I A-Ant', *The Academy*, February 16 and March 1

Bray, L. 1986. *César-Pierre Richelet (1626-98)*, Tübingen: Niemeyer

— 1990. 'Les marques d'usage dans le *Dictionnaire françois* (1680) de César-Pierre Richelet', *Lexique* 9, 43-59

Bronstein, A.J. 1986. 'The history of pronunciation in English language dictionaries', in Hartmann 1986, 23-33

Browne, Sir T. 1643. *Religio Medici*, London: Printed for Andrew Crooke

— 1646. *Pseudodoxia Epidemica, or Enquiries into very Many Received Tenents and Commonly Presumed Truths*, in Keynes 1964, II, 17-548

Brunot, F. 1924-43. *Histoire de la langue française des origines à 1900*, Paris: Armand Colin

Burchfield, R.W. 1973. 'The treatment of controversial vocabulary in the Oxford English Dictionary', *Transactions of the Philological Society* 1973, 1-28

— 1980. 'Aspects of short-term historical lexicography', in Pijnenburg and De Tollenaere 1980, 271-86

— 1987. *Studies in Lexicography*, Oxford: Clarendon Press

Catach, N. 1989. 'L'orthographe dans le dictionnaire monolingue', in Hausmann *et al.* 1989-91, I, 501-8

Chapman, R.W. 1952. *The Letters of Samuel Johnson*, Oxford: Clarendon Press

Claes, F. 1974. *Lijst van Nederlandse woordenlijsten en woordenboeken gedrukt tot 1600*, Nieuwkoop: De Graaf

— 1977. 'De lexicografie in de zestiende eeuw', in Bakker and Dibbets 1977, 205-17

— 1980. *A Bibliography of Netherlandic (Dutch, Flemish) Dictionaries*, Amsterdam: Benjamins

Clifford, J.L. 1979. *Dictionary Johnson. Samuel Johnson's Middle Years*, New York: McGraw-Hill

Clifford, J.L. and Greene, D.J. 1970. *Samuel Johnson. A Survey and Bibliography of Critical Studies*, Minneapolis: University of Minnesota Press

Congleton, J.E. and Congleton, E.C. 1984. *Johnson's Dictionary. Bibliographical Survey 1746-1984*, Terre Haute: Dictionary Society of North America

Corbin, P. 1989. 'Les marques stylistiques/diastratiques dans le dictionnaire monolingue', in Hausmann *et al.* 1989-91, I, 673-80

DeMaria, R. 1986. *Johnson's Dictionary and the Language of Learning*, Oxford: Clarendon Press

Dobson, E.J. 1957. *English Pronunciation 1500-1700*, Oxford: Clarendon Press

Dolezal, F. 1985. *Forgotten but Important Lexicographers: John Wilkins and William Lloyd. A Modern Approach to Lexicography before Johnson*, Tübingen: Niemeyer

— 1986. 'How abstract is the English dictionary?', in Hartmann 1986, 47-55

Drosdowski, G. 1989. 'Die Beschreibung von Metaphern im allgemeinen einsprachigen Wörterbuch', in Hausmann *et al.* 1989-91, I, 797-805

Glatigny, M., ed., 1990. *Les marques d'usage dans les dictionnaires (XVIIe-XVIIIe iècle)*, Lille: Presses Universitaires de Lille

Goetz, D. and Herbst, T., eds, 1984. *Theoretische und praktische Probleme der Lexikographie*, München: Hueber

Grindsted, A. 1988. 'Geographical varieties (and regionalisms) in bilingual lexicography', in Hyldgaard-Jensen 1988, 181-92

Hartmann, R.R.K., ed., 1979. *Dictionaries and their Users*, Exeter Linguistic Studies 4: University of Exeter

— ed., 1983. *Lexicography: Principles and Practice*, London: Academic Press

— ed., 1986. *The History of Lexicography. Papers from the Dictionary Research Centre Seminar at Exeter, March 1986*, Amsterdam: Benjamins

— 1994. 'Bilingualised versions of learners' dictionaries', *Fremdsprachen Lehren und Lernen* 23, 206-20

Hausmann, F.J. 1990. 'Das Wörterbuch der schweren Wörter', in Hausmann *et al.* 1989-91, II, 1206-10

Hausmann, F.J., Reichmann, O. and Wiegand, H.E., eds, 1989-91. *Wörterbücher/Dictionaries/Dictionnaires. Ein internationales Handbuch zur Lexikographie*, Berlin: De Gruyter [Vol. I 1989, Vol. II 1990, Vol. III 1991]

Hayashi, T. 1978. *The Theory of English Lexicography 1530-1791*, Amsterdam: Benjamins

Heddesheimer, C. 1968. 'The authorship of *A New English Dictionary (1702)*', *Notes and Queries* 213, 444-5

Hobbes, T. 1651. *Leviathan*, London: Andrew Crooke

Householder, F.W. and Saporta, F. 1962. *Problems in Lexicography*, The Hague: Mouton

Hulbert, J.R. 1955. *Dictionaries: British and American*, London: Deutsch

Hull, W.I. 1933. William Sewel of Amsterdam 1653-1720, Swarthmore: Swarthmore College

Hüllen, W. 1986. 'The paradigm of John Wilkins' Thesaurus', in Hartmann 1986, 115-25

— ed., 1990. *Understanding the Historiography of Linguistics. Problems and Projects*, Münster: Nodus

Hyldgaard-Jensen, K. and Zettersten, A., eds, 1988. *Symposium on Lexicography III. Proceedings of the Third International Symposium on Lexicography May 14-16, 1986 at the University of Copenhagen,* Tübingen: Niemeyer

Hyldgaard-Jensen, K. and Pedersen, V.H., eds, 1994. *Symposium on Lexicography VI. Proceedings of the Sixth International Symposium on Lexicography May 7-9, 1992 at the University of Copenhagen*, Tübingen: Niemeyer

Ilson, R., ed., 1986. *Lexicography. An Emerging International Profession*, Manchester: Manchester University Press

— 1990. 'Present-day British lexicography', in Hausmann *et al.* 1989-91, II, 1967-83

James, G., ed., 1989. *Lexicographers and their Works*, Exeter Linguistic Studies 14: University of Exeter

— ed., 1994a. *Meeting Points in Language Studies*, Hong Kong: Jilin University of Technology

— 1994b. 'Towards a typology of bilingualised dictionaries', in James 1994a, 184-96

Kabell, I. and Lauridsen, H. 1989. *Frideric Bolling's Engelske Dictionarium (1678)*, Copenhagen: Faculty of Humanities, University of Copenhagen

Kastovsky, D. and Szwedek, A., eds, 1986. *Linguistics across Historical and Geographical Boundaries*, Berlin: Mouton de Gruyter

Keast, W.R. 1957. 'The two Clarissas in Johnson's Dictionary', *Studies in Philology* 54, 429-39

Kerling, J. 1979. *Chaucer in Early English Dictionaries*, Leiden: Leiden University Press

Keynes, G., ed., 1964. *The Works of Sir Thomas Browne*, London: Faber & Faber

Kirkness, A. 1980. *Geschichte des Deutschen Wörterbuchs 1838-1863. Dokumente zu den Lexikographen Grimm*, Stuttgart: Hirzel

Kolb, G.J. and Kolb, R.A. 1972. 'The selection and use of the illustrative quotations in Dr Johnson's *Dictionary*', in Weinbrot 1972a, 61-72

Kolb, G.J. and Sledd, J.H. 1953. 'Johnson's Dictionary and lexicographical tradition', *Modern Philology* 50, 171-94

Landau, S. 1986. *Dictionaries. The Art & Craft of Lexicography*, New York: Charles Scribner's Sons

Littré, E. 1897. *Comment j'ai fait mon Dictionnaire de la langue française*, Paris: C. Delagrave

Lodge, R.A. 1989. 'Speakers' perceptions of non-standard vocabulary in French', *Zeitschrift für Romanische Philologie* 105, 427-44

Long, P.W. 1909. 'English Dictionaries before Webster', *Bibliographical Society of America Papers* 4, 30

Lounsbury, T.R. 1909. *English Spelling and Spelling Reform*, New York: Harper

McAdam, E.L. 1970. 'Inkhorn words before Dr Johnson', in Bond 1970, 187-206

McCracken, D. 1969. 'The drudgery of defining: Johnson's debt to Bailey's *Dictionarium Britannicum*', *Modern Philology* 66, 338-41

Mackenzie, L. 1985. 'Metaphor in contemporary semantics', *Dutch Quarterly Review* 15, 52-72

Mathews, M.M. 1933. *A Survey of English Dictionaries*, London: Oxford University Press

Mencken, H.R. 1923. *The American Language*, New York: Alfred A. Knopf (3rd edn)

Molhuysen, P.C. and Kossmann, F.K.H. 1911-37. *Nieuw Nederlandsch Biografisch Woordenboek*, Leiden: Sijthoff

Murray, J.A.H. 1900. *The Evolution of English Lexicography*, Oxford: Clarendon Press

Murray, K.M.E. 1977. *Caught in the Web of Words. James A.H. Murray and the Oxford English Dictionary*, New Haven: Yale University Press

Nencioni, G. 1989. 'The dictionary as an aid in belles lettres', in Hausmann *et al.* 1989-91, I, 146-51

Niebaum, H. 1989. 'Diatopische Markierungen im allgemeinen einsprachigen Wörterbuch, in Hausmann *et al.* 1989-91, I, 662-68

Noyes, G.E. 1941. 'The development of cant lexicography in England', *Studies in Philology* 38, 462-79

— 1943. 'The first English dictionary, Cawdrey's *Table Alphabeticall*', *Modern Language Notes* 58, 600-605

— 1954. 'The critical reception of Johnson's Dictionary in the later eighteenth century', *Modern Philology* 52, 175-91

Nuccorini, S. 1988. 'The treatment of metaphorical and idiomatic expressions in learners' dictionaries', in Snell-Hornby 1988, 149-60

O'Connor, D. 1991. 'Bilingual lexicography: English-Italian, Italian-English', in Hausmann *et al.* 1989-91, III, 2970-76

Osselton, N.E. 1958. *Branded Words in English Dictionaries before Johnson*, Groningen: Wolters

— 1973. *The Dumb Linguists. A Study of the Earliest English and Dutch Dictionaries*, Leiden: Leiden University Press

— 1983. 'The history of English-language dictionaries', in Hartmann 1983, 13-21

— 1985. 'Spelling-book rules and the capitalization of nouns in the seventeenth and eighteenth centuries', in Arn and Wirtjes 1985, 49-61

— 1993. Review of The Oxford English Dictionary, Second Edition, *IJL* 6, 124-31

— 1994. 'Dr Johnson and the spelling of *dispatch*', *IJL* 7, 307-10

Potter, S. 1973. Review of A Supplement to the Oxford English Dictionary ed. R.W. Burchfield, Vol. I A-G, *Review of English Studies* 24, 460-4

Quemada, B. 1968. *Les dictionnaires du français moderne 1539-1863*, Paris: Didier

— 1972. 'Lexicology and lexicography', in Sebeok 1972, 395-475

Rasmussen, J. 1991. 'La lexicographie bilingue avec le danois', in Hausmann *et al.* 1989-91, III, 3051-61.

Read, A.W. 1935. 'The contemporary quotations in Johnson's Dictionary', *English Literary History* 2, 246-51

— 1962. 'The labeling of national and regional variation in popular dictionaries', in Householder and Saporta 1962, 217-27

Reddick, A. 1990. *The Making of Johnson's Dictionary. 1746-1773*, Cambridge: Cambridge University Press

Reichmann, O. 1990. 'Formen und Probleme der Datenerhebung I: Synchronische und Diachronische historische Wörterbücher', in Hausmann *et al.* 1989-91, II, 1589-1611

Riddell, J.A. 1974. 'The reliability of early English dictionaries', *Yearbook of English Studies* 4, 1-4

Riemens, K.-J. 1919. *Esquisse historique de l'enseignement du français en Hollande du xvie au xixe siècle*, Leiden: Sijthoff

— 1921. *Les débuts de la lexicographie franco-néerlandaise*, Paris: H. Champion

Roe, K. 1977. 'A survey of the encyclopaedic tradition in English dictionaries', *Papers of the Dictionary Society of America* 1977, 16-23

Rypins, S. 1925. 'Johnson's Dictionary reviewed by his contemporaries', *Philological Quarterly* 4, 281-6

Samuels, M.L. 1983. Review of A Supplement to the Oxford English Dictionary ed. R.W. Burchfield, Vol. III O-Scz, *Notes & Queries* 228, 483-7

Schäfer, J. 1970. 'The hard word dictionaries: a re-assessment', *Leeds Studies in English* 4, 31-48

— 1980. *Documentation in the OED: Shakespeare and Nashe as Test Cases*, Oxford: Clarendon Press

— 1982. 'Chaucer in Shakespeare's dictionaries: the beginning', *Chaucer Review* 17, 182-92

— 1983. 'Tod und Winterschlaf der Lexikographischen Tradition: ein Problem moderner Lexikographie', Anglistentag 1981, 35-44, Frankfurt/M: Jörg Hasler

— 1984. 'Glossar, Index, Wörterbuch und Enzyklopädie: der Beginn einsprachiger Lexikographie zur Zeit Shakespeares', in Goetz and Herbst 1984, 276-99

— 1989. *Early Modern English Lexicography*, Oxford: Clarendon Press

Scheurweghs, G. 1960. 'English grammars in Dutch and Dutch grammars in English in the Netherlands before 1800', *English Studies* 41, 129-67

Schmidt, G.D. 1989. 'Diachronische Markierungen im allgemeinen einsprachigen Wörterbuch', in Hausmann *et al.* 1989-91, I, 657-61

Sebeok, T.A. 1972. *Current Trends in Linguistics. Vol. 9. Linguistics in Western Europe*, The Hague: Mouton

Segar, M. 1931. 'Dictionary making in the eighteenth century', *Review of English Studies* 7, 210-13

Sheard, J.A. 1954. *The Words We Use*, London: Deutsch

Simon, I. 1960. 'Saxonism and the hard-words dictionaries', *Revue des langues vivantes* 26, 411-20

Simpson, J.A. 1990. 'English lexicography after Johnson to 1945', in Hausmann *et al.* 1989-91, II, 1953-66

Sledd, J.H. 1947. *The Alvearie of John Baret.* Unpublished dissertation, University of Texas

— 1949. 'A footnote on the inkhorn controversy', *University of Texas Studies in English* 28, 49-56

Sledd, J.H. and Kolb, G.J. 1955. *Dr. Johnson's Dictionary. Essays in the Biography of a Book*, Chicago: University of Chicago Press

Snell-Hornby, M., ed., 1988. *ZüriLEX Proceedings. Papers read at the Euralex International Congress, University of Zürich, 9-14 September 1986*, Tübingen: Francke Verlag

Stanley, E.G. and Gray, D., eds, 1983. *Five Hundred Years of Words and Sounds*, Cambridge: Brewer

Starnes, D.T. 1940. 'Literary features of renaissance dictionaries', *Studies in Philology* 37, 26-50

— 1954. *Renaissance Dictionaries English-Latin and Latin-English*, Austin: University of Texas Press

— and Noyes, G.E. 1946. *The English Dictionary from Cawdrey to Johnson, 1604-1755*, Chapel Hill: University of North Carolina Press.

— 1991. *The English Dictionary from Cawdrey to Johnson, 1604-1755. New edition with an Introduction and a Select Bibliography by Gabriele Stein*, Amsterdam: Benjamins

Stein, G. 1983. Review of A Supplement to the Oxford English Dictionary ed. R.W. Burchfield, Vol. III O-Scz, *Anglia* 101, 468-75

— 1984. 'Word-formation in Dr Johnson's Dictionary of the English Language', *Dictionaries: Journal of the Dictionary Society of North America* 6, 66-112

— 1985a. *The English Dictionary before Cawdrey*, Tübingen: Niemeyer

— 1985b. 'Forms of definition in Thomas Elyot's *Dictionarie*', in *Kontinuität und Wandel. Aspekte einer praxisoffenen Anglistik. Festschrift für Leonard Alfes*, Siegen, 195-205

— 1986. 'Definitions and first-pronoun involvement in Thomas Elyot's dictionary', in Kastovsky 1986, 1465-74

— 1988. 'The emerging role of English in the dictionaries of renaissance Europe', *Folia Linguistica Historica* X/1, 29-138

Steiner, R.J. 1991. 'Bilingual lexicography: English-Spanish, Spanish-English', in Hausmann *et al.* 1989-91, III, 2949-56

Stenberg, T. 1944. 'Quotations from Pope in Johnson's Dictionary', *University of Texas Studies in English* 23, 197-210

Sterkenburg, P.G.J. van 1983. *Johan Hendrik van Dale en zijn opvolgers*, Utrecht: Van Dale Lexicografie

— 1984. *Van woordenlijst to woordenboek. Inleiding tot de geschiedenis van woordenboeken in het Nederlands*, Leiden: Brill

Tollenaere, F. de 1977. 'De lexicografie in de zeventiende en achttiende eeuw', in Bakker and Dibbets 1977, 219-27

Trench, R.C. 1857. 'On some deficiencies in our English dictionaries', *Transactions of the Philological Society 1857*, 1-70

Vooys, C.G.N. de 1934. 'Iets over oude woordenboeken', *Nieuwe Taalgids* 28, 263-72.

— 1947a. *Verzamelde Taalkundige Opstellen, Derde Bundel*, Groningen: Wolters

— 1947b. 'Matthias Kramer als grammaticus en lexicograaf', in De Vooys 1947, 259-67

Wakelin, M.F. 1987. 'The treatment of dialect in English dictionaries', in Burchfield 1987, 156-77

Weinbrot, H.D., ed., 1972a. *New Aspects of Lexicography,* Carbondale: Southern Illinois University Press

— 1972b. 'Johnson's Plan and Preface to the Dictionary: the growth of a lexicographer's mind', in Weinbrot 1972a, 73-94

Wells, R.A. 1973. *Dictionaries and the Authoritarian Tradition*, The Hague: Mouton

Werner, R. 1991. 'Die Markierungen im zweisprachigen Wörterbuch', in Hausmann *et al.* 1989-91, III, 2796-803

Wiegand, H.E. 1989. 'Aspekte der Makrostruktur im allgemeinen einsprachigen Wörterbuch: alphabetische Anordnungsformen und ihre Probleme', in Hausmann *et al.* 1989-91, I, 371-409

Wimsatt, W.K. 1951. 'Samuel Johnson and Dryden's Du Fresnoy', *Studies in Philology* 48, 26-39

Wimsatt, W.K. and Wimsatt, M.H. 1948. 'Self-quotations and anonymous quotations in Johnson's Dictionary', *English Literary History* 15, 60-68

Wrenn, C.L. 1949. *The English Language*, London: Methuen

Zgusta, L. 1971. *Manual of Lexicography*, The Hague: Mouton

— 1989a. 'The Oxford English Dictionary and Other Dictionaries', *IJL* 2, 188-230

— 1989b. 'The role of dictionaries in the genesis and development of the standard', in Hausmann *et al*. 1989-91, I, 70-79

Zöfgen, E. 1991. 'Bilingual learner's dictionaries', in Hausmann *et al.* 1989-91, III, 2888-903

Index